Following Old Fencelines

NUMBER TWO:
C. A. Brannen Series

Following Old Fencelines

TALES FROM RURAL TEXAS

Lee Winniford

TEXAS A&M UNIVERSITY PRESS
COLLEGE STATION

First edition

The paper used in this book meets the minimum requirements

of the American National Standard for Permanence

of Paper for Printed Library Materials, Z39.48-1984.

Binding materials have been chosen for durability.

LIBRARY OF CONGRESS CATALOGING-IN-PUBLICATION DATA

Winniford, Lee, 1932–

Following old fencelines : tales from rural Texas / Lee Winniford. — 1st ed.

p. cm. — (C.A. Brannen series ; no. 2)

Includes bibliographical references.

ISBN 0-89096-802-0 (alk. paper)

1. Winniford, Lee 1932– —Childhood and youth. 2. Hopkins County (Tex.)—Social life and customs. 3. Hopkins County (Tex.)—Biography. 4. Winniford family. 5. Alexander family. 6. Ward family. 7. Wolfe family. 8. Folklore—Texas—Hopkins County. I. Title. II. Series.

F392.H67W56 1998

976.4′274063′092

[B]—dc21 97-34586

CIP

As part of a legacy that may guide them through their wanderings in geography and time and spirit, this book is dedicated to my grandchildren: Bethany Jade and Jennifer Lynn Decker, Regan Delane Gardner, and Devin Michael Colvin.

Table of Contents

Illustrations

Foreword

Lee Winniford knows hundreds of stories. I have heard perhaps a hundred of them, and I want to hear the rest, because she tells them powerfully and persuasively. After she tells her stories, she will—equally powerfully and persuasively—tell what they mean to her.

"Folk" who are in equal measure both folklorists and artists—those who combine creative imagination with scrupulous ethnography to explore their own traditional communities—are extremely hard to find. Lee Winniford is one of the few.

Following Old Fencelines reverses the processes and exceeds the achievements of the most creatively evocative autoethnographies of the past. Pierre-Jakez Hélias in *The Horse of Pride: Life in a Breton Village* and Jean Ritchie in *Singing Family of the Cumberlands* recast translations of experience into romantically artful narrative. What Lee Winniford has effected in her life and in the process of making this book—a process that shows through the framework of these tales—is the translation of artful traditional narratives into richly contextualized experience.

Hélias and Ritchie employ a language of nostalgia, a nostalgia learned from and shared with a larger, distant world—a readership that never shared the experiences that these two artful "former folk" describe. For all the beauty and truth of their visions, Hélias and Ritchie speak with the voices of outsiders and win our sympathies largely because they sound the way that we, as outsiders, expect them to sound.

But the sound that governs Lee Winniford's book is the language of tale-telling in Hopkins County, Texas. For her, both by chronology and priority, the stories came first. She wrote the rest of the book around them, in an effort to convert her readers into listeners, to bring them to a place where the stories would sound and mean the same to them as they do to her. She has struggled to maintain the traditional voices that she learned as a child. Winniford offers us the voices she heard from others and developed herself, listening to her grandmother, mother, father, aunts, and uncles. Although she modestly and accurately insists that she has failed to reclaim the exact words of her elders, I believe that she has come remarkably close, for the tales in this book play as well to their native community as to the sympathetic outsider.

One of the reasons that Lee Winniford has been able to strike this balance is that she lived with the stories inside her for decades after most of their first tellers had fallen silent. She left the rural world so lovingly restored here and went to the city. She became a high school teacher, a college teacher, and a social worker. She mastered many urban and formal languages extremely distant from the dialects of these tales. Yet through all her travels she kept the stories of Cumby, Texas, alive in her mind. Most often retold only to herself, the stories became in effect her most palpable link with her past.

The author's subsequent learning and teaching gave her the perspective to cast this book in two broad dialects: that of the insider artist and that of the outsider evaluator. Lee Winniford has written poetry, published literary criticism, and counseled troubled people from many backgrounds. Nurturing internally her native voices and mastering new ones that could ultimately frame these tales for outsiders, she acquired an improbable range of descriptive skills. All of them find important places in this book, which, as a result, satisfies the intellectual curiosity of the academic, engages the interest of the layman, and, through it all, remains as true as possible to the speech and values of those who gave her their stories.

After Lee had already produced several masterful autoethnographical studies and narrative performances drawn entirely from her own memory, she prepared to go back to Cumby to study the sites of the storytelling and collect the tales, memories, and impressions of others. As she was leaving, I repeated for her my cardinal rule for folklorists: "The goal of fieldwork, as impossible to achieve as it is necessary to pursue, is to represent the other in the other's own terms." She looked straight at me and replied, with absolute conviction but with no hint of condescension or self-effacement, "I *am* the other."

How many of us can say that? Those who are truly "other" seldom possess the interest to learn the codes through which the academy characterizes them as such. Those who master the codes most often bury their otherness so deeply in academic trappings that they widen the distance between their outsider and insider selves—a distance that inevitably binds them much more closely to other academics and creates in the process a whole new community of others. Their speech engages only the scholar's side of the growing gulf. In Ronald Grimes's brilliant *Marrying and Burying: Rites of Passage in a Man's Life,* the autoethnographer displays a stunning mastery of many genres: confessional, humorous, social-scientific. But the voices that he blends are all those of a tight community of intellectual others. Even in his own community, Grimes reports, one of his colleagues, upon reading part of his book, told him, "If I had just read this . . . and saw you walking down the street, I'd cross to the other side" (xi). Postmodern ethnographers may seek to "evoke" the other, but the ironic result is a deification of the otherness of the academic and a text that is, as Stephen Tyler puts it, ultimately "unspeakable."

Lee Winniford has learned much from the soul-searching of postmodern ethnographers. At first, her family stories possessed for her an almost scriptural authority, and her early attempts to recapture them were driven by a quixotic yearning for the exact restoration of times and tales that will never be lived or heard again. Her readings of recent works on the problems of representation convinced her of the impossibility of this task, but they did not dissuade her from her purpose of making this book primarily a statement of, by, and for the storytellers who gave her so much. Thus, although she has not compromised the rigor of today's folklore scholarship, she has refused to surrender her stories to an insular academic dialect.

Few have found ways to bind rather than drive apart the traditional and scholarly worlds. One of the most successful was Zora Neale Hurston, whose work has been for Lee a model and an inspiration, lovingly acknowledged in the early pages of this book. Like Lee, Hurston lived in many worlds and mastered many voices. But even Hurston did not attempt to put as many of them together in one place as Lee does here. In *Mules and Men,* Hurston presents a spectacular summa of her hometown's storytelling, easily and naturally attained. But we learn in *Dust Tracks on a Road,* Hurston's autobiography, that her reentry into the traditional arts of Eatonville, Florida, was in reality an awkward and painful process. Hurston had lived too long in other worlds—some of them academic—to return with ease and grace. In *Their Eyes Were Watching God,* Hurston revisits the same traditional past as a novelist, retelling some of the same stories we have heard in the other books—but in a poetically evocative form. In these three books, Hurston presents herself, by turns, listening, confessing, and artfully recreating. Reading the three together, we discover the remarkably rich and multifaceted traditional life of a young girl in Eatonville.

It is not, I believe, too much to suggest that Lee Winniford has captured her version of all three of Hurston's voices in this one book. Lee's stories flow with ease, even as we feel the agony of her attempts to reenter this vanished world. A hard-earned blending of voices allows us to experience the art of the past, the pain of the present, and the beauty of both.

I admit my bias. Having witnessed firsthand the sincerity, the reverence, the almost frightening conviction, and the sometimes overwhelming sense of urgency with which she has struggled to reach this balance, I cannot believe that this book falls short of the arts and efforts that went into its creation.

The select few will read Grimes and Tyler with awe. Lee Winniford wants everybody to share her stories and her past. If they don't, it's not her fault. If they do, they would never cross the street to avoid her. I know of no book truer to what an ethnographic biography ought to be.

Carl Lindahl

Acknowledgments

My rediscovery of the rich legacy of lore developed through both branches of my family and through the people who settled and continue to populate the little Texas town where I was born and grew up began when I enrolled in a folklore course at the University of Houston in the summer of 1990. To Professor Carl Lindahl I am indebted for introducing me to the field of folklore, for suggesting the importance of the memories that I retain from my childhood, for motivating my study and fieldwork over a period of four years, and for guiding and encouraging me through the long, often discouraging, process of shaping the materials I gathered into this collection.

Completing this project would probably have been impossible without the help of my brother, James Winniford, who not only assisted in the collecting process but also in reconstructing a "past" that could serve as part of the context for the stories in my collection. My niece, Shannon Winniford McCraw, was an enthusiastic participant in fieldwork expeditions and an invaluable research assistant.

I have drawn strength and inspiration from the fact that my long-term friend, Bert Kellar, never lost faith in me, even in the worst of times; I also appreciate the many instances when another friend, Carla Davis, came to my rescue supplying whatever seemed most needed—paper, tapes, typewriter ribbons, words of comfort. My friends Jo Ann Simms and Susan Cooper performed the practical service of proofing (and critiquing) my copy when my eyesight failed—and the more crucial spiritual service of believing in me and my project when my courage failed.

Because this project explores family, and because I felt that I needed to be open and candid in that exploration, I am especially grateful for the loving and unwavering support and encouragement of my children, Jay Flowers and John and Leann Decker. I am also grateful to the many informants ("sharers"), living and dead, who either directly or indirectly supplied the stories that constitute my collection.

Following Old Fencelines

Chapter One

Introduction

RETURN OF A PRODIGAL DAUGHTER

Moving in a northerly direction through East Texas, the traveler watches as hills and creeks and thick piney woods give way to ever-broader stretches of flat grasslands and a relative scarcity of trees of any kind, especially evergreen. At significant junctures along the main highway, impressive road signs announce that the region the visitor has entered is the Dairying Capital of the World, and indeed one catches glimpses of cattle grazing on the open expanses of pasture and of occasional clean but weathered dairy barns and feed sheds. But in the dead of winter when the pastures are mostly brown and stubby and the herds of cattle are huddled somewhere out of the weather (and out of sight), nothing seems on a scale that suggests worldwide preeminence.

On the outskirts of Sulphur Springs, the seat of Hopkins County, the traveler encounters modern urban sprawl: flashy motels, gas stations, office buildings, and fast-food joints with their abundant neon signs and outdoor lighting. The encounter, however, is abrupt and brief—for in whatever direction one continues, the temporary illusion of plenty, ease, and extravagance succumbs to an older order of rural restraint and parsimony reflecting hardship and limited good.

This traveler's destination is Cumby, a little town that people generally have never heard of. Cumby is located in western Hopkins County six miles west of Brashear and sixteen miles west of Sulphur Springs on the LA & T Railroad and on Highway 67 and Interstate 30. Farm-to-Market Road 275 passes through the town, connecting

Miller Grove, ten miles south, with State Highway 11, six miles north of Cumby. Two Hunt County towns are within easy driving distance of Cumby: Commerce, some ten miles northwest on State Highway 11, and Greenville, twenty miles due west on Interstate 30.[1]

From Sulphur Springs, one can reach Cumby either by traveling the superhighway (Interstate 30) or by driving along old Highway 67. These two routes run parallel to each other, lying perhaps a half-mile to sometimes a mile apart, and they set up the contrast that distinguishes so many places in Hopkins County: the modern, high tech, and fast moving as opposed to the old, slow, and decaying. I choose to drive along old Highway 67, the only route open during the years when I was growing up in this part of Texas—an area I left as a teenager in the early 1950s. In the decades that separate me from this place where I was born and spent my childhood and adolescence, I have realized accomplishment and loss, have experienced victories and failures, have known great joy and deep sorrow. I have struggled to continue my formal education, taught in the Texas public schools for thirty years, married, and had children and grandchildren. I have weathered a failed marriage, a bout with alcoholism, and the disintegration of the "world" that I had left Cumby and Hopkins County to find.

In the wake of these most recent setbacks, I determined to pursue a dream long deferred, earning a doctoral degree. And it was in my first graduate-level folklore course at the University of Houston with Professor Carl Lindahl that I awakened—not all at once, for the process has been gradual—to the importance of the hundreds of stories that I had heard during my childhood and that were as significant as any other aspect of my youth to my sense of identity. Certainly I did not initially think of these childhood stories as folklore. I began my first folklore course with the notion that folklore comprised the exotic traditions of any culture but my own. However, as I came to an understanding of folklore as the integral, unofficial, and deeply interpersonal fabric of stories and traditions through which communities express their ideas on their environment, identities, and values, I also became committed to what has been an ongoing effort to collect and recollect this material from my childhood (or, if I may indulge momentarily in the poetic, to rescue what seems to me a beautiful and powerful part of human experience from imminent oblivion). As a self-appointed community folklorist and "prodigal daughter," of sorts, I am returning to this area as I have not returned to it before—with a motive and a mission.

Nothing that I pass is actually recognizable in any specific way, although I am aware that certain buildings and other landmarks must date back to the period when I would have been familiar with them. But the overall impact of the landscape is the same, wrenchingly familiar in its starkness and its subdued neutrality. Even under a clear, blindingly blue January sky, the fields and pastures and patches of scruffy brushland are an unrelieved gray and brown and black. Bare branches create a grim lacework against the hard blue horizon, and one senses the biting cold though one is protected from it. The land is the same. It is land that was not easily won, and it yields grudgingly to the human hand and heart. Survival on it was a struggle that in the past (as well as the present) involved dedication, compromise, and keeping expectations well in check.

That no building or tree or bridge or country lane actually jogs my memory is, however, disappointing. Furthermore, this circumstance emphasizes my dilemma with regard to the project I am attempting: gathering and interpreting within their context the folkloric materials that I associate with my childhood. My memories of Hopkins County and of Cumby are vivid and charged with emotion. More than that, this particular part of Texas has been a consistent dreamscape throughout my lifetime. For several decades, any meaningful dream I have had, whether happy or troubled, was invariably set in my hometown and county. It was in finally recognizing this phenomenon that I came to acknowledge the significance of this place and of what I must have learned here in shaping the person I have become. At a subconscious level, no matter where I have traveled, what lifestyle I have pursued, or what conditions I have confronted, the issues of any given moment have been worked out against this backdrop or within the recollected environs of this place and the perceptions of truth and reality it engendered. Many of these insights of truth and reality were, I became further convinced, transmitted through the body of lore that I have decided to gather and interpret.

But memories and dreamscapes can become warped, exaggerated, surreal. It was with the implications of such distortions in mind that I planned my return visit to Cumby. My purpose was to reestablish a contact with the past, with Cumby and the country around it as it really had been instead of as it had come to seem to have been in memory and in dream. I hoped to find clues to such an "objective past," as I called it, by experiencing the place as it is in the present. In the very process of getting here, I am discovering that even such an indirect approach will not really be feasible. Remnants from the past still in place will not necessarily be recognizable to me because my own perspectives have changed. Things shrink with time and disengagement. Heights are not as grand, distances not as great, rooms not as large. Uncle Bernice's peach and crabapple orchard is gone, but more disturbing than that, the wonderful hillside along which it sloped in graceful rows turns out to be only an uneven little piece of ground draining off into the easement for the city waterline.

Thus, although one finds and sees and touches some tangible thing from the past, one does not enter that past again or resurrect the same feelings and responses that the object, whatever its former importance, once aroused. Any reconstruction of the past will be, at best, a weird hybrid: a conglomeration of memory and dream, of new perceptions of old things and of new things and their relation to the old. All this will be bounced off other people's memories, facts, and data as they are recorded and preserved in a variety of sources. I am headed for Cumby, already at least vaguely conscious that I am attempting the impossible.

Having passed through Brashear, I begin to search in earnest for landmarks, signs of the past that must surely remain. There are a few. Far out among buff-colored fields and pastures, all formidably fenced and cross-fenced and prominently posted with No Trespassing signs, hulks a big, wood-frame way station that used to service travelers along the Old Jefferson Trail on the way to Dallas, Fort Worth, and points beyond. The old building was already often in disuse when I was a child, so it is amazing that the structure still stands, appearing—at least from this considerable distance—relatively intact. I strain to catch a glimpse of an elegant old house, some generations ago the home of a well-known, wealthy doctor whose guest lists impressed local historians. Famous people ate and slept there, or so the story goes. I cannot be certain that I am correctly identifying this landmark, so changed is the lay of the land. Then, straight ahead but still a couple of miles away, I see the Cumby water tower. I experience the first real tug at memory and feel the first jolt of emotion. I recall climbing the tower one night during my senior year in high school and painting my initials on the tank.

Just outside the Cumby city limits, old Highway 67 breaks off, and traffic is routed into a loop and overpass in the interstate system. From the overpass, one can look down Interstate 30 toward the west and see the new, modern section of Cumby as it strings out along either side of the six-lane highway. Cumby is, thus, now bisected by the roadway and by the railroad that, when I was a child, marked its southernmost boundary. On the south side of the railroad near the superhighway are scattered new businesses, gas stations, and fast-food establishments. On the north side is a ghost town, caught in a time warp. But the ghost town is not as I remember it, not as it was, because it is now nonfunctional, like a museum exhibit or a movie set.

It is, nevertheless, the old Cumby to which I am returning, and from the overpass, traffic is routed finally to a narrow asphalt road that leads into what used to be the main part of town. I notice the little frame church where I attended summer revivals and where I was baptized; its windows and doors are boarded up, and apparently the building is now used for storing hay. Several of the old homes along the way look much as they did in the past, although I have trouble remembering who lived in them then.

Along the old town's main street—a piece of Highway 67 now dismembered by the imposing interstate system—many of the old business buildings still stand, most of them empty and boarded up. Where a building has burned or collapsed and fallen in, debris has been cleared away and an empty space remains. In the residential sections of the town, occasional new, modern brick homes have been built where the originals were torn away. But in the old business district, there seems to have been little inclination to replace destroyed buildings with new. The buildings that remain are the same ones I knew as a child, but they seem squat and cramped, not exactly in the right place or in the correct alignment with or proportion to each other. Which one was Smith's Grocery, which the dry goods store? I locate what I think must be the old motion picture theater, and it houses—what else?—a dinky little video shop. I recognize the old post office and Manning's Garage, although it is not a garage anymore and it no longer belongs to Manning.

In the Cumby of my memories, I can move about freely and with confidence, knowledgeable about the secret nooks and crannies as only an insider can be, certain of where I am going and what I will find there. In the Cumby of the present, even to the extent that the past is preserved, I feel disoriented, awkward, and claustrophobic—and almost totally distanced. I am at the moment an outsider here. My name and my origins here mean that I have "a foot in the door," as the old folks might say, but becoming an insider again will take tact, tenacity, and a sort of insight that I hope I can still exercise. Becoming an insider again could, in fact, take more time than I have left to me in this life: earning trust and acceptance can be a very slow process.

Three or four buildings down from the old post office, which stands on a corner by Farm Road 247, there is a space where one or possibly two of the original buildings have disappeared. In this tiny space, townspeople—specifically, the Masonic Lodge, according to a prominent metal placard—have constructed a miniature park, curbed and framed by three-globed street lamps. The park is equipped with a little bandstand and a number of wrought-iron benches. A historical marker notes momentous events in Cumby's history: its founding, its first post office, the coming of the railroad and of the Masons, and its most distinguished writer, Ben Green. In its very incongruity, the little park is a startling discovery; the presence of the marker, with its belated attempt at recognition, comes as a minor revelation, at least. The town, I realize (something I have always known but have never seriously considered before), has always worked and still works at creating its own legend. Probably individuals involved in this process would be better satisfied with a phrase like "establishing its historical significance," but there is much appropriation, exaggeration, and omission. The legend of "place" that they create and the "historical significance" that they work to establish maintain the "high tone"[2] that permits the psychic and spiritual survival of people living in a still somewhat isolated area where work

The ghost town

is hard, profits are few, and recognition or credit or acclaim is rarely forthcoming.

Certain local families have been especially active in promoting this concept of past. The Green family comes immediately to mind. Wilson A. Green settled in Cumby (then Black Jack Grove) in 1852, operated a tavern and mill, and in 1870 erected the town's first cotton gin. He was the father of M. M. Green, whose son Ben F. "Doc" Green, the area's most dependable veterinarian, preserved and displayed family artifacts. Ben was also a popular storyteller, especially among the assortment of men who gathered on pretty days in front of the barbershop or Callan's Grocery Store. The wonderful woman who, through four years of high school English, demanded that I develop a clear, grammatically correct style of writing and showed me the might and magnificence of great literature was a Green—Ruth Green Bowden —and she was a critic, a storyteller, and a contributor to local histories.

My own family, on the paternal side (the Winnifords and Alexanders), likewise promoted the idea of family as enacting a continuing tradition and as functioning significantly within larger movements of history. Great-uncle Sam Winniford was a traveling fiddler renowned as much for his storytelling as for his fiddling; his brother, Great-uncle Norve, a county commissioner and for years a rural mail carrier, frequently wrote for local newspapers and was documented by local historians.[3] Cousin Jesse Alexander made regular contributions to Greenville newspapers, and Aunt Ella Winniford Taylor and Cousin Bessie Winniford McRae were often called on to co-write articles dealing with local history.

To me, it is still somewhat of a revelation that the Greens and Winnifords and Alexanders and other storytellers with whom I am less familiar were transmitting and in some cases preserving "lore." Nevertheless, I came to understand through my study with Carl Lindahl that folklore is a community-based process through which people express and negotiate their shared understandings, beliefs, and concerns. Folklore is the unofficial culture of any group, not just the product of the poor or old-fashioned. No matter what their social background, groups like families share beliefs, attitudes, gestures, behaviors, and tales that they, as Lindahl expresses it, "create and reshape as unofficial expressions of group identity."[4] It is not difficult for me to see that the storytellers and writers I have mentioned were negotiating group identity; that is, they were selecting and transmitting stories that created the sense of past history, present status, and future influence that they wanted associated with their families and their community. The tellers gave presumably accurate accounts—based either on their own memories of events or on anecdotes related to them by other family members—of "historically significant" episodes in which family members had participated.

These family legends add up to the town's folkloric or legendary history, and they propose a concept of mission and accomplishment too grand for the meager land and its diminishing potential to accommodate. The vision of both past and present is out of proportion to what an outsider can perceive as either historical or present reality. But the important thing, as I came gradually to realize, is that the framework of values inherent in this vision maintains order and dignity despite poverty and focus and identity in the face of change and chaos. I have lived for many years in a fast-moving, progress-driven culture in which such order, dignity, focus, and identity are not operative and are in fact sadly missing; and yet, in some elemental way, they operate for me—probably because Cumby, or at least the Cumby of the past, remains my dreamscape.

In the little park that seems a concrete manifestation of the town's legend making, I run my fingers across the inscription on the historical marker and consider how many of the stories that constitute my own heritage are extensions of, or elaborations or variations on, the events that the marker commemorates. From the gradual accumulation of this folk information throughout my formative years—told according to each informant's memory of it and interpreted through that narrator's special experiences and observations—I formulated my ideas about what mattered in life and of how human beings managed to meet life's demands and retain their humanity. It was the durability of the values transmitted in large part through my family's and my hometown's legend making that, even before I arrived at any coherent explanation for it, had convinced me of the importance of the folkloric materials that are part of my heritage.

It occurs to me in touching the tangible marker with its powerful, intangible message (which only someone who had been an insider in this community could really decipher) that what I am proposing to do in collecting and interpreting the stories I remember is not very different from what all these other tellers of tales have done. I will be no more personal and subjective than they have been. It is reassuring at this moment to recall that Barre Toelken singles out as an important unifying characteristic that "all folklore participates in a distinctive, dynamic process" which he describes as constant change or "variation within a tradition." He further portrays the materials of folklore as "tradition-based communicative units informally exchanged in dynamic variation through space and time."[5] I know that each of the stories from my childhood was told at least a little differently from the way I now remember it.

Nevertheless, some of the narratives—my grandmother's, for example—have, over the years, assumed an almost scriptural status for me: I will never tell them as well as she did, though part of me always wants to, because in my mind they remain *her* stories. Although even my strongest recollections do not allow me to retell her stories as powerfully as I remember her to have told them, what

I have learned about the dynamics of folklore has finally allowed me to accept the value of my own tellings. That my memories and perceptions may be somewhat different from those of individuals who told the tales to me (or from those of persons who presently reconstruct those times past) does not necessarily constitute a misrepresentation or betrayal of the place and the people. I may add another facet or dimension to a body of material that has been evolving and accreting since the area's earliest settlement—and I may, perhaps, make much of it accessible to a public outside that limited area's boundaries.

But even with my fingers still spread against the face of the inscribed marker, even as I come to see with greater clarity and to accept with greater equanimity my peculiar role as folklorist, I come to a new and significant realization. The type of storytelling, or the storytelling mode, that the little park with its historical marker represents for me involves specifically the lore of the paternal side of my family, the Winnifords and Alexanders. The Winnifords and Alexanders created a family saga that corresponds to and often dovetails with the "legend" of the little town. Many of the stories that I have remembered and cherished from my childhood do not, however, fit into this mode. They are not stories about events, or family participation in events, such as the marker commemorates. They are instead stories about human needs and emotions, about reward and punishment, about sin and retribution, about faith and hope, about human contacts with the unexplainable and the supernatural. These are, for the most part, stories told by the maternal side of my family, the Wards and Wolfs, and they seem to me to represent another storytelling mode altogether.

From the outset, I feel a strong obligation to distinguish between the two storytelling modes as I perceive them, out of a sense of fairness both to the folkloric materials I am collecting and to the people who transmitted them. Yet I am conscious that making such a distinction involves serious complications. What distinguishes one body of lore from the other is less a matter of genre or type than it is of how the tales in each body functioned for tellers and listeners and of how the situations in which the stories were told affected a given tale's expected impact (and, hence, the manner in which the tale was performed and the attitude with which it was received). Form, subject, and theme were often less distinguishing factors than was context.

Certain generalizations can be made, rather spontaneously, on the basis of my most vivid memories of storytelling sessions. The Winnifords and Alexanders told their anecdotes at family gatherings on holidays, during farm activities such as hog killings and cotton picking, and while taking refuge down in the storm cellar from vile Texas weather. The storytellers were frequently men, the audience boisterous, and the mood one of hilarity. The Wards and Wolfs sometimes told their stories out on my Grandmother Ward's sleeping porch in town but most frequently at graveyard workdays at Long Cemetery, the rural graveyard where members of four generations of the two families were buried. The storytellers were predominantly women, the audience quiet and intense, the mood serious and secretive.

The foregoing is, however, an oversimplification of the two storytelling modes as I have come to recognize them: the gender distinction, for instance, is not as exact as these descriptions suggest, since there were both men and women storytellers in each mode; storm-cellar storytelling might be earnest and personal rather than rowdy and humorous. The key, perhaps, to the difference between the two modes lies in what the people in each style thought they were doing when they told stories. The Winnifords and Alexanders, I am certain, regarded their storytelling as creating and transmitting a family "history"—a saga, if you will. They were convinced that they were dealing with absolute, objective truths. These families had occupied their land for three generations and expected to remain there, so "facts" could be checked out and errors duly noted. More casual storytelling was, for them, a source of entertainment and encouragement while they performed arduous tasks that enabled them to survive and to continue their history. Their stories were rarely religious or moral in content or intent and, with a notable exception or two, never contained elements of the supernatural.

The Wards and Wolfs were, on the other hand, more mobile, and they were evasive and close-mouthed about family history. They told stories to teach moral lessons, to emphasize warnings against misconduct, and to inspire listeners to remain strong in faith and good works. Their storytelling helped sustain a value system and a lifestyle that was essentially "portable"—that is, as applicable to one place as to another. They were careless about "factual" details, were attracted to stories that were not necessarily about family members, and frequently employed religious and supernatural elements. Their audiences often contained people who were not family members.

Certainly, I feel challenged to become a part of the storytelling tradition that the park and the historical marker seem to me to represent. After all, the Winnifords and Alexanders were among the settlers the marker mentions. Later, the menfolk went off and fought in the Civil War or joined the gold rush—while the womenfolk stayed behind to struggle with loneliness and the elements in order to hold onto the land. The thought of retelling these "historical" stories is exciting. Yet many of the tales that exerted a subtle but powerful influence throughout my life belong to the other storytelling mode. And I am far enough along in my collecting process to sense that this body of lore is the more fragile, the more controversial, the more likely to be forever lost. Attempting to do justice to both storytelling modes is a daunting prospect.

Keenly aware as I am that what I am proposing to do in collecting and representing the lore from my childhood bears little resemblance to other folklore collections with which I am familiar, I am drawn to Zora Neale Hurston and her *Mules and Men*.[6] The attraction could be a treacherous one, of course. As a collector of folklore, Hurston has not received scholarly acclaim from folklorists, primarily because she only partially adhered to scholarly standards. And while it appears that Hurston may now receive more recognition as a folklorist than she has in the past, her status in the field is still shaky. For instance, Rosan Jordan's 1992 paper in *Southern Folklore* is a splendid defense of Hurston as a "holistic folklorist" against detractors like John Dorst, who criticizes her participant-observer fieldwork and claims that *Mules and Men* represents a failure to fully connect with the Other.[7] Clearly, Hurston's reputation as a folklorist is open to controversy; she was and is a controversial figure.

On a personal level, I can identify with Hurston, who described herself as a wanderer, "not so much in geography, but in time. Then not so much in time as in spirit."[8] Perhaps I too qualify as a "prodigal daughter," to use a term originated by Lucinda M. MacKethan in her critical study of this black woman anthropologist and folklorist of the 1930s.[9] Hurston left her hometown, and, after an absence during which she continued her education and had new and varied experiences, returned to that community with a different perspective and an increased awareness of the richness of its culture. Hurston, however, had been away from Eatonville, Florida, only a few years when she returned as an anthropologist and folklorist. For me, the time lapse is much greater, which poses special problems—but the basic scenario is the same.

The communities in which Hurston's lore and my own lore originated had important characteristics in common. Both were insular, rural communities considered backward, primitive, and economically deprived by the culture at large. To the extent that both towns were aware of being affected by the larger culture, they perceived it as essentially hostile, as *other* than their own, as strange and potentially threatening. In both communities, folklore contributed to a sense of cultural cohesion and individual self-worth. The tales clarified the behavior that the group approved, instilled the values perceived as essential to the community's lifestyle, and, as Robert Hemenway points out, "suggest[ed] strategies necessary for the preservation of the group in a hostile environment."[10]

Finally, Hurston's relationship to her community and its lore seems similar to my own link to the little Hopkins County community in which I was born and to the stories that I remember from my childhood. As Karla F. C. Holloway notes, Hurston "held a linguistic as well as cultural identity with and empathy for the 'informants' and accepted a responsibility to celebrate their cultures through her double vision." This feeling of responsibility affected Hurston's decisions regarding the format that she used for reporting her collected materials. Hurston returned to a community that was still very much as it had been when she left it and was probably able to collect information from the same storytellers who so impressed her as a child. I, on the other hand, am attempting to re-create a community as it existed forty or fifty years ago and as it is remembered by participants or by their children and grandchildren. Cumby and the farming communities around it have changed. This section of Texas may still be "backward" as compared to more urban areas, but much of its insularity has vanished. Because I, like Hurston, hold a "linguistic as well as cultural identity with and empathy for [my] 'informants,'" I, too, feel a responsibility to represent their culture—as it was in the past—as fairly and accurately as possible.[11]

But Zora Neale Hurston's works can serve me as models only in a most rudimentary fashion. Her role remains that of the folklore collector and anthropologist of the early decades of this century. She is essentially an accepted and trusted outsider who merely listens and records and who does not permit her own thoughts and feelings to intrude in a way that would affect the detachment of her collections. Hurston's stance of detachment cannot be duplicated in my project, of course. Although a few of the stories in my compilation are taped, a great majority of them are reproduced from memory—memory that is often based on hearing the story told several times and perhaps by more than one storyteller.

As a first-person narrator, I must attempt to reproduce storytelling situations in the past when I participated as an insider who was involved both intellectually and emotionally in the circumstances that produced the stories and in the audience response to the storytelling process. My "double vision" involves not only examining how the story seemed to affect narrator and audience at the time it was told (when I was a child and an insider) but also contemplating how I (as a more distanced and experienced adult outsider) now perceive those dynamics to have worked. Such a procedure involves providing historical, social, economic, religious, and even psychological context, and it involves interpretation. At the same time, I know that I must avoid the trap of seeming to imply that some overarching functional model explains all storytelling situations and the stories that were told at these gatherings, large and small. I must resist any temptation to "tie things up in a neat little package." Because I was there as observer and participant, I can attest with certainty that some of the stories can be explained in terms of function. I am aware, however, of the complexities of human interrelationships; thus, context is frequently a more reliable guide to analysis and interpretation.

I make no claim to be discovering absolute or objective truths. I am more interested in the truths that each version of a story conveys for its teller and listeners. What I expect my collection to do, most pointedly, is to show the intensity, accuracy, and redundancy with which many of the most popular tales from both storytelling modes—and some of the most important ritual occasions during which they were told—reflect the major values and complex interactions of the community in which I grew up. Many people have written ethnographies of tale-telling communities, but my project will be an ethnography *in tales* of a community. The tales constitute the primary ethnographic material.

What I bring to the collecting task, and to the task of providing context and interpretation, is the perspective of someone who left the Cumby-Hopkins County area, continued her education, and experienced other people, places, and things. I can speak, or write, as one who accepted or rejected the "truths" of the stories but who still believed them integral to the idea of self. I am someone for whom the old values worked (or perhaps at times did not work) in preserving the integrity of soul. I have been broke and have not resorted to theft, have been hungry and have chosen not to beg, have wavered through sorrow and loss but have not disintegrated, have failed and lived on the streets without being drawn into crime and violence. That I have always known who I am has much to do with the dreamscape against which all conditions of mind and body and soul are invariably measured. This knowledge accounts for my survival and my return, both to the abstract concept of mission and to the concrete place of my birth. I know of no more powerful validation of the lore I am recollecting than this.

Chapter Two

Getting a Handle on the Past

Four days into my allotted time of exploration, research, and fieldwork, I return to the little town with my brother, James Winniford, and my niece, Shannon—all three of us "hell bent," as the old farmers around that part of the county used to say, on "reconstructing the past." But we are not as naive as we were in the beginning about the complications involved in such reconstruction, nor are we 100 percent optimistic about the degree of success we can expect.

The present visit to Cumby and Hopkins County is, admittedly, not "fieldwork" in the conventional sense. It is more in the nature of an aide-mémoire for both my brother and me, ventured upon with a sense of mild desperation because we have realized how limited are my other human resources: most of the people who comprised the folk groups we remember from childhood are dead. Moreover, even when I locate someone who may be able to provide information, I am not attempting to mine current oral tradition: I am asking them to recall traditions from the past, traditions connected with a particular time, place, and circumstance. My experiences have been and are, therefore, highly personal, individual, and peculiar to the kind of project I am attempting. Collecting from people with whom one has had a lifelong association and strong emotional involvement can be daunting. There is no way of remaining unaffected by the nature of previous relationships and by the ways in which the collecting process may influence such ties in the

Author with brother, James Winniford, in front of his favorite pecan tree

future; there is no way to avoid feeling that sitting down around a tape recorder stultifies, trivializes, and even kills the very thing I am trying to revive.

Early in my work on the Hopkins County material, I began to discover the unexpected and disturbing problems that collecting can create. Memories of three collecting debacles, in particular, haunt me as my brother, niece, and I begin our day of exploring the Cumby area. The first occurred shortly after completing my first graduate-level folklore course—the course that inspired me to pursue the project of collecting and recollecting the stories from my childhood—in late August of 1990. I arranged a conventional taping session with Cousin Mamie Winniford Robertson, whose story about Great-aunt Becky's tragic Civil War romance appears in chapter 5. We met at her little house in Cumby, and the taping session went smoothly, with none of the hitches I might have anticipated. I was relieved and delighted. By the time I got around to attempting to transcribe the tapes, however, Cousin Mamie had died. I discovered to my horror that the recorder had picked up all the distractions of which I had been mostly unconscious because I was focused on Cousin Mamie's physical presence: her lively face, her body movements, her positive energy. Clearly audible were the false starts, the sometimes labored breathing, the searching pauses, and the inadvertent sounds of pain and fatigue that escaped from throat and chest—and there was no visual Cousin Mamie to counteract them. I could not at first bear to listen to the tapes in their entirety, and for some months I could not even contemplate working on the transcription. (I made no attempt to reproduce the painful distractions in my transcriptions.)

An emotional reaction to a taping session, sufficient to interfere with the transcription and use of the material taped, would be unlikely to result from interaction with informants less intimately known and intricately involved in the collector's own life. I do not, as a matter of fact, like the term *informant* because it does not evoke the kind of relationship that I as a collector of folklore prefer to have with the person from whom I am collecting. Bruce Jackson, in *Fieldwork,* acknowledges that there are connotative problems with "informant" and offers a number of designations used by other folklorists: "respondent," "participant," "interviewee," "source," "consultant."[1] "Sharer" would suit me better, but it is a word that looks better in print than it sounds when spoken aloud. Therefore, it won't quite do. Still, I like to think that the person from whom I am collecting shares what he or she knows with me. Sharing implies certain conditions that I consider important: willingness on the part of the sharer; an acknowledgment that I have made a valid claim on his or her store of information; and a reciprocal interaction between the two of us, collector and provider of lore.

My convictions in this regard further complicated my second unhappy collecting experience, certain emotion-charged taping sessions with Aunt Minnie Foster, who supplied one of the Uncle Fate stories used in chapter 8 and some items of cemetery lore in chapter 6. Aunt Minnie is actually my Grandmother Ward's orphaned niece, whom she reared from infancy. Minnie had for years been a close companion to my grandmother and had always participated in my grandmother's audiences during Sunday afternoon storytelling sessions out on the Ward sleeping porch as well as on graveyard working days at Long Cemetery. She seemed an ideal source for the materials I was collecting: she would be able to correct childish misconceptions I might have about my grandmother's storytelling methods and the stories she told; she could also probably supply details I had missed and might know tales I had never heard.

During two winters when I was going about my taping in earnest, Aunt Minnie was living with my brother on his farm near Longview. I considered this arrangement fortuitous indeed. Aunt Minnie was also willing to have our interviews taped. In a bitter and depressed old age, however, she had determined that, as an orphan foster child, she was excluded from the intimate Ward family circle. She had thus formed the habit of repressing or denying memories that conflicted with this negative interpretation of her girlhood. I filled two and a half tapes during my longest session with her but got little of the information for which I was probing. Eventually, Aunt Minnie did make a passing reference to some superstitions connected with Long Cemetery, and she told the story of the deaths of the bois d'arc trees used in chapter 6. Her Uncle Fate story, found in chapter 8, was obtained almost by trickery. She interposed the anecdote while my brother and I were casually discussing the Uncle Fate material, and I happened to have a tape recorder handy. Although Aunt Minnie readily agreed to my using the story thus taped, I could not help wondering if she were truly a willing "sharer" or if I were pressuring her into relinquishing tidbits of information she did not really want to supply. These circumstances considered, the scanty material that I got from Aunt Minnie posed ethical problems almost as difficult as the obstacles of collecting.

Surprisingly, in my work with my brother, James, I have encountered even more unsettling complications than with the previously mentioned sharers, despite his good-humored support and tireless efforts on behalf of my project. My first taping session with my brother was probably the most discouraging of my early fieldwork experiences. To begin with, my brother and I discovered that, although we grew up in the same family, our experiences with the family's folklore differed markedly. This is probably explained by gender differences. As a male, he was exposed to entirely different materials—or to contrasting versions of the same lore—from what I as a female heard and presumed to be the prevailing tradition.

Astonished as we were at this discovery, we were equally amazed that we had not been aware of these differences before. We realized that we had both been much more *passive* carriers of the family's lore than we had believed ourselves to be. Although James and I are both teachers and public speakers, we had not created storytelling situations that would have made our conflicting experiences and information apparent. We had not, for instance, told stories during the gatherings of our two families, where we might have shared the tales from the past with our children. Furthermore, we had not retold the stories to each other. We often made references or allusions to various of the old tales, assuming that our memories of such anecdotes were basically alike. It was a shock to find out that when one of us had jokingly asked, "Remember those stories about Great Uncle Fate?" and the other had laughed and nodded, we were both, in fact, deluded: my brother recalled one set of stories; I recalled another.

Early on in our collecting and recollecting of the family stories, we had lengthy discussions and debates—sometimes quite heated—about how these differences happened and what they might mean. Our discoveries and the explanations we eventually settled upon were emotionally disturbing. There was a gathering uneasiness that the past was not as "cut and dried" as we had believed it to be and a nagging guilt that we had not been "tradition bearers" in exactly the same way as had our parents, grandparents, and other kin as well as the communities of which they had all been a part.

My work with James has been wonderfully productive and positive. Yet at various times during our collaborations, I have had serious reservations about what we might accomplish. I suspect that these reservations have resulted more from the closeness of our relationship, the nature of that relationship in the past, and my often unrealistic expectations than from technical or logistical hurdles we have had to overcome. I began my first taping sessions with my brother in late December, 1991, and early January, 1992, during a Christmas break visit at his farm close to Longview. The weather was bad, which created endless distractions: the fire in the wood-burning heater in the room where we worked needed rekindling; the dairy cattle needed to be let into the lot and fed; ice must be scraped from the back stoop. But more unnerving than the constant interruptions was the fact that the taping did not proceed as I had planned. My brother was not comfortable with the interview format, no matter how carefully I imagined I was handling it. When he "got on a roll," as he put it, he found my efforts to guide the discussion merely irritating, causing him to "lose his train of thought" or taking "the wind right out of his sails."

Midway through the proceedings, my brother barricaded himself behind a table, appropriated both recorder and microphone, and talked nonstop. I settled for being an appreciative, if somewhat nonplussed, audience, for I felt some guilt about not doing my "job," whatever I naively perceived that to be. It did occur to me that my brother's approach was entirely appropriate to the storytelling mode used on my father's side of the family, where the dominant male or patriarch held forth without interruption. My brother was offering authentic Winniford discourse, though it might be moving in unanticipated directions. Although it is true that James provided a lot of information that did not relate to my project, it is also significantly true that he told stories and described customs and events that I would not have known to ask about. It was because he was free to meander verbally through memories that were important to him that I became aware that he knew stories I had not heard and that his versions of many of the "familiar" stories were quite different from my own.

Toward the end of that first collecting visit in the winter of 1991–92, my brother suggested, "Why don't you just let me tape whatever else comes to my mind and mail the tapes to you? That'll save us a lot of trouble. The weather's bad, and I'm having to jump up every five minutes and tend to things—and I can tell it's making you nervous. Let's just relax and enjoy these last few days." Relax and enjoy we did. I may have had some misgivings about James's commitment to supplying whatever additional information he possessed, but he is a man of his word. A few weeks later the tapes arrived, a treasure trove of personal experiences and reminiscences, family history, nearly forgotten agricultural practices, jokes, songs, and miscellaneous bits of gossip and "tomfoolery."

What I have discovered while working with my brother is the importance of flexibility, both in my methods of collecting and in my expectations for what there is to collect. I prefer painting with watercolors to painting with oils because the former medium provides surprises, sometimes disastrous but often potentially glorious. The test of the artist's skill is the ability to incorporate the glorious surprise so that it lends sublimity to the entire painting. Collecting, even re-collecting, lore is a similarly chancy and exciting process. The keen disappointment of not finding some item where one expected to find it—one of collecting's disastrous surprises—can be offset by discovering what one never suspected might be there.

However positively I may have come to regard my work with my brother, the truth is that my first few ventures in fieldwork proved enormously disappointing. This was because the few remaining storytellers either had not kept the stories alive within themselves (or given them any real significance), or they suffered from physical and psychological afflictions that interfered with their recalling and sharing information. I had begun the project with a body of internalized and remembered stories that were important to me. I therefore assumed that reawakening and sharing the tales, specifically with people who had heard the stories told in the original contexts, would be the best way to reconnect with the Cumby and Hopkins County of years past and with the body of folklore that I believed had evolved there. I had realized that I would be collecting what folklorists call "salvage folklore," which, as Bruce Jackson comments, "is always collected in radically different contexts than the ones in which it was formerly learned and performed." I could not join the same group of storytellers that I remembered from the graveyard working days of my youth; I could not listen to the same rugged farmers tell jokes and regale each other during chilly hog killings. But I had hoped to be able to gather what Jackson rather poetically describes as "bits and pieces about a world of another time or a life in another place" from a substantial number of "sharers."[2] I had imagined that so doing would give my project the sort of authenticity I wanted it to have.

As my experience in gathering information revealed that this substantial number of sharers was no longer available, I was faced with the scary prospect of doing the bulk of my fieldwork in the remote and treacherous "fields" of my own memory. During those remembered times, I interacted as an "insider" in that place and that culture and among the people living then. Just as I am now an "outsider" in the Cumby and Hopkins County of the present, so is my present self an outsider in the remembered place and culture and among those remembered people. The recalled place is "other" because its topography has now been rearranged and buildings erased; the culture is other because it has not remained static or even precisely ongoing; the people are other because they are dead or irrevocably changed by sickness, age, and circumstance. Great chunks of place, culture, and people are lost, and the bits and pieces I can salvage are imperfectly representative. Further, the self who was an insider then is now other. Bright, curious, and observant as that girl was, I have to question what she saw and heard as well as how she perceived and interpreted all that was going on around her. Ultimately, I have to examine how much the stories I remember were, in fact, a part of the old community. I feel threatened, first by the absence of sharers who might validate or reinforce my perceptions and second by input from sources like Aunt Minnie, who seemed not to value the stories in the same way that I do.

My image of myself as folklorist has certainly been altered by the realities of my circumstances and the nature of my project. Kenneth S. Goldstein's very readable *A Guide for Field Workers in Folklore* intimidates me: his approach to fieldwork is so beautifully structured, calm, and almost scientific that it hardly seems applicable to the emotion-charged encounters, dead ends, and soul searching that mark my labors with my project.[3] It would have been reassuring, for instance, to follow the directions given in Edward D. Ives's detailed manual for field workers, *The Tape-Recorded Interview: A Manual for Field Workers in Folklore and Oral History,* in which he discusses how a tape recorder works, how to select the right equipment for the job at hand, how to set up and effectively record interviews, and how to process what one has collected.[4] But Ives's common-sense manual presupposes an adequate budget and a field in which informants are alive, available, and healthy.

My own low-budget operation allows me few options: I have to make do with the equipment at hand. I have a little Emerson tape recorder that was, I think, a Mother's Day gift from my son some years back; friends gathered up and donated their blank tapes, and I accepted them gladly without much attention to quality or tape length. I take a lot of photographs, mostly for my own reference, and I have used my handy Kodak S 100EF with donated film. I may fantasize about being a well-equipped, well-organized folklore collector—a Richard Dorson type, efficient, aggressive, and always productive. In practice, I am a sort of collector-bum. At least my folklore mother-figure, Zora Neale Hurston, had a little car in which she could comb the countryside. I find myself hailing the Greyhound and hitching rides from my sympathetic brother, niece, or any other kind soul who appears to be headed in a promising direction.

My idea of the final shape my project can take has been likewise transformed through my attempts at traditional fieldwork; through sessions with my brother in which we sometimes taped, sometimes analyzed and debated the materials from our childhood; and through my gradual comprehension of the fluidity and elusiveness of the stories I am attempting to collect and recollect and of the culture in which they evolved and were told. My original plans for the project were based on my initial, quite "unfolkloric," notion that the stories I remember had a fixity that transcended context. My unexamined conviction that the stories had an unchanging, nearly scriptural quality and exhibited much the same meaning and influence for all tellers and listeners made me feel insecure in my own memories and perceptions of the past. I wanted the experience of finding sharers who could validate my assumptions that there existed only one authentic version of each of the stories. This was a version that some sharer would remember in its detailed and accurately structured wholeness or that could be assembled from the memories of several sources.

I knew that I could not tell the stories through the voice of my grandmother, the storyteller from whom I had heard most of the stories I originally planned to gather. I imagined, however, that I could substitute the voices of sharers whose memories reinforced or "documented" my own. I had in mind that I could amass the stories—as "things" that existed in some sort of stable, timeless, and spaceless rigidity—and by collecting them somehow be able to portray the cultural essence of a time, place, and people that were integral to my sense of self. I thus envisioned a text from which I as collector and writer could withdraw, or in which I could and probably should participate minimally or at most dialogically.

My plans for such a text emerged naturally from my misconceptions and insecurities, not from any self-conscious literary, folkloric, or anthropological stance. I did not, as do George E. Marcus and Michael M. J. Fischer, for instance, weigh the relative merits of producing a realist or modernist or postmodernist (or positivist or structuralist or poststructuralist) text.[5] By the same token, necessity rather than literary taste or folkloric-anthropological conviction dictates that I modify my original plans for presenting my project. A paucity of sharers makes such a text an impossibility. Either I must resign myself to producing no text at all or produce a text in which mine is the pervasive voice and over which I exert obvious and certainly subjective control. If the stories are to be told, I must tell them—a matter of salvaging bits and pieces of the original narrative experiences that so affected me during my growing up.

Hence my decision to attempt to lend these fragments meaning and authenticity by telling them in context, and hence my rather inadvertent venture into ethnography. Hence therefore, too, my present visit to Cumby and Hopkins County. My gut instinct that I could not write with authority about Cumby—past or present—while sitting in an apartment in Houston corresponds to a commonly held principle of ethnographers. This precept is, as David Jacobson succinctly states, that "the ethnographer's presence in the field is the basis for establishing the credibility of an ethnographic account."[6] Jacobson cites authorities on this topic such as Marcus and Cushman (1982), Clifford (1983), and Gerta (1988). My gut instinct puts me in good company, although my presence in Cumby may serve psychological as well as literary needs.

My brother's strong interest in the stories told by the paternal side of our family convinced me to enlarge my project to include those stories. I am sure that his renewed enthusiasm for all the family stories, paternal and maternal, has to do with their function as family history. James is concerned primarily with stories for which he *can* find accurate and authentic versions; that is, versions that can be documented by public records. This makes his search and his goals different from mine. My niece, Shannon, is interested specifically in tracing family genealogy, and she has perfected her research skills in that pursuit. She finds the stories fascinating and enjoyable; more pointedly, they provide clues and leads she can follow in tracing complicated genealogy. We travel together and they are, we all agree, my "helpers"—but we are hunting subtly different game. Sometimes our purposes and methods complement each other, sometimes they contradict.

❧ "This part of town was sure different then," James recalls ruefully. We are standing once again on a worn sidewalk in old downtown Cumby, the ghost town as we have come to think of it. Shannon stands with us, hunched against the January cold. For me, this will be a second day of attempting to resurrect the past, phoenixlike, from its ruined remnants. For my brother, it will more likely be a nostalgic journey like several we have previously taken traveling not-quite-familiar roads to not-quite-familiar places where we spent our childhood.

My brother does not have to clarify what he means by *then*. We are both remembering when the faded hulls of buildings were in good condition and housed thriving small businesses, when the sounds of the overburdened cotton gin throbbed in a purple autumn haze, when Saturday afternoon sidewalks were crowded with farm folk and their shy, sun-baked children, and when, even on weekdays, clumps of impatient people gathered out in front of Sommers' Drugstore waiting the arrival of the Greyhound.

The paternal side of my family—the Winnifords and Alexanders—were cotton farmers, so the little town of Cumby was pivotal to their operations. It was the place where they came to buy flour, sugar, and other staples; where they purchased seeds for planting; and where they brought their wagon loads of cotton to be ginned and baled, graded and auctioned. My mother's immediate family (my grandmother, an uncle, and two aunts) lived within the city limits, only a short walk from the old downtown business district. Ironically, however, the town probably functioned less meaningfully in their lives than it did for the families of farmers. The womenfolk on the maternal side were reclusive, seldom socializing with other people in town and refusing to attend local churches even during revival season in the summer.

Uncle Bernice, my mother's older brother who had been shell-shocked in World War I, took a daily morning walk into town and sat in front of the barbershop or the feed store talking or sometimes arguing bitterly with other men who gathered there. One of the grocers occasionally ordered special cuts of beef for Uncle Bernice, and whatever other grocery shopping was done for the family locally my uncle did, trudging home with the sack at noon. Both families—farm folk and city folk—did their "important" shopping in Sulphur Springs (sixteen miles to the east) or in the Hunt County towns of Commerce (ten miles to the north) or Greenville (some twenty miles to the west). Nevertheless, however tenaciously both sides of my family may have clung to the values and customs they brought with them from their places of origin, they conformed at least superficially to the lifestyle of this tiny Texas town.

And Cumby was indeed small, though it did not seem so to a little girl accustomed to the isolation of the farm. It is strange to remember nights out on my Grandmother Ward's sleeping porch, when the "sounds of the city" so impressed me: the groaning of the big trucks on the highway, the whistle and rumble of the freight train, the crowing of roosters in a couple of dozen back yards. It seemed to me that I was in a hub of teeming human activity. The truth was that a half-century ago this part of Texas was a great, slow, silent space where noise startled the ear.

The settlement of Cumby dates back to the first half of the nineteenth century. For information concerning the settlement of the Black Jack Grove-Cumby area, I have relied on accounts given by three local historians, Gladys St. Clair, Florene Chapman Adams, and Sue Via Brazell.[7] In or about the year 1839, the Texas Rangers (or Indian fighters, as they were called locally) selected a little grove of blackjack timber on a hill just west of the business district of the present town of Cumby as a camping place. The grove of trees was surrounded by open territory, which offered the Rangers the advantage of preventing a surprise attack by the Indians from any direction. The Rangers designated this camping place as the Black Jack Grove.

The first settlers began to pitch their tents near this camp to give them protection from invasion by the Indians. The blackjack tree, incidentally, is a type of small-leaf oak, whose dark bark and rock-hard acorns have a pungent, musty smell, especially when wet. It was probably this noticeable odor that convinced both settlers and Indians that the leaves, bark, and acorns from the tree were poisonous. The Ranger camp was also a camping place for wagon trains on the Old Jefferson Trail from Jefferson, Texas, to places west.

This was mainly because "the Black Jack trees also served as protection from the Indians. When the Indians got on the warpath, they would chase the settlers back into the Black Jack trees, but the Indians would stop at the edge of the grove of trees because they were superstitious of the Black Jack trees."[8] Most people believed that the Indians feared this particular spot because of the presence of evil spirits.

Who gets credit for being Cumby's first settler depends a lot on whose descendant is compiling the personal history of the town. Indeed, representation is uneven among the more reputable historians, as well. Wash Cole, who settled in Cumby in 1842, is often mentioned as Cumby's first settler. Actually, he may have been preceded in 1841 by a man named Stewart who located seven miles northwest of the Ranger camp. Sue Via Brazell comments that the man and his wife had lived there almost a year before the wife "had the pleasure of seeing another woman," so it was "a lonesome life." A wave of settlers arrived before 1852, including the Smiths, Rippys, Brighams, Coles, Bakers, Arnolds, Branoms, Jordans, Findleys, and Mathewses. In 1852 several other families moved in, including W. Y. Box, Urbane Alexander (my great-great grandfather), C. Garouth, Robert Greaves, Wilson A. Green, and James Brown. The Alexanders came to Texas from Illinois, the Winnifords from Virginia; other early settlers migrated from the Carolinas, Mississippi, and Alabama, as well.

The early history of the little settlement that would eventually be named Cumby highlights the acquisition of the things that made survival possible for the hard-working people who were settling there. Settlers like the Bakers, Greens, Coles, and Browns owed their prominence in the town to the fact that they operated businesses and provided services necessary to the farming community. Before the windmill was built in 1861, the nearest mill was a water mill located at Sulphur Bluff. A round trip to this mill usually took ten to fifteen days. The first steam mill in the Cumby locality was operated by John R. Baker in 1867. The first cotton gin was erected by W. A. Green about 1870. This gin was a horse gin, as they were called, since horses furnished the power to run the machinery. The gin had a capacity of four or five bales a day. Later, Bill Cole and his father bought the property and replaced the horse with steam, installing a small boiler that held about 250 gallons of water. The Coles also owned a grist mill to grind corn for bread. In 1875 M. D. Brown erected a flour mill, cotton gin, and sawmill combined, originally located a mile east of town and later moved into town.

Getting a post office established is considered by local historians as a crucial juncture in the history of Black Jack Grove-Cumby. The post office in Black Jack Grove, established in 1848, was one of only seven in the county before the Civil War. In connection with its post office, the town went through a series of name changes. Its name was changed to Theodosia in 1857 and then back to Black Jack Grove in 1858. Then, in 1896, new difficulties cropped up. There were two Black Jack Groves in Texas, each with a post office. This resulted in problems with the mail. According to Florene Chapman Adams, "The name was changed to Cumby in 1896 to comply with requests by both the railroad and the Post Office Department. Congressman D. B. Culbertson suggested the name in honor of his friend, Colonel Bob Cumby."

Two other events regarded as evidence of Cumby's progress in the last half of the nineteenth century were the building of the railroad and the organization of the Masonic Lodge. Actually, the organization of the Masons in Cumby predated the arrival of the railroad. The Masonic Lodge was organized in 1856. An article in the *Commerce Journal* in January, 1956, states that the early-day Masonic history predates the charter, as Cumby Masons met under a special dispensation as early as April, 1854. The *Journal* article covers a two-day centennial program at which the 100-year-old charter of the lodge was officially retired. A new, duplicate charter was then issued to replace the faded document that gave the Cumby Masons authority to operate their lodge. The article goes on to explain that the original charter, issued at Galveston on January 24, 1856, survived two fires that destroyed the lodge hall and twice was blown away in storms, only to be found and returned.[9]

The railroad was built in 1880 and was called the East Line and Red River Railroad. It was a small type, being narrow gauge, and only light locomotives could travel it, at a speed of eighteen miles per hour. This made it about a day's run from Greenville to Jefferson. The Cotton Belt Railroad wanted to build a roundhouse at Cumby, but the city fathers believed that it would bring in a rough type of people, so they refused to grant the railroad's request. Already, during my childhood, the narrow East Line and Red River Railroad had been supplanted by a heavier track, the LA & T.

The one event in the history of Black Jack Grove-Cumby to which local historians assign most importance was the ladies' march on the saloons in 1896. Before 1896, Black Jack Grove was a place of open-bar saloons, and many of the men wore six-shooters on their hips. (The family legends about Great-uncle Fate and Great-uncle Wood, which figure in later chapters of this book, date back to this era.) In a *Dallas Times Herald* article, "Ladies' March on Saloons Still a Legend in Cumby," writer Tommy Ayres explains: "Cumby then was named Black Jack Grove. And Black Jack Grove was about the roughest, toughest little town on the old Jefferson-to-Dallas road. Fist fights, knifings and shootings marred most every weekend. Three men were killed in a gun battle one day and 'a nice woman wouldn't be caught on the streets on Saturday.'" Ayres quotes Bessie McRae, who was one of Great-uncle Norve Winniford's daughters, as saying, "I've heard all kinds of lewd things went on in those places back then—and a lot of women were worried because their sons were going to them."[10]

What was perhaps even worse, *husbands* were frequenting these "lewd" establishments, too, and serious complications sometimes developed—the upshot of which was that men were not the only ones packing guns. Great-uncle Sam Winniford used to enjoy telling the story about the day a Mrs. Cross came to town to check out reports that her husband was "messing around" with one of the not-so-nice women who patronized the saloons. Convinced the reports were true, Mrs. Cross sought the woman out, challenged her, and shot her dead there in the middle of the main street with the boisterous weekend crowd looking on.

Finally, a group of disgusted citizens forced a local-option election, which amazingly resulted in the town being voted dry. Although all saloons were closed, however, two men continued to sell whiskey in places called "blind tigers." Angry townswomen resolved to do something about the blind tiger saloons that continued to sell booze illegally, but the owners of the blind tigers declared that no woman was going to put them out of business. Their defiance prompted the women's raid on the saloons. The story of this raid varies somewhat from teller to teller, with the point of view depending on the role each narrator's relatives played in the incident. Certain basic details are consistent. On the afternoon of February 6, 1896, twenty-five bonnet-clad women were joined by three local college girls at the home of a Mrs. Goodjohn. There they formulated a plan of action, after which they met at the Baptist Church and prayed over what they were about to do. Then they marched into town, forced their way into the rebel saloons, and disposed of the booze in an orgy of hatchet throwing, overturning and breaking bottles and jugs, and otherwise intimidating saloon owners and patrons.

Historians are probably correct in emphasizing the importance of the rejection of the old open-bar-saloon lifestyle to the people in the Cumby area. From that point on, people around Cumby developed an increasingly moral and straitlaced attitude toward drinking and all activities generally associated with its selling and consumption. During my childhood, both Hopkins and Hunt counties were dry, and old rounders looking for fun hitched the train into Dallas or paid the price demanded by notorious but carefully low-profile bootleggers. So self-conscious were these people about their town's "clean, dry" reputation that when, for instance, drinking was mentioned in any of the stories told at graveyard workings or other gatherings, the narrators always made clear that what was being imbibed was "bootleg booze"—the drinkers did not buy it in Cumby. This was the case even when the tales concerned events that must have happened before 1896.

Although I heard the account of the prohibitionists' raid many times while I was growing up, even then the stories of saloons and shootings and rampaging, angry women did not have much immediacy regarding the street where my brother, niece, and I are now standing. Certainly, impassioned action seems totally remote from the empty "movie set" that old downtown Cumby has become. Such once-violent issues have long since been resolved and perhaps committed to record, as on the marker in the placid little park a few yards down the street. I decide that we need to move on to other remnants of the past. The church we attended as children is still standing, although it is empty and boarded up; the school building that once housed grades one through twelve is still in use; and the old Winniford homeplace where our grandparents lived and died (and where our Aunt Lynna spent her stubbornly independent last years) is still in the family. Some of the buildings remain, although the dwelling burned down. These places should revive thoughts and emotions, bring back memories; perhaps, I suggest to my brother, visiting them would be productive.

The three of us crawl back into the Rambler and drive around the corner to what was once our church, choosing this site as our first stop because it is closest and because, as we already know, there is less to see and investigate. The one-room frame building with its simple pitched roof occupies a narrow city lot. Even when the building was in use and in good repair, it was not an imposing structure, lacking both the steeple and the stained-glass windows that often distinguish Protestant churches. Now the windows are boarded up, and the paint has peeled to reveal the gray old lumber underneath. My niece comments on how small and bleak the building is, concluding that it is hard to imagine it was ever a church at all. My brother and I assure her that we recall a time when the place seemed both stately and holy, when there were bright lights and excitement and, especially during summer revivals, people standing outside or visiting or milling about. "And dodging bugs!" my brother laughs. "Or swatting them with those funeral parlor fans! The bright lights drew them. June bugs and candle flies and sometimes worse—zooming around like dive bombers, landing in people's hair or lodging in their collars!" We chuckle at memories of people and events that we associate with the unattractive little building.

During most of the year, people in and around Cumby honored their denominational affiliations and, from time to time, argued energetically about "scriptural baptism," whether dancing was a sin, and whether a person could "fall from grace." For the most part, one inherited both church affiliation and political party from one's parents, and one "belonged" to both more out of loyalty than conviction. This fact became especially evident in summer, when all the churches held their revivals. The revival schedule was somehow worked out so that no two churches held their meetings simultaneously. Thus, everyone in town had a chance to attend all the revivals, making for an extended season of spiritual inspiration and social activity. The summer revival season was anticipated with much enthusiasm and many preparations. Summer clothing suitable for church must be assembled and, as my mother used to say, "spaced out," so that one did not appear to be wearing the same outfits to every series of meetings. If a family offered to provide food and lodging for the evangelist and the song leader for a night, this could mean rearranging sleeping quarters so that these strangers could have adequate privacy. People on outlying farms had to make sure of transportation.

Religion was a strong but subtle influence in the Cumby in which I grew up. Churches were organized in each community in Hopkins County almost as soon as there was a settlement. "The Methodists and Baptists, who organized in many communities before the Civil War, were followed by the Presbyterians and Christians," Gladys St. Clair explains. About religion in the early history of the county, E. B. Fleming comments: "Religion was far more universally respected than now [1902]. In fact everybody believed in it. The author does not remember of hearing of a skeptic or infidel in the whole county as far back as forty-five years ago. Everybody who could get religion was a member of some church, and those who could not get it rarely ceased to try, and never seemed to doubt the reality of heaven and hell, the existence of God and the inspiration of the Bible."[11]

In 1948 there were six churches in the Cumby city limits—Baptist, Methodist, Presbyterian, Church of Christ, and First Christian—plus, more than likely, what my brother calls an "off-brand" Baptist congregation of some sort. These groups are all, of course, Protestant. Although people imagined that their doctrinal differences were of great import, the teachings of these various denominations produced an amazingly homogenous moral and spiritual lifestyle.

In religion, as in certain other aspects of their lives, people in the Cumby area harked back to the nineteenth century, or, as they would probably have expressed it, they were "old fashioned." Religion provided a frame of reference within which everyone could operate with a comfortable degree of certainty. There were basic tenets or "givens" that everyone accepted, no matter with which religious group they had aligned themselves. Under a humorous heading, "Cussedness, Pure Meanness, Sin and Crime," David Hugh "Dick"

Hare offers a tongue-in-cheek list of the activities that people in Hopkins County considered morally, spiritually, and ethically wrong:

> Stealing, Lying, Not Paying Debts; Murders and Robberies; Shooting Dice and Playing Poker; Drunkedness; Wife Beating; Drinking in Presence of Ladies; Cussing before Preacher, Women and Kids; Talking in Church; Playing Hooky from School; Women Riding a Horse Astraddle; Bobbed Hair for Ladies; Ladies Wearing Dresses above the Knees; Eaves-Dropping (on phones); Drawing a Gun or Knife on a Person; Sunday Picture Shows; Placing a Buggy on a Roof; Not Giving Handouts to Tramps and Beggars; Turpentining Dogs, Cats and Horses; Not Saying Please, Thank You, Goodbye, Howdy and How Are You; Not Keeping One's Word or Cheating; Not Bowing Head for Prayer in Church; Working on Sundays (Ox Not in Ditch); Whistling at the Girls; Slapping or Pulling Girls' Hair; Playing Marbles or Tops "For Keeps"; Matching Money (Heads or Tails); Throwing Eggs at People; Tin-Canning Dogs or Horses; Bobtailing or Castrating Dogs and Cats; Throwing Paperwads and Erasers in School; Shooting a Buzzard and Pot Shotting Quail.[12]

Much of the humor of the above list stems from its satiric method, which suggests problems with prioritizing and, hence, a skewed value system. The list is accurate in covering many of the actions that were regarded with disapproval on moral and religious grounds by people in the Cumby area in the first half of the twentieth century. The implication of a skewed value system is also more or less accurate, at least concerning the society at large. My niece, for instance, ventures a guess that in spite of the strong church presence in the town, people in Cumby and Hopkins County were prejudiced and intolerant, especially with regard to race. My brother laughs. "People were so prejudiced that we grew up not even knowing what prejudice was. There was never any occasion to see it in action. There were just no blacks around, or Mexicans, either."

This is no exaggeration. Blacks, as a rule, were not permitted in the area at all. In order to see a black person, even at a distance, it was necessary to travel to Commerce or perhaps to Greenville, twenty miles away, where the sign at the city limits read "The Blackest Land, the Whitest People." (This sign has now been removed.) It was a standard joke among the menfolk that every time they drove into Greenville, a bunch of blacks would be lounging beneath that sign.

The rare exceptions to the "no blacks" rule are perhaps worth mentioning. The man who for years owned the largest and finest house in Cumby kept quarters for blacks, a hovel down by a little gully in back of his place. From time to time he brought in a family of blacks to tend his house and grounds, but they never stayed long. They were probably driven away more by loneliness and isolation than by actual harassment. People looked the other way when the blacks approached them on the streets, never speaking, never acknowledging that the dark-skinned people existed. But there had been at least one instance when overt intimidation had been used to rid the town of a black family. Certain Cumby old-timers occasionally bragged that a group of them "had chased them niggers clean over Massey Hill."

There was another interesting exception to the no blacks policy. Saint Paul's, an all-black school between Commerce and Greenville, did not have an inside gym—but the school had an excellent basketball team almost every year. Saint Paul's was permitted to use the Cumby gym on Saturday nights, in order that it might host other black basketball teams in the region. Almost certainly, very little tolerance or generosity was involved in this gesture. Probably the Cumby school system was paid for the use of its facility. Perhaps more important, the games provided Cumby residents with a unique sort of entertainment, for blacks were regarded as highly humorous curiosities.

In fact, a strong cultural trait of the people of this little town was a distrust of and a hostility toward strangers in general, or persons entering the area from outside its social, economic, and moral sphere. There was little incentive for outsiders to come even to Cumby, much less to the rural communities that surrounded the town; nor were the town and outlying communities equipped to accommodate drifters or persons casually "seeking their fortunes." Small farmers and their families (both landowners and sharecroppers) were accustomed to hiring out to their more landed neighbors once their own crops were laid by—or to rotating between their crops and the crops of men with bigger farms. The wages thus earned allowed them something beyond mere subsistence, the only cash money they might see all year. A hard-working outsider was competition that local people feared and resented. Migrant workers (white, as a rule) were not welcomed, either, although in bumper years they might be needed. The places where these workers camped or were otherwise housed were declared strictly off-limits out of a conviction that such people were given to violence, filth, and thievery.

There is a certain unavoidable melancholy as my brother, niece, and I examine the faded lettering under the front eaves of the tiny, boarded-up, cracker-box building, the only remaining sign that it was once a church. While we are standing there, a man pulls up in an old Chevy, gets out, and comes to ask if we need help. He is a grizzled, leathery-faced fellow wearing a heavy denim work jacket and scuffed boots. We tell him we used to attend church here "a long time ago." The man has the good grace to be obviously regretful that our church is boarded up and full of hay, and he assures us that a couple of the other old churches in town are still "in business" and that we probably could arrange to visit them. We thank him, but none of us really wants to prolong our venture into the town's—and our—spiritual past, as it were.

The drive back through the old downtown and then onto the bumpy street leading to the school takes less than five minutes. I am aware once again of a sense that space has become strangely cramped; I find myself struggling to readjust dreamscapes. The old school building and the gym, however, are immediately recognizable: shabbier and dingier, perhaps, but very much intact. A number of prefab buildings have been added in an area behind the gym, housing—judging from construction paper cutouts on all the windowpanes—elementary classrooms. I am not surprised that the people in Cumby have cared well for their school building and grounds and have made additions; education has always been important in Cumby.

The first school in Cumby was a little log structure, the next a vacant storehouse used also as a place of worship. The school was taught, about the year 1869, by Miss Molly Sayle. From 1895 to 1905, the population of 673 (a larger population than I recall in the Cumby of my childhood) could boast of a college called Independent Normal College with Professor R. L. Taylor in charge. Later the college was run briefly by a Professor Curlee and was renamed Curlee College. Eventually, the college was moved to Commerce, partly in response to the city fathers' refusal to grant the railroad's request to build a roundhouse in Cumby. The school then became East Texas State University. In an article in the *News Telegram* Fall Festival Section, September 6, 1977, Bessie McRae is quoted as declaring that the town of Cumby started to die in 1910 "because two wealthy old men kept the Cotton Belt Railroad out because they didn't want a tax increase."[13] Perhaps this near-sighted, selfish failure to invite progress did result in the loss of the college—and there is some evidence that the little town did come to a standstill with regard to population growth and attracting businesses. Adams writes that in 1948, "there were 12 stores [in Cumby], a broom factory, telephone exchange, mill and gin, several other small businesses, 6 churches, a 9-teacher school, and a water system supplied by a deep well." It was this nine-teacher school that I attended during the ten years of my primary and secondary education.

The school building and its grounds occupied (as they do currently) what now seems a cramped space on the south side of town between old Highway 67 and the railroad track. All twelve grades were housed in one building, a structure that was regarded, during my childhood, as quite adequate and up-to-date. The lower grades were apportioned two grades per classroom: first and second, third and fourth, fifth and sixth, seventh and eighth. These rooms were on the west end of the building. At the east end, the rooms for high school students were set up according to subjects offered: an English room, a math room, an ag-science room, a typing room, a home economics lab. There was an auditorium that did double duty as a "study hall" with a fair-sized proscenium stage that served for all kinds of school and community activities.

The library was a kind of "floating" affair, a collection of donated books that settled sometimes in an alcove in the principal/superintendent's office, sometimes in a corner of the auditorium. I had read all of these books by the time I was in the sixth grade, so keeping me supplied with reading matter was an ongoing task that tested my teachers' resourcefulness and dedication. At the time I entered school, a gym with a rounded roof (Quonset-hut style) had just been built, and when I was in fourth grade, a small cafeteria in back was completed—serving meals that were partially subsidized by the government. I recall that the menus were characterized by

Cumby rhythm band

foodstuffs like wieners and sauerkraut and pinto beans and rice and that even at twenty-five cents a plate, many of the students—myself included—could not afford the luxury of a hot meal.

My brother eases the Rambler into a parking space. We are visiting on a day when classes are not in session, and the buildings and grounds have that hollow, deserted feel that schools get when noisy, energetic children are not there. The three of us get out of the vehicle, but we are hesitant about appearing to be "snooping around." The next Cumby native we encounter may not be as obliging as the man at the church. It is strange to be an outsider in the one place where, in those growing-up years, I always felt I belonged. My family might move from farm to farm, so that "home" was a portable thing, but the school was dependably here, in this same spot, year after year. Now, however, I am trespassing, and I am for the moment displaced and sad.

My brother and I comment on the additions to the school facility, with which my niece is, of course, less impressed than we are.

There are no school buses in sight, my brother notes, and he wonders if the system has also increased its fleet of buses. We recall that when we were children, the school operated with only two old rattletrap buses and that each bus had to make two or three different runs, both in the morning and again in the afternoon. If we had to ride the first run in the morning, we would get to school before dawn; if we rode the last run in the afternoon, depending on the weather, we might still be on the grounds at sunset. My astute niece sympathizes with the teachers who had to provide supervision during those times.

So far as I can recall, some sort of supervision was nearly always provided. There were, however, occasional lapses—and the results could be disastrous. On April Fool's Day when I was in second grade, a high school boy driving his dad's truck arrived at school to show off in front of the early arrivals. He and his girlfriend resolved to play hooky that day and—on the basis of who knows what kind of reasoning—decided that their venture could succeed only if they took *everyone* with them. So after some discussion and persuasion, we all took our lunches, and someone filled a couple of jugs with water. The high-spirited lad loaded us into the back end of his truck, and we took off for a section of a creek with shade trees and water suitable for wading. When the principal and teachers got to school, they found a substantial portion of their student body missing, and the search began. It was noon before somebody located us. By that time we had waded the creek (which would have been rather chilly at that time of year) till our clothes were wet and muddy and eaten our lunches (and got sick on green dewberries to boot). The boy and his girlfriend had compromised themselves to the point that they were married soon after. It was a sorry crew that was marched back all dirty and straggling into the school building under the disapproving stares of students who had avoided such delinquent behavior.

This incident turns out to be another that my brother does not believe actually happened, at least not as I have recounted it. I remind him that he would not yet have started school at the time when these events took place, but he remains dubious. As my brother and I argue over the details of this story I have just recounted, I am rather startled to realize that in trying to provide context for and verification of the old stories that I recall from my childhood, my brother and I are telling other tales of a more recent vintage. Some of these are stories that we have not told before, even to each other, as is clearly evidenced by James's surprise at my account of the April Fool's Day escapade and his skepticism that it happened as I remember it. Certainly, we have not told these tales to our children or created opportunities for sharing our experiences with our combined broods, as I feel confident our parents and grandparents and other kinfolk would have done.

I mention the strange fact of our neglect to my brother, and we comment dourly on how we have allowed ourselves to be caught up in fast-paced lives that have not prioritized that kind of sharing. "Isn't it strange," I insist, "that in trying to figure out how the old stories ought to be told, we are discovering new stories about ourselves, about each other?"

"I guess that's what life is, what history is," my brother muses. "Just layer upon layer of stories." But he still finds it hard to believe that he never heard about the hooky-playing incident. He is forced, however, to own up to participating in a childhood project that backfired—for both of us.

Because the school buses were not dependable and, further, often could not even attempt to make runs down muddy, icy country roads, walking the proverbial three miles to school was a part of reality. For a (thankfully) short period of time during our school years, James and I walked nearly five miles from one of the Alexander farms at the very back of the land grant. On winter mornings, we left home before daybreak, cutting through pastures and wooded areas, crossing the creek (always pitch dark), and listening to the howling of wolf packs holed up in the bottom land. After such a journey, the school room with its groaning old steam heater seemed a warm and friendly refuge.

The problems with transportation often caused real frustration, however. It irked everyone that the county was consistently indifferent to needed repairs of rural roads. Two of the Winniford homeplaces were on a dirt road that made a U down from black-topped Farm Road 275. A bridge over a small branch of a creek not far from the house where my family lived at the time deteriorated so badly that the bus driver decided the heavy school bus should no longer attempt to cross it. My brother and I were therefore forced to walk up to Farm Road 275 in the mornings and wait for the bus.

One afternoon, when as chance would have it both my parents were gone from home, the county grader leveled the road up to the bridge. But—maddeningly—instead of repairing the bridge, the road crew retraced its path and graded up to the bridge from the other side, leaving the bridge as it was. Motivated more (I hope) by righteous indignation than by purely criminal impulses, my brother and I decided to take action. We hauled a load of old wood shingles down to the bridge and filled in all the potholes. Then, with hoes, we spread dirt over everything until the bridge looked as if it, too, had been graded. When our parents came home, we told them that the county had done its work and that they could notify the bus driver that he could make his regular rounds.

The next morning, we stood out on the front porch with our armloads of school books, watching happily as the big, yellow bus lumbered up the road toward us with its cargo of wrestling, screaming school kids. The front part of the bus made it across the bridge without a hitch, but when the heavy back end of the bus hit the bridge, it went through the old boards and settled into the creek bed. The bus, thus upended, just stood there on its rear with its front wheels dangling in the air. There were some alarming moments until finally the bus driver pushed the front door open, heaved himself up and out, and jumped to the ground. He was followed one by one by the schoolchildren, none of whom was hurt beyond a few bruises and skinned places. The next day, the county put in a new bridge. It would have been gratifying to my brother and me to have been able to take credit for getting a move on the county, but we maintained a discreet silence.

James and I argue good-humoredly about whose idea it was to fix the bridge. That seems to be the only detail open to question. My niece laughs at the sheepish expression on her father's face as he confesses to taking part in this escapade. "Don't get the idea that we were up to pranks like that all the time," my brother defends our youthful selves. "Really, we were very serious about school. We knew we had to be." He is right about that.

One blistering hot day around noon out in the cotton field, my dad turned to me and said, "Well, Lee girl, if you don't want to spend the rest of your life out here, you'd better make hundreds in school and stay out of the bushes with the boys." I stood there with sweat running down my neck and with shoulders aching from pulling a heavy cotton sack and decided that I definitely could make hundreds in school and avoid the bushes for a while. I suspect that for my brother and for many of my classmates, a commitment to learning stemmed from similar admonitions. Education was perceived as a sure route out of the hard conditions with which we were familiar and into a degree of comfort and security. Certainly, not all Cumby students at this time finished high school: the hard life, hard times, and nature took their toll, and there were dropouts. Nevertheless, the idea that finishing school—and finishing with a good record—was the desirable route to take remained, I think, intact.

Since most families farmed, the school system geared itself to the seasonal schedule of essential farm work, for young people were an important part of their families' work force. It was customary, for instance, for Cumby schools to open the new school year sometime in August, run for six weeks, and then dismiss for four to six weeks for cotton picking. An article in the August 29, 1954, *Times Tribune,* titled "Going with Summer Term," opens with the statement "Cumby schools will be going strong with a summer term when the regular fall opening date arrives for most Hopkins County systems."[14] The Cumby superintendent of schools, L. B. Click, who was officiating during much of the time I was in school, defends the practice in this same article. With no air conditioning, no ceiling fans, and no cold water in the fountains, it seems in retrospect that those summer terms must have been grueling indeed. No one was accustomed to being cool in summer, however, and so discomfort was accepted without complaint.

In spite of the difficulties involved in attending school, and despite what would be considered limited facilities by present-day standards, students were offered a solid grounding in basic subject matter. The conviction that even a small town can compete with larger cities in educating its youth was—and apparently still is—an important part of the people's thinking. An article in the April 18, 1978, *Commerce Journal* titled "Cumby Enjoys Neighbor Cities" actually devotes most of its space to the town's school system. It makes the point that "stressing education over athletics is the policy of the Cumby Independent School District" and emphasizes new teaching methods and evidence of student achievement.[15] As my brother and I recall, the school was integral to the town, and getting involved was not an unpleasant duty for people back then. They looked forward to school activities that were open to the public and had fun being there. Christmas programs, the senior play, and graduation exercises were enthusiastically attended.

The three of us load back into the Rambler and, after maneuvering the bumpy streets, pull onto Farm Road 275, going due north. This is a road my brother and I have traveled hundreds of times—walking, riding the school bus, hauling cotton to the gin in a horse-drawn wagon—and stretches of it are very much as we remember. We note old landmarks with satisfaction and regard new developments with an anxiety that would be difficult to explain. Nowhere has such drastic change occurred as in the very area that should seem like "home" to us. Here the contrast between the old and decaying and the new and progressing is strikingly evident. Sporadically, where owners have managed to hold onto all or part of their land, there are scruffy little fields and pastures and shabby old houses, and memory is validated. But often only yards away, land has been subdivided and sold, and trim, modern houses have been built with citified lawns and pickups in their drives. The topography itself has changed. Hills, gullies, and narrow creeks have been smoothed away, and neat brick houses with level lawns have camouflaged whatever geological remnants of harsh, demanding Texas soil and rock may lie beneath. I cringe at how tame it all is, at my doubts that the earth could ever reclaim itself.

"Do you think they get blue northers still?" I ask. "Like the three or four we watched blow in—or the really bad ones that Uncle Sam and Grandpa talked about?"

"A blue norther wouldn't stand a chance around here," my brother concludes after a silent, thoughtful pause. "These folks would just ignore it. They have lost respect for blue northers."

The homeplace where my grandparents lived, and which had always seemed a nucleus of extended-family activities, is located on a piece of land still owned by someone in the family. Except for the ravages of time and the elements, this place remains unmolested in its quiet decay. This homeplace is in the north corner of the U along which, when the land was first settled, several Winniford and Alexander families built their homes. We enter the U from Farm Road 275, driving slowly and carefully to allow ourselves time to get our bearings. There is anguish in the obliteration of tangible signs of the past.

For a long time, the large, rambling house that my grandfather built, adding rooms as his family increased and needed them (and once considered one of the finest homes in the area), stood, defying heat, cold, storms, and vandals with its sturdiness. My Aunt Lynna stayed there as long as she could, "maintaining the home and keeping up the Winniford name," as she put it. Almost symbolically, shortly after her death a powerful bolt of lightning struck the dwelling, and it burned to the ground. A couple of barns still remain, squatting closer and closer to the ground with each season, and there are some henhouses, coops, and broken fences. Everywhere the lumber is silver-gray and hollow with age, so that one wonders, on touching it, how it musters the strength to hold together, length on length, to bear some dim resemblance to the structure built when it was new and smelling strong of pine.

❧ We sit quietly in the Rambler for a considerable time, gathering courage to walk the grounds and investigate. From this distance, the black splotch where the house burned down resembles an old wound that is healing over—for rough grass, briars, and vines are reclaiming the charred ground. A part of the old fireplace and chimney still thrust grotesquely skyward, and the bois d'arc trees near the storm cellar—singed by the blaze—must have put out new growth in the spring. We emerge at last and move tentatively about. Without the house and other buildings, perspective is alarmingly altered. There is that sense that the geography is shrinking, surrealistically, nightmarishly. Remembered places that once seemed spread out toward horizons—east, west, north, and south—now seem crammed together around some invisible center.

"It's like everything is being pulled closer and closer in," I comment in real dismay. "It's like there is a black hole, and everything will soon be swallowed up." My brother does not laugh at the black hole analogy.

So how can I re-create the past?

Old Winniford homeplace, 1993

We find the debris-filled holes where the old wells were and the hump of earth and air vent that mark the storm cellar where, toward the end of her life, a determined Aunt Lynna did combat with a nest of rattlesnakes down in its damp darkness. I locate the clump of stunted trees where the pigpen stood, and I know that in the corner of the barnyard where the barbed wire fence is torn and tangled, hogs were drawn and butchered every year after the first hard freeze. Men joked and sang and told stories as they did the butchering or stood around the fires where they scalded and scraped the carcasses and rendered fat for lard. I linger for a long time at the crumbled remains of the fireplace and chimney and assure myself that my grandfather sat just here, exactly over this spot, surrounded by his sons and brothers and nephews and cousins. There, confident in their rapt, good-humored attention, he told his stories or listened sometimes to theirs.

Black holes can swallow barns, fences, and chicken coops; geography can shrink past recognition. Eventually there will be nothing here, nothing meaningful to me, that can be perceived through sight or touch or smell or sound. But I have the stories that were told here—and I recall who told them, and when, and the manner of their telling.

Chapter Three

Picking Cotton, Killing Hogs, and Stretching the Truth

The farming lifestyle of the paternal side of my family offered a number of storytelling situations. Perhaps it would be more accurate to say that these vigorous, hard-working people had discovered early in their experience as settlers how to turn necessary and arduous tasks such as potato diggings and hog killings into celebrations of sorts by sharing the work with extended family and neighbors, providing good food for the workers, and joking, singing, and telling stories while they worked or during brief rests. Granted, the most important storytelling sessions—meaning those that were relatively formal, lengthy, and conducted by the dominant male—occurred during family get-togethers on Sundays and holidays. Stories were told while the group was still sitting around the table after a big meal or when they retired to the parlor and gathered around a crackling blaze in the fireplace in winter or escaped to the cool of the front porch in summer. It was during these formal gatherings that the most involved and treasured of their family stories were told and retold, corrected and embellished.

Both my brother and I, however, recall hearing songs, jokes, and stories during hog killings and out in the cotton field while the pickers rested or ate lunch in the shade of the cotton wagon. Stories told in these informal settings were likely to be short and often humorous anecdotes about family members—frequently members still living—because part of their intent might be to regale or tease various persons present. It was during these sessions that the less-admirable exploits of the family, past and present, were acknowledged and put into good-humored perspective.

For cotton farmers, all the planning and hard work that began each year with the turning-under of the old crop in late fall or early winter climaxed when the new crop of cotton started opening along in late September. As previously mentioned, cotton was still the major money crop during this time—a fact that even the school respected by closing for the cotton picking season. Farmers often mortgaged their cotton crops, borrowing money from the banks in order to finance the operations of their farms in the months before harvest time. Mortgages were paid off in the fall, and the sale of cotton and wages earned for picking it provided the only sizable inflow of cash that most farmers were likely to enjoy during the year. Cotton crops were important, and the cotton picking season was marked either by flushed success or by dismal failure.

The cotton field—or "patch," as it was called—was part of every farm child's reality, almost from birth. Parents took small children to the field with them, for women usually chopped and picked cotton along with the men. Toddlers were put on a quilt, frequently in the shade of the cotton wagon, to entertain themselves as best they could while the parents worked. The mother would pick or chop her two rows, turn around and pick or chop back, and at that juncture check on her children. Farm kids were punished severely if they wandered away from their designated spot, so they usually remained where their parents had left them—fighting, scratching, and throwing dirt on each other for lack of anything else to do. Disasters could occur in the time it took the mother or father to pick or hoe up and back down two sets of rows. On one occasion, for example, my mother picked her way back to the wagon and found my brother and me peacefully asleep on our pallet with a big chicken snake curled up between us.

Children, however, did not remain idle in the shade of the wagon very long. I was fortunate in having to serve as a babysitter for my little brother, which postponed my cotton picking career for a couple of years. Most children learned to pick cotton before they started first grade in school. At first, a child picked in one of the parent's rows, under close supervision. Instructions were given about not leaving tags, not getting leaves in the cotton, and being certain that the stalk was picked clean. Childish hands could become swollen and cut from handling the sharp cotton burrs. My mother always made gloves for everybody out of old socks, but the fingers had to be left free and uncovered. One's fingers, therefore, were always sore from cuts and from the abrasive, acidic effect of cotton on the skin. My hands, I am convinced, never recovered from this early abuse that left them permanently rough-looking and red (a condition that caused me much dismay back in my hand-holding days). But I had long, nimble fingers, and I could out-pick many of the men.

When a child had mastered the art of cotton picking, he or she graduated to picking one row, always beside the parents. In preparation for that step up in the profession, a child-size ducking sack would be sewn for him or her. A full-fledged cotton picker picked two rows at a time. Children were warned not to climb on the cotton wagon and not to sit on their full sacks; this could result in dirty, wasted cotton and, it was believed, also affected the length of the staple when the cotton was judged and priced. Most important was the repeated warning not to get rocks or other hard objects in the cotton. A stray rock or two could cause a bale to catch fire in the separator while ginning and result in its loss.

When cotton opened in the fall, small farmers and their families (both landowners and sharecroppers) did what was called a "first picking" in their own fields, unless they had got off to a late planting in the spring. In that event, they would hire out to other farmers until their own crops came in. In the early days, the blackland prairie on which the Winniford and Alexander farms were located easily produced a bale and a half of cotton per acre. This was much more than the 350 pounds claimed by Gladys St. Clair in her history of Hopkins County, which would have been less than a bale (a bale was 500 pounds of lint).[1] In order to gin out this amount, a farmer took 1,500 pounds to the gin if the cotton were picked and 2,000 pounds if his hired help had pulled bolls. "Picking cotton" involved disengaging the staple or lent from the opened boll (called a burr) and leaving the empty boll on the stalk. "Pulling bolls" involved snapping the cotton from the stalk boll and all—and was resorted to generally when insects or bad weather had kept the bolls from opening properly. Usually, having to "pull bolls" meant the crop was bad.

Despite the wistful bragging of old men in the family and of other locals that the land had in bumper years once produced three bales per acre (with the second picking weighing in as much as the first), by the time of my childhood, even a bumper crop was less than a half-bale an acre. People joked rather grimly about "bumble-bee cotton," a term for which my brother, James Winniford, offers a humorous explanation: "Bumble-bee cotton is cotton that's grown in poor, old East Texas soil. The cotton is so doggoned short that, as farmers joked, a bumble bee could 'sit on his hiney' and take the nectar out of the one blossom that the sickly cotton stalk might produce. And if that one blossom made a boll, you were lucky, and it was about the size of a marble. That's where you drug the bottom out of the cotton sack, because you had to walk awfully fast in order to get a weighing of cotton."[2] By the late 1940s, farmers who had once made a fairly good living raising cotton and who held on stubbornly to the notion that someday, somehow, the land would be productive again were beginning to either sell out or turn their land to pasture.

The Winniford families belonged to the stubborn group. During my childhood, their philosophy was that if one just plowed deep enough and kept the Johnsongrass from taking over, good crops would finally make their reappearance. Ironically, plowing deep was part of their problem in the first place, for the practice permitted the rich, black soil to wash away and left the clay beneath. Contrary to their belief, the soil was not richer deeper down. At any rate, my family plowed and planted cotton in the early spring, chopped it in the late spring, finished the first picking, hauled the loads of cotton to the gin—and then hired out to other farmers in the area who planted more acres and had larger crops to gather. In the mornings, often before sunup, the landed farmer would drive around the neighboring country in his truck, picking up families of cotton pickers who would clamber into the back end of his truck with their sacks, lunches, and water jugs, much like cattle being hauled to market.

Cotton picking involved strange rearrangements in human relationships, a fact that my brother and I discussed during a taped interview (one of the rare occasions when he submitted to this format) on his farm between Longview and Gilmer in January, 1993.

Lee W.: You know, it used to amaze me when we'd hire out to pick for someone else—though they were neighbors or sometimes even our kinfolks. There was this change in your social status all of a sudden. All of a sudden, no matter what the relationship had been previously, you were *hired help.*

James W.: All of a sudden you became hired help. It must have gone all the way back to the slave days.

Lee W.: Yes, that must have been when it originated.

James W.: And the cotton picker became the hired hand, the field hand—I won't say that other word—but he no longer held the status that he did as cousin or even, sometimes, brother or whatever be the case. Suddenly you were a cotton picker there.

Lee W.: The lowest rung of the social and economic order.

James W.: Lowest man on the totem pole! And so when you started picking cotton for these folks, they immediately had what you could call attitude adjustment. Up until that time, you could have been the best of the folks, and yet when it comes down to the time to pick cotton, well, then you just about *stayed* in the field. Now then, they would let you come up to the *yard* . . .

Lee W.: At noon.

James W.: At noontime to eat your dinner.

Lee W.: But not always.

James W.: Sometimes. Yes, a lot of times we ate it in the field under the wagon over there.

Lee W.: Yes, I remember that.

James W.: But, anyway, this attitude thing was really strange because people that were even your own kinfolk, when you started picking cotton, well, you'd find yourself either eating under the wagon or maybe out in the yard under a tree—somewhere—and you brought your own. By crackies, if they fed you dinner, why they charged you for it, you know.

Lee W.: You bet!

James W.: And so you became the chief laborer, the worker. You lost a good portion of your human dignity, you lost your status, right then and there. Because you were in the cotton patch.[3]

People endured these subtle and sometimes not-so-subtle indignities because they needed extra money. From the time I entered school, I paid for my own school clothes with money I made picking cotton (that my mother was a fine seamstress helped me stretch my money). I also usually set money aside for school lunches, supplies, and other incidentals. But escaping from the cotton patch was what motivated me to study hard, make high grades, and have a chance of leaving Cumby as soon as I could.

Joking and telling stories probably helped cotton pickers keep their spirits high and maintain their dignity and self-esteem (especially when they were hiring out to pick on other people's land) while they put up with a string of minor insults and worked under a broiling Texas sun. The cotton field was a highly specific and seasonal, or temporary, cultural context in which people interrelated in a way that would have been unacceptable to them elsewhere. Thus the system of ideas, symbols, and behaviors that, as Elliott Oring suggests, a cultural context "encapsulates" tended to be specific to their temporary situation.[4] This situation required submitting to the extreme discomforts of heat, dirt, insects, and vegetation that tore the flesh and nettled the skin as well as to disturbing shifts in social status. Stories told in the cotton field often implied layers of meaning different from or beyond what the stories might mean when and if they were told elsewhere.

Pickers would gather at the cotton wagon, weigh in and empty their sacks, and then sit in the shade of the wagon and enjoy a cool drink from the water jug (kept "refrigerated" by being wrapped in heavy, wet cloth and buried in cool earth or under a bush). At midday they would eat the lunches the women had prepared by lamplight in the predawn darkness while the men were doing the milking: the morning's leftover biscuits, fried sweet potatoes, Vienna sausages, or sometimes cold fried chicken.

Tales often concerned cotton pickings of times past, when the soil was rich and virgin and the crops were bountiful. One of the men would likely tell a story like the one I call "Shittin' in Tall Cotton."

Shittin' in Tall Cotton

Back at the end of the nineteenth century and during the first quarter of the twentieth, the blackland soil of the Winniford and Alexander farms produced bumper crops. Cotton stalks grew nearly as tall as a grown man's head, covered from ground to top with big, fluffy bolls of cotton. It took dexterity and an eager, muscular reach to strip the stalks from top to bottom without missing any cotton and without getting any of the big, green leaves into one's sack. Men and women prided themselves on developing sufficient skill to pick two rows at once quickly and efficiently. Family members took credit for being among the best pickers in the country.

One year—a particularly good year—a man showed up in Cumby who was an expert cotton picker. He had picked cotton down in the Rio Grande Valley and out in West Texas as well. He was what you would call a professional cotton picker. He bragged that he could outpick any man in any cotton patch anywhere—and farmers who hired him soon discovered that he wasn't just "spoutin' off." My grandfather and some of the young men in the family ran into this fellow one Saturday in Smith's Grocery, and the professional picker had the nerve to challenge them. If he couldn't outpick any man among them, he would pick a week for my grandfather for free. My hot-tempered grandfather hired him on the spot.

Early Monday morning, the hired man showed up, and they all went out to the cotton field. The professional picker was completely bowled over. He couldn't believe his eyes! He had never seen cotton that tall before and had never worked in cotton any taller than waist-high. Naturally, he had trouble with the tall stalks and the big, green leaves, and trying to develop new skills slowed him down considerably. At the end of the day, even some of the women had weighed in more cotton than he had.

My grandfather was too kind and honest a man not to pay the fellow for his week's work, but the braggart's failure to measure up to his brag was a family victory. As the storyteller always concluded, "We told him, 'Things are just a little bit different around here. You're shittin' in *tall* cotton now!'"

This tale reminded pickers, especially family members, of the tradition of hard work and of excelling in that work that was their heritage. Like many stories, it described a time when life was better and kept the hope alive that some day, somehow, there would again be cotton so high and bushy that it was hard for a stranger to pick. The colloquialism with which the story always ended bounced off the literal emphasis on the height of the cotton. It employed the popular figure of speech used to describe someone who was enjoying especially good fortune or had moved a rung up the social ladder and was "rubbing elbows" with his or her erstwhile superiors.

This story could take on different layers of meaning, depending on the situation and the manner in which it was told. If the narrator was merely reminiscing about better times, the tone might be wistful, and the speaker would demonstrate how tall the cotton was, how large the bolls, and how wide the pickers would have to spread their arms in order to encompass the stalk. But if, for instance, the teller and his listeners were pulling bolls in "bumble-bee" cotton and the landed farmer was criticizing them for insufficient weigh-ins, the tone could become rebellious and satiric. The teller would emphasize details that belittled the employer's crop and his farming abilities and justified the pickers' inability to achieve their customary weigh-ins.

An important element in the story, of course, is the outsider, the "professional" cotton picker. If teller and listeners felt especially threatened by the prospect or the reality of competing with migrant or other workers from outside the community, then the narrator would emphasize the sinister character of the professional picker, fleshing out his villainous qualities and assigning him long speeches in which he was blatantly egotistical and insulting. Mody Boatright makes the point that in order for a tale to enter the oral tradition and survive, "it must afford emotional satisfaction to the hearers."[5] The foregoing tale was popular among members of the farming community because it provided such satisfaction on many levels and in many circumstances.

Other stories explored the common anxieties of pickers and told of mishaps when tragedy either occurred or was narrowly averted. My father was the hapless hero of one of these misadventures. He told the story himself sometimes, as a personal experience which he represented on some occasions as humorous and on others as admittedly harrowing. Other family members, male and female, also told the story, each from his or her point of view.

Hurrying Home to Corn Mash

One of the fears of cotton farmers, especially those who still used teams of mules or horses to haul their wagons of cotton to the gin, was that they would not manage to get their load pulled sufficiently out of the way of an approaching vehicle—or that the driver of a fast-moving car might not see them in time to swerve—and there would be a collision. Such an accident occurred at least once or twice each fall. The driver of the car or truck was rarely seriously injured, but the farmer perched precariously on top of the bale of cotton was vulnerable, the mules or horses could be crippled or killed, and the cotton would be scattered and lost. There was always some anxiety as the womenfolk watched their men drive off on a wagon load of cotton—and general relief when farmers returned safely.

Once when he was young and still unmarried, my father took a bale of cotton into Cumby behind a team of vigorous young horses. The trip to the gin was without incident, but when my father started back home with the empty wagon, he found the team harder and harder to control. Euphoric because of their lighter load and eager to return to the barn where they knew they would be fed the corn mash with which my grandfather pampered his horses, the team strained at its bits while my father braced himself and fought to hold back on the reins. At last, as they rounded a curve, a wheel came off the old wagon. The wagon careened wildly and overturned, pinning my father under it. Unhurt themselves, the horses broke free and followed the familiar road home, their trace chains clinking behind them.

My father's mother and sisters were terrified when they saw the team arrive at the barnyard gate minus the wagon. Weeping, they climbed into the family's Model A and retraced my father's route, not knowing what ghastly scene they might come upon. Their worst fears seemed realized when they spotted the overturned wagon, its wobbly wheels still spinning idly. But my father was regaining consciousness after his fall and had suffered no injuries except the blow to his head. The women were able to pull the wagon aside enough to free him.

❧ Like many of the stories, this tale lent itself to more than one interpretation. My father sometimes—and other male storytellers always—told this tale as a lively, highly humorous series of events demonstrating my father's ineptness in handling the team of horses: he was the only person they had heard of who had had a one-vehicle accident in an empty wagon. When this interpretation was intended, the tellers—my father included—did comic pantomimes of my father struggling to hold back the horses, of the team prancing happily up to the barnyard gate, and of my father staggering dizzily to his feet when his womenfolk eased the wagon off him. There were times, however, when my father told the tale as a harrowing experience that taught him the necessity of checking out and repairing equipment and of familiarizing himself with the dispositions of farm animals with which he worked. Women storytellers—my father's sisters and female cousins—interpreted the story as an emotional near-tragedy, dwelling on their feelings of shock and alarm when the runaway team arrived, their anxiety as they set out to find the wagon and my father, the momentary terror when they did, and their relief when they discovered my father alive and stirring.

Since cotton pickers brought their children to the fields—even when the children were toddlers too young to work—there was always some uneasiness about how well the children would fare when they were left behind at the wagon or in the shade of a bush at the end of the rows. Stories frequently gave indirect expression, at least, to these parental worries.

A Nest of Thieves

A woman called Aunt Mattie, a determined, termagant female who was married to one of my grandfather's cousins, figured in several family stories. She was a hard-working, no-nonsense, strong-willed farm woman but a loving, protective mother nonetheless.

One hot summer, her entire brood of children came down with whooping cough, and at cotton picking time they were all still weak, sickly, and demanding special care. Their throats were still sore and their appetites poor, and Aunt Mattie despaired of getting them to eat well enough to regain their strength.

But her help was needed in the cotton field, so she brought her sickly offspring along and made them as comfortable as she could under the shade of the wagon. The children had been willing to ingest little else than milk and soft-scrambled eggs, so Aunt Mattie brought along these items in order to satisfy their finicky appetites. At midday, she said, a tiny fire would suffice to scramble a pan of eggs.

When the pickers broke at lunch, however, Aunt Mattie discovered that the milk had been overturned and spilled and the eggs were gone. The ailing children had been napping and had noticed no intruder. The same thing happened on the second day, and again the children had seen nothing. Aunt Mattie was the suspicious type, and she decided that two strapping boys who had hired on to earn pocket money were the guilty parties: the mean, sneaky rascals had slipped in and stolen her poor, sick children's special treats. Although the boys stoutly denied that they had committed the crime, she took off after them with a cotton stalk. The boys outran her and didn't come back.

On the third day, certain that she had chased off the thieves and all was secure, Aunt Mattie came back to the wagon at midday to prepare a meal for her children. But her store had been raided again! This time, however, the guilty party was close at hand. Aunt Mattie spied a large chicken snake, his long body lumpy with the unbroken eggs he had swallowed. When he slithered away at her approach, she followed him to a whole nest of similarly loathsome creatures under some big rocks. Aunt Mattie yelled for someone to fetch her a hoe, but hoes were not usually brought to the field at cotton picking time. Not to be outdone, she grabbed the coal oil that she would have used for starting her campfire, threw the fuel on the snakes, struck a match, and set the squirming robber reptiles ablaze. This proved a rather gruesome spectacle, but Aunt Mattie wasn't squeamish.

There was always some concern that snakes, rats, and other vermin might pose a threat to small children left unguarded in the field, as well as some guilt on the part of their mothers for leaving them unattended. My mother had experienced a similar confrontation with a snake, but she had not managed to apprehend and destroy the reptile. She relied instead on my father to hurry across the field and do the honors, thus permitting the snake to get away. But Aunt Mattie's rough-and-ready approach to motherhood left no doubt that her maternal instincts were operative. Her quick-thinking handling of what she perceived as danger was doubtless reassuring to teller and listeners.

On the other hand, pesky, curious children could themselves create trouble. One story that was often told—each time with a different cast of characters who, whatever their identities, had conveniently moved away—concerned a prank played by two young boys.

Burning the Bale

One fall some kinfolk—a man, his wife, and two young boys—hired out to pick for one of the "big" cotton farmers once they had finished their own picking. The landed farmer was known for his ill temper, arrogance, and general lack of consideration.

From the first, the farmer lived up to his bad reputation. He deducted pounds at weigh-in for every imaginable reason: dew in the morning, dirt on the staple, leaves in the sack. He declared the best shaded area off-limits to pickers for rest breaks and lunch at midday. He shouted at everyone and used foul language. He was especially abusive to the father of the two boys—going so far on a couple of occasions as to shove him around in a bullying, insulting way.

The boys were devoted to their father, who they understood was enduring the abuse because they all needed money. Familiar with the dangers posed by rocks in the bale, they formulated a daring plan and watched for an opportunity to slip unnoticed to the cotton wagon. In their pockets, they carried rocks of a size and sort that they considered most likely to strike a spark—and they had decided exactly where to place them in the wagon load of cotton so that the entire bale would burn before the gin could be shut down.

So the bale burned, and the boys got their revenge. The farmer couldn't prove who sabotaged his bale, but he had a pretty good idea. Obviously, the perpetrators had to be boys who had moved out of the area and were safe from implication.

The bale-burning story was another that lent itself to more than one interpretation. If the story was told, as it sometimes was, to warn children not to play on the cotton, the two boys were depicted as young villains whose mischief caused serious trouble. If, on the other hand, the narrator and listeners were working in the fields of an employer who was taking advantage of them or who was otherwise abusive, the two lads could become heroes. The story emphasized the boys' love for their father, their justified resentment that he was ill treated, and their cleverness in devising and implementing a plan to get even. Told in this way, the tale served to empower teller and listeners. They were not entirely helpless in their situation. There were ways of striking back if they chose to use them; that fact made endurance a matter of choice, as well.

Cotton picking was tiring, rest breaks and midday meals were brief, and spirits could sag, so jokes and stories tended to be succinct and audience reaction good-humored but muted. The strength and overtness of the undercurrent of resentment and rebellion that generally characterized cotton picking stories varied according to how tight money was, how good the crops were, how hot or wet the weather, and, of course, the dynamics of interpersonal relationships. Stories told at hog killings, in contrast, were usually playful and humorous and were told with more verve and gusto because tellers and listeners were excited about what they were doing and were in high spirits.

Hog killing was one of several practices carried over from pioneer days into the mid-twentieth century. Of early days in Hopkins County, Gladys St. Clair writes: "There were hog-killing days in the winter. On these occasions several men went with dogs in search of the range of the hogs. The best marksman of the crowd would shoot the selected ones. The hog was then tied with the rope to the horn of a saddle or the horse's tail and dragged to the place where it was to be dressed."[6]

St. Clair is, of course, describing hog killing when hogs were raised on the open range. Many farm families during my childhood still raised turkeys on the open range, but hogs were kept in pens and fattened on grain, slop, and other refuse. Every farm place had a "smokehouse" for storing meat, but the meat was seldom actually smoked. For the most part, meat was preserved by salting it down immediately after it was butchered. Due to the lack of refrigeration, farmers had to wait until the first norther to kill hogs. Everyone hoped that the eagerly awaited cold snap would come before Christmas because whole boiled hams were an anticipated Christmas delicacy. My brother describes a typical hog killing.

> On that morning when it was real nice and cold, you'd get busy. And this took *everybody*—we're talking about little bitty children all the way up. Everybody participated in the hog killing! Well, they would take a shovel and dig a hole in the ground and set a barrel on about a

forty-five-degree angle, and they would heat up a big batch of scalding water. Then they'd get out the wagon frames and lay them down on the ground—side boards, they were called—and fix a place where we could lay the hog to scald him. Because these hogs were *big*.

So the grownups—papa, grandpa, or whatever—would go down to the hog pen and they'd first shoot this big old hog and then get in there and stick him so that he would bleed. Then they'd get a horse and a singletree down there—now that's the deal that goes on the trace chains behind the horse—they'd hamstring this old hog and hook him up to that singletree and let the horse pull him and drag him back up to where the butchering was going to take place. You dragged him out over and laid him on top of those side frames—these were one-by-twelve boards that made a clean place to lay the hog—and then you took all of that scalding hot water that was boiling out there in that barrel and you poured it on him, and everybody got busy and started scraping that hog. That means you take your butcher knives, and you have them razor sharp, and you go out there and you—it's literally *shaving* that old hog. By the time you pour that rip-snortin' hot water on that hog and you've got him scalded out good and scraped him down—well, he'll be just as clean as a whistle.

After that, you have a scaffold, and you raise the hog up and hang him up there, and you gut him. In the process you clean him out, and you throw more hot water on him, scald him down. That's the cleanest that hog has ever been!

Well, of course, there was not a thing wasted. Back in those days, they didn't waste a thing in the world. Oh, you might throw the tail away for an old dog to eat, or you might throw the ears away or something like that. Some of the folks that would be there working with the hog killing, they would take the lungs out of that hog—they called them "lights"—but they would put them on a stick and put them over the fire and roast those lungs over the fire. And then they'd take their pocket knives or whatever and cut out chunks out of that and eat it. But they'd be standing around the fire, you know, and of course working a little bit, talking a little bit, and this thing and that, and you'd have those people standing there eating those lights.

Now this story wouldn't be complete if I didn't mention one of the prime items that comes from a good hog killing—and that is that they would render the lard out of that stuff. They would take the fatty portions of the meat, including the hide, and they rendered lard out of the fat. They cut it up in little chunks and put it in one of those great big old pots with a fire going under it. That would melt the fat—or grease—out of the meat.

They called the meat that came up to the top, floated on top, cracklins. That lard was hot, and those little cracklins would just be sizzling and sailing across the top of that hot lard, and it smelled pretty good, you know. Usually, they had a strainer or dipper of some sort, and as those cracklins would come to the top, they would watch until they got nice and brown and juicy looking, and they would lift those cracklins out and put them over in another container. Then from those cracklins Mama or Grandma would make cracklin cornbread. That cracklin cornbread was fine stuff![7]

My brother gets somewhat diverted from hog killing as a social function by his memories of the event as the prelude to a month or so of good eating. Neighbors in a farm community always took turns helping each other kill hogs. While the men worked outside, the women worked in the kitchen grinding sausage, stitching up sacks from cheesecloth to store it in, preparing cuts of meat for salting down, and chopping up the fat to be rendered into lard. They kept coffee perking, to brace the men against the cold. A huge pot of backbones and ribs would be cooked off, and this dish was served with hot biscuits about midafternoon. Once the meat was salted away and the neighbors were ready to leave, each family was given a sample of the sausage and organ meat as well as a portion of whatever might be their favorite cut.

Hog killings were bloody, boisterous affairs. The weather was brisk and cold, people were full of energy, and spirits were high because everyone looked forward to a supply of fresh meat. Songs, jokes, and stories tended to be of an equally boisterous nature—loudly declaimed and accompanied by laughter and horseplay. Stories about human foibles—which gave men and women opportunities to laugh at and to tease each other—were especially popular.

The men in the family had a little ditty with which they regaled each other at various gatherings, and they were likely to burst into snatches of it at hog killings: "All the Winnifords have big feet / The more they work, the less they eat." Feet symbolized for them what noses represented in Sterne's *Tristram Shandy;* they, as well as neighboring men helping with the butchering, enjoyed the ribald insinuations of the song. A certain amount of ribaldry was, incidentally, permitted at hog killings. The second line of the ditty could be varied to suit the occasion or to fit the antics of some kinsman: "We'll crack some heads at the county seat," "Ev chases every girl he meets," or "Sam left his cows out in the sleet." The men took delight in spontaneously supplying clever rhyming lines.

Many of the stories told at hog killings concerned incidents involving family members that, if not exactly ribald, were off-color enough to be unsuitable for other, more formal, occasions. My brother relates a story that the men liked to tell about my grandfather.

Up in Smoke

> In the wintertime, especially, the folks would take ashes from the fireplace or the heater, and they would go down and they would pour it into this old toilet [an outdoor privy] to sanitize and keep down the bad odors.
>
> Well, my grandpa—he seemed to have been quite a little character—but one day he took the bucket of ashes down, you know, and he poured them into the old two-holer to sanitize and cut down on the odors and what have you, and he comes on back to the house. Everything is fine. But he looks back down in a little while, and, lo, smoke is ascending into the heavens!
>
> Poor old Grandpa, he had taken some ashes down there that still had some live coals in them—and he set his privy on fire.[8]

Younger men in the family liked to razz my grandfather with this story. Especially if there were neighbors listening, he managed to look suitably sheepish and declared that the storyteller was exaggerating—though, according to my grandmother, the little building burned to the ground. More than likely, however, it was my grandfather himself who first told the story of this bizarre, if also embarrassing, adventure. Winniford men, in particular, got a kick out of their own mishaps if these accounts elicited hearty laughter from their audience.

Men in the family and throughout the neighborhood took pride in their physical strength and in their ability to handle strenuous tasks such as hog killing, as well as in the practical know-how needed for getting the job done right. Stories about individuals who lacked strength and expertise—or who were just plain lazy—were gratifying to these hard-working, capable men, probably because such stories made them look especially good by comparison. Great-uncle Sam, who was a notoriously bad farmer, was the central figure in several humorous stories. He was the black sheep of the family, primarily (it seemed to me) because he was not enthusiastic about farming. Sam was a traveling fiddler and a scholar, of sorts, and—at least while he was relatively young and before he lost his eyesight—he preferred bright lights and the open road to following a turning plow. Accounts of his agricultural debacles were enjoyed by both men and women. One tale told of a hog-killing venture.

Sausage on the Run

Uncle Sam had a big old hog called Lucifer—long, tall, and hump-backed—that grew to unwieldy proportions. People said the animal wasn't shaped right for butchering and the meat wouldn't be any good, for sure. The hog was mean as the dickens. On occasion, when Sam would be away on a fiddling gig, the hungry hog would break out of his pen and terrorize the whole community.

Uncle Sam planned to butcher his hog during a family hog killing, but when the first good norther hit, Sam was off fiddling somewhere, and old Lucifer escaped the sausage grinder. Uncle Sam took offense at the sarcastic, critical remarks of some of the men in the family, so he and a couple of his musician buddies decided they'd show the whole bunch of them and butcher old Lucifer without those "smart alecks'" help. (No one ever intimated that Uncle Sam and his friends were drinking, but their actions suggest they may have been under the influence.)

Their first mistake was using a little handgun. They shot old Lucifer a couple of times somewhere around the head, and the big hog went down. Then, instead of slitting the animal's throat, they "finished him off" by whacking him on the head with a sledgehammer. The three men had prepared a trough full of steaming—but not scalding—water, and they soon tired of attempting to scrape the hair off the animal's tough hide. So, eager to get the whole thing over with, they trussed old Lucifer up and, with the help of a mule, hoisted the big hog up onto the scaffold so he could be gutted and cleaned.

Suddenly, all hell broke loose. Old Lucifer regained consciousness, and he wasn't a bit happy about the situation in which he found himself. He gave a couple or three mighty heaves, broke the ropes, and fell to the ground squealing and squalling like a whole den of devils. Red-eyed and foaming blood at the nostrils, old Lucifer charged the men who had abused him so severely. Uncle Sam and his two buddies were in such a state of shock that they barely managed to dodge the big hog. They just watched dumbfounded as he ran through the canebrake and down to the creek.

A couple of days later, circling buzzards led some of the menfolk to the place where Lucifer had finally succumbed to his mistreatment. The general opinion was that the hog would not have made good eating, anyway, but there was no getting around the fact that Uncle Sam had botched the hog butchering.

This story lent itself to lively narration, with the teller, usually one of the men, dramatizing Lucifer's squealing and lunging and then the shock and amazement of the inept musician-butchers as they scurried to escape from the resurrected hog. Other Uncle Sam stories were told by women, as well: by my aunts or my father's female cousins. The indomitable Great-grandma Sarah—who had raised my grandfather and his two brothers after she was widowed by the Civil War—is the real heroine in a story about Uncle Sam's irresponsible farming.

Mending Sam's Ways

Great-grandma Sarah took pride in having held onto the family land during the tragic wartime and strenuous Reconstruction. When her three sons came of age, she happily divided the land among them, but she expected them to work with the same dedication she had to make the land productive. My grandfather and his older brother, Great-uncle Norve, measured up to her expectations, but Great-uncle Sam was often an exasperating disappointment.

One spring, Uncle Sam got most of his planting done. But when an opportunity to travel around the country and play his fiddle presented itself, Sam could not resist. He hired a family of tenant farmers to live in his house and see that his crops were laid by—and he took off.

No one in the family approved of this arrangement, especially as it became increasingly obvious that Uncle Sam's judgment with regard to tenants was sadly misguided. The yards grew up, the horses and cows were clearly not properly tended, and there were no signs that the cotton was being chopped or the corn thinned. Finally, someone reported that the tenants, who were evidently too lazy to go to the timbers for firewood, were destroying the cross-fencing so they could burn the posts in their cookstove. For Great-grandma Sarah, this was the last straw.

She and her sister, Great-aunt Becky (a headstrong spinster with a reputation herself), loaded their guns, climbed into the buggy, and drove down the road to Uncle Sam's place and evicted the feckless—and thoroughly frightened—tenants. My grandfather and his older brother stubbornly refused to leave their own crops in order to help save the absent Sam's, and Great-grandma Sarah humored them in their indignation. She and Aunt Becky and a couple of teenage nephews managed to get Sam's crops laid by.

When Great-uncle Sam eventually showed up again, Great-grandma Sarah informed him that if she was still woman enough to get his crops harvested, she was woman enough to "whale the livin' daylights out of him" if he didn't stay at home and mend his ways. Whether out of chagrin or fear, Sam stayed on his farm, at least long enough to get the crops harvested that year.

Such stories, familiar through repeated retellings, nevertheless continued to evoke guffaws and appreciative comments from listeners, whether the tellers were men or women. Hog killings were active affairs, with much moving about and continual interaction between the men doing the slaughtering out in the barnyard and the women salting down the meat and stuffing sacks of sausage in the kitchen. There were not, so far as I was aware, long storytelling sessions among the women as was the case with the maternal Ward-Wolf side of the family.

The Headless Rooster

Grandmother Winniford—who had been a Lantroupe—was a quiet, authoritative, hard-working woman and not much of a storyteller. I remember only one story that she told, and her manner of telling was so brusque and literal that for a long time I did not doubt that it was fact. Just a few days ago, she told my brother and me and some cousins, she had been wringing a frying chicken's neck, and something had diverted her attention so that she didn't do it exactly right. Well, the head came off and the chicken flopped out into the yard. Before she could grab him, however, he jumped up and ran off into the bushes in back of the barn. She had heard the headless fowl several times in the past few days, she declared, although she hadn't caught sight of him. The headless young rooster couldn't cackle or crow, of course, but you could hear the air wheezing through his headless neck and the sounds of his feet scrambling around in the brush. When one of my cousins suggested hopefully that the rooster would soon die of hunger, Grandmother Winniford said she wasn't so sure of that. After all, the headless rooster didn't have a brain, so how was he to know that he was hungry?

Stories about runaway half-butchered livestock were obviously popular among these farm folk, although I am not certain whether my grandmother's headless chicken story was ever told at hog killings. In fact, the story may have been concocted for the specific instance I remember, intended to discourage an audience of gawking, curious children who were interfering with her preparations for Sunday dinner. But while that may have been her only telling, the story had uneasy currency among children in the family for many years. My brother recalls another story of my grandmother's that, to my surprise, I had not heard before. This tale would have been somewhat out of season at hog killings, but its bizarre subject matter fit comfortably into the lively repertoire.

Watermelon Boy

I guess, first of all, I would tell you one of the old stories that my grandmother told me when I was little. It seemed as though a lot of times the old folks—or even our mamas and daddies—would tell us stories that

> were intended to cause us to not do things they didn't want us to do, and so a lot of times they would tell us some pretty good yarns.
>
> My grandmother was always worried about us children swallowing watermelon seeds and maybe getting choked or something of that sort. And so she told me one time that if I ate my watermelon too fast and swallowed a seed—she said she knew a little boy that did that, and the watermelon seed sprouted, and he walked around dragging a watermelon behind him because the vine grew out his little hiney and it had watermelons on it. And he went walking around dragging that watermelon around on the ground.
>
> I know that was a yarn—but for a little kid, it gave you something to think about. Maybe it caused us to listen to granny, you know, and not eat the watermelon too fast and swallow the seed.[9]

My brother most likely is correct in assessing the intent of this story. It may be said that the performance of folklore can be among other things an exercise in behavior modification. Whether one agrees with this broad generalization or not, my paternal grandmother's brief forays into storytelling were obviously intended to modify behavior. Her practical, no-nonsense persona and her abrupt, poker-faced delivery enabled her to depict, as Oring says legend often does, "the improbable within the world of the possible."[10] This left her audience off-balance—full of wonderment but hardly daring not to believe. Perhaps if my Grandmother Winniford had been an enthusiastic storyteller, her material would have been very similar to that of my maternal grandmother (whose stories fill a later chapter in this collection). The two women did, in fact, have certain things in common, despite their tendency to give each other a wide berth. Gender, of course, was primary; in addition, both were part Indian, and both belonged to families that, if for no other reason than that the males were rather wild and unruly, were regarded as socially marginal.

The paternal side of my family had strong ties to the nineteenth century, to the frontier customs of their forebears, and to the values that had enabled these pioneering ancestors to persevere. These ties can be explained, in part, by their storytelling. By constructing and accreting a family "history," they brought ancestry from the past into the present and ensured that at least some of their traditions would be ongoing. Many of the people with whom I come in contact both socially and professionally do not know who their great-grandparents were, much less what their personalities were like, what they believed, or how they led their daily lives. For me, personages like Great-grandma Sarah and Great-aunt Becky are familiar, vital extensions of my perception of family. That perception offers me a niche in the scheme of things that is comforting in my prodigality, my "wanderings."

When my daughter, Leann, read the first draft of this chapter, she was amazed by these people she did not know and these stories she had never heard. I realized how inadequate a storyteller I have been. Life is too fast paced; the occasions do not present themselves. These excuses are sad. My father's family made time for telling, while they picked cotton and killed hogs and sat out Texas tornadoes down in the storm cellar. Theirs is a legacy worth sharing.

Chapter Four

Telling Storm-Cellar Tales in Cyclone Country

One of the strongest images from my youth is of my family hunched together in the damp darkness of the storm cellar with the flickering flame of the coal-oil lantern highlighting their features. The storm cellar during bad weather was another of the rural settings in which the stories that I associate with the paternal side of my family—the Winnifords and Alexanders—were often told. Although my father generally deferred to my grandfather and the other older Winniford men at family gatherings, assuming the role of enthusiastic listener, in our immediate family he was, of course, the dominant male and chief storyteller. In no place were we more conscious of his skills than down in the cellar with the wind and rain and thunder whistling and rumbling above us. We made countless visits to the cellar, and the memories of these family times together tend to meld. One experience, however, does stand out from the rest: the time when a dangerous little twister hit our farm.

It was May. The day had started out partly cloudy and rather balmy, but by four o'clock that afternoon, when the school bus dropped my brother and me off at the end of our drive near the mailbox, the temperature had dropped. As my father would say, "Bad weather was building up in the west." There was a play of lightning in a dark bank of clouds on that horizon, and little ragged bits of cloud scurried across the sky high above us.

Our parents were already out tending to evening chores, we

noticed, as we walked toward the old farmhouse. My mother was hurrying across the yard with an armload of dry clothes that she had taken off the clothesline, and she was obviously relieved that we were home. She called to us to change out of our school clothes quickly and to get our own assigned tasks done. We were going to get a storm out of those clouds in the west, she told us, probably a bad one. The sudden drop in temperature was an ominous sign. My brother and I nodded and waved to indicate that we understood as we ran across the front yard and up the front steps to the porch.

"What do you want to bet we spend the night in the storm cellar!" my brother grumbled.

"Maybe not," I reassured him. "It's early yet. The storm may be over by dark—or by bedtime, anyway."

"Or it could just go around us," my brother suggested. "It wouldn't hurt God a bit to let this storm go around. Just this once, when I have arithmetic homework and a map in geography."

I agreed: one day's respite in view of these complications did not seem an unreasonable expectation. Neither of us, however, would have voiced these opinions in the presence of our parents. They did not tolerate criticisms of the deity's handling of the weather.

We went through the house, deposited our schoolbooks on the dining room table, changed into our work clothes, and met briefly at the water bucket in the kitchen for a cool drink of well water. Then we rushed across the screened-in back porch, down the back steps, and out into the increasingly menacing-looking weather. I was in junior high and James was only a couple of years younger, so we were old enough to carry an important part of the family's workload. We understood what had to be done and took our tasks seriously. May was a critical time in the cycle of farm work. New spring plantings of cotton, corn, and hay would be at full stand and generally would have been thinned or chopped, but the plants were still tender and easily damaged. Most of the cows dropped their calves in the spring, and these animals had to be tended carefully. There would always be several chicken hens with broods of young chicks.

For my family, turkeys were almost as significant a source of income as cotton. Turkeys would lay throughout the early spring. Eggs were collected and stored during the laying season and then finally carried to a commercial hatchery in Commerce, so that we would be tending two or three hundred freshly hatched turkeys sometime in late April or early May. The season's big "hatching" was divided into flocks, and each flock was assigned to one of several brood hens and trained to run the open range.

That May afternoon, my family was concerned with getting all this vulnerable livestock—on which our livelihood depended—into some sort of shelter where there was protection from rain, wind, and hail. While my brother went to the barnyard to help my father, I gathered eggs from the henhouse and other known laying places. I then shooed a couple of old hens and their chicks into coops and closed the doors so they could not get out until the storm had passed. After that, my mother and I joined my father and brother down past the barnyard at the turkey "brooders," the long, low sheds in which we sheltered the young turkeys. Turkeys are not so docile as chickens and are harder to pen.

While we worked, we shared our worries about the approaching storm. My father was respected among the neighbors for his ability to "read the weather," so we relied on him to predict what the elements might do. That afternoon there were many things about the ugly, darkening sky that alarmed him. There was a rim of light under the bank of clouds, which meant strong wind was behind them. Dad called our attention to how the clouds were rolling and boiling. "We need to get these turkeys in the brooders and get back to the house," he warned. "That storm may hit quicker than we think." My brother and I exchanged meaningful glances. We were conscious that we worked under the threat of the approaching storm and that we were almost certainly faced with a prolonged stay in the storm cellar.

Probably the one place during my childhood where I felt safest and most secure was the storm cellar. I realize this only in retrospect, for when I was growing up, trips to the storm cellar were dreaded and endured as stoically as possible in spite of the discomforts involved. But it was in the storm cellar that my family came together for long hours of close, uninterrupted contact, where intimate thoughts were shared and plans for a future were made once the storm was over. I do not think any aspect of modern life offers a comparable opportunity for families to have time to communicate and to get to know each other.

Around Cumby, almost everyone had a storm cellar, even many families in town. Certainly, most farm places were so equipped. Electrical storms were frequent, and the area was famous as a "cyclone alley." Farmhouses, in particular, tended to be rattletrap frame structures that could not withstand a strong wind. Most people were afraid to sit out a bad storm in their dwelling.

Although all cellars were basically a hole in the ground with a dirt roof on top, there could be important differences in their construction. People who were situated permanently on their own land, especially those who had managed to build a fairly presentable house, usually tried to provide themselves with an equally presentable storm cellar. Such cellars would be relatively large, deep enough that adults could stand up once inside them without cracking their heads on the roof, and dry. Bricked-in and mortared walls were a desired feature. Floors were never bricked because of a concern that water might seep in and stand, but a board platform raised two or three inches from the floor was a welcome luxury.

My Grandmother Ward's storm cellar in Cumby was a large, rectangular affair, which my Uncle Bernice had furnished with long, reasonably comfortable benches and rows of neat shelves for storing jars of canned fruits and vegetables. He had devised a pulley-operated door that always impressed people who showed up to take refuge from the weather. "Going to the cellar" at Grandma Ward's was usually a social event. Neighbors up and down her street came when the weather was especially threatening, and everyone filed down into the cellar and sat quietly gossiping while the storm raged on.

Cousin Jesse Alexander was a retired seaman who had picked up a number of skills, including mixing and pouring cement. He constructed a cement cellar that was the talk of the countryside, truly the last word in comfort and convenience. But for reasons that were never clear, the thing leaked like a sieve, and water rose quickly on the cement floor to the alarm of the occupants. To alleviate this problem, he purchased a pump and hose, which he installed through the cement roof. During the time when my family lived close to his place and shared his wonderful cellar, I recall many instances of sitting huddled in the cellar with the door thrown open and Cousin Jesse standing outside in the wind and rain, for all the world like a brave sea captain, whistling and manning the pump.

Most cellars, however, were more humble affairs. My family moved around a lot, from one family farm to another as well as to a couple of tenant farms, and my mother was especially nervous about bad weather. Therefore, after he had straightened sagging porches and jacked the house up on its blocks, my father's next job was always to dig a cellar. For him, this was generally a one-man operation. The cellars he dug were therefore small, with barely enough room for the four people in our family and with roofs that were so low that he had to stay hunched over when he stood up and moved around.

Dad would select a high place with good drainage far enough from the house and outbuildings that they were not likely to be blown over onto it but close enough that it could be reached in a hurry. Then he would mark off a square with string and begin work with a spade and shovel. The digging got harder the farther down he went, and my mother, brother, and I usually helped him lift the dirt out with buckets. When the square in the earth was deep enough, he would dig a trench sloping down into one end of it. This is where the steps would be built and the framework for the door laid out. Heavy posts (railroad crossties were his favorite) were set in each corner and additional ones placed along the side if they were available. To these posts, my father attached whatever siding he had been able to acquire: old boards or sometimes tin roofing. Once the interior of the cellar was finished, the roof was put on. Heavy posts or crossties were laid across the excavation from side to side, partially braced by the standing posts in the corners and at the sides. Over these were laid strips of tin roofing that, it was hoped, would keep the roof from leaking. Finally, the dirt that had been removed from the excavation was spread on top in an oval mound. My father was a good carpenter, so the steps and door that he built would be works of art, even when all he had to use was old scrap lumber. Such cellars were dark, damp, and musty and attracted a variety of vermin: rats, snakes, spiders, and, on one occasion, a family of skunks.

It always seemed that most of my family's trips to the storm cellar happened at night. Usually just after sundown, my parents would note dark clouds on the western or northwestern horizon, the direction from which most of our "weather" came. If there was a faint play of lightning among these clouds, that was a danger sign, and my mother made preparations. First, she would lay out our coats (we always wore coats, even in summer—whether because these were expensive garments that she did not want blown away or because, Texas weather being what it is, she considered it entirely possible that we could emerge into a blizzard, I do not know). Next, she would fill the lantern with coal oil, and finally she would fill an old jug with water. My father, for his part, would make certain that an ax and shovel were in the cellar just in case we had to dig out. Then we waited for the storm to either "come up" or "go around." Sometimes my brother and I would enjoy a few hours of fitful sleep while our parents kept watch on the developing storm. At whatever point they felt certain that we were all in the storm's path, they would awaken us. We would don coats and shoes and rush through the dark and the first puffs of wind and rain to the cellar, where my father would stand, holding the door up and open while we scrambled down the steps.

Thus, that late-afternoon May storm was different. It is my theory that we visited the storm cellar more frequently at night because by daylight the elements, generally speaking, do not look and sound so frightening as they seem in the dark when the lightning flashes across the sky and the winds whistle and roar in the stillness. Quite possibly, however, had the May storm hit at night, it would have caught us unawares because most of the danger signs would not have been visible. We noticed agitation among the livestock: the cows started coming in from the back pasture, some of them at a run, lowing for their calves; the chickens took to their roosts, although it was nowhere near sundown, and they stirred about restlessly, clucking and cackling in muted alarm. Jagged flocks of birds skittered across the sky ahead of the storm, which now seemed, indeed, to advance rapidly.

My father had the storm-cellar door propped open, and he was filling the lantern with coal oil from a barrel in the smokehouse—a preparation my mother would usually have already completed had there not been so much to do and so little warning. My father exclaimed rather breathlessly that he had never seen a sky with quite the same greenish hue as this one. He was sure that must mean hail, wind, and maybe even a cyclone.

Great-uncle Sam was living with us at the time, and the blind old man had pulled a rope-bottomed chair out onto the front porch and was tuning up his fiddle. With the filled and lighted lantern in hand, my father walked around the house and warned my great-uncle, "You'd better not try to sit this one out, Sam. It looks bad. I think it may be a cyclone or something."

"You know I can't stand being holed up in that cellar. Having to feel my way around, not knowing what's going on. If it's my time to die, I'd rather be out in the open. I'm not one to hide from the Grim Reaper. He can come get me right out here, if he's a mind to—while I'm sitting on my porch playing my fiddle like a man!"

"Well, I'm not going to try to force you—but I want you to know that it could get bad. There's a greenish hue all across the west, and the clouds are boiling and tumbling like smoke from a brush fire."

"The sky is green?" My old great-uncle sensed that my brother and I were standing beside our father, and what he said was mostly for our benefit. "Then it likely is another cyclone. I sat out the last one that hit here. Watched it blow away the barn. Picked it up, set it clear on the other side of the barnyard fence, and smashed the whole thing flat. Kind of systematic—picked it up, set it down, smashed it. They used what lumber they still could and just built a new barn right there—that barn that's standing now. They built it where the cyclone had set the old one and went on and moved the fence line a little."

My mother interrupted by calling from inside the house. She ordered my brother and me to come in and get our coats and go on to the cellar. She was putting all the windows down.

Big, solitary drops of rain were kicking up dust here and there on the scraped dirt yards, and unexpected little gusts of wind whipped about, jerking the branches of the ancient cedars and blowing loose objects across the ground. My brother and I obediently fetched the coats that my mother had waiting for us, and my father preceded us down the steep steps into the cellar with the lighted lantern. Once we were seated and he had hung the lantern from its hook, he ascended the steps to check on my mother.

On this occasion, my mother took an inordinately long time with her above-ground precautions. Not only did she lower the windows throughout the house but she, too, paused to plead unsuccessfully with my blind great-uncle to join us in the cellar. My brother and I sat in the flickering lantern light and listened uneasily to the sounds of the now-pounding rain and of our stubborn old uncle fiddling wildly out on the front porch.

At last my mother came down the steps, followed by my father, who moved much more slowly because he was lowering the cellar door as he came. When the door was closed, he fastened the chain so that gusts of strong wind could not lift the door and blow it open. To our astonishment, both our parents' faces and clothes were mud-spattered.

"It's raining mud balls!" my mother gasped as she seated herself. This development was both exciting and unsettling. I recall that we sat in awe for a time, trying to comprehend what was happening.

The storm cellar had its own protocol, and periods of respectful silence were sometimes in order. Behavior was restricted, of course, by the confined, limited space. Excessive movement on the part of anyone could have made other occupants uncomfortable, so one was expected to sit very still whether one was awestruck or not. I always thought that we behaved in the cellar much as we did in church and with much the same motivation: a feeling that we were, in that place, in especially intimate contact with the Almighty. The perception of god-in-nature, which most farmers shared to some extent, was very strong in my parents, meaning that the "god of farmers" spoke to them in the fierce lightning and crashing thunder and howling winds. Thus, at the peak of a storm, when the divinity's "voice" was most clearly heard, we were expected to sit in silence. That silence might be literally prayerful if my parents feared for their crops and livestock. The mood—and behavior—was permitted to become more relaxed when the critical moments passed and we settled in to wait out the storm. The cellar was a cramped place where discomfort and boredom set in quickly. Both my parents utilized whatever skills they had to keep us all entertained. If we were all wide awake and full of energy, we might sit and sing songs together. Often we sang hymns, or "church songs," as we called them. But there were other favorites.

"Old Dan Tucker" was a song that my father sang with wild facial expressions and gesticulations.

Old Dan Tucker, well he come in drunk
And he fell in the fire and he kicked up a chunk

And a red-hot coal got down his shoe
Then, oh, oh, oh, how his coattail flew!
Get out of the way for Old Dan Tucker
He's too late to get his supper!

There was another song he sang to try to reassure us when we noticed an especially vicious-looking spider lurking in some dark corner.

See that spider in the air?
He ain't got on no underwear.
See that spider on the wall?
He ain't got on no drawers a'tall.

If we could laugh at the improperly-clad spider, our fears subsided.

Often, once it seemed that the worst was over, a period of prayerful silence would be broken by accounts of bad weather, usually (though not always) accounts of Texas bad weather.

Possession is Nine-Tenths of the Law

There was the story of an ambitious farmer—one of the kinfolk, an Ellis or Alexander, maybe—who came into some land and set to work immediately getting his crops planted and laid by and sprucing up the house and outbuildings. The house was not in bad condition except for needing a new roof. The ambitious kinsman bought high-grade cedar shingles and with the help of a brother did a truly professional job putting a new roof on his dwelling. He took great pride in thinking that the roof would last another twenty years.

One afternoon while he was working in one of the far fields, he glanced over toward his homeplace and saw a black, mean-looking twister zigzagging over the countryside, heading toward his house and barns. Well, the man threw down his hoe and started running home. He was kind of crazy, of course, for what could he really do once he got there? But he felt that somehow, some way, he must keep the twister from dismantling all his hard work.

Suddenly, everything got dark, and he was stopped dead in his tracks, half-stunned by the pounding rain and hail. The farmer heard that proverbially awful sound, like an approaching freight train. There was a breathless second, and he looked up. He must have been standing directly under the eye of the twister. Swirling high above his head, the cedar roof was still intact as it was being carried away by the storm.

As soon as the storm was over, the kinsman started looking for his roof. He was certain that if it had stayed in one piece long enough for him to recognize it, the roof was still around somewhere if he could find it. He located it the next day in a cantankerous neighbor's pasture. This neighbor refused to allow the roof to be removed from his property. Possession, he declared, was nine-tenths of the law, and the roof was in his pasture through an act of God.

The matter was never happily resolved. The kinsman put another roof on his house, and the neighbor raised the roof that had blown onto his property and made a cowshed out of it. But relations between the two households were strained, to say the least.

Another story, most often told by my mother since it concerned an older brother, describes yet another twister—one that may have landed in Arkansas rather than Texas.

Room with a View

Uncle Elmer and Aunt Nora moved around a lot, and their circumstances were often dire indeed. At one point they moved to a small, run-down farm on which the only dwelling was the original, one-room log cabin. Uncle Elmer hustled up lumber here and there and attached lean-tos on either end of the log structure. Aunt Nora appreciated the extra space, but she was disappointed that the additions covered the log room's only window. Because this room contained the flue and chimney, she had to use it for her kitchen, and she hated a kitchen without a view.

Uncle Elmer was much less interested in digging a storm cellar than he had been in providing extra living space. Therefore, when bad weather came, Aunt Nora took her babies and crouched down with them in the log room, which everyone assured her was strong enough to hold during a storm.

One day a twister ripped through their section of the country. It splintered Uncle Elmer's lean-tos but, as had been predicted, left the log structure standing—with Aunt Nora and her babies safe inside. Uncle Elmer was devastated that all his carpentry had come to naught. Aunt Nora, however, insisted that "every cloud had a silver lining": there was a window in her kitchen once again.

In addition to cyclonic winds, northeast Texas was subject to other meteorological disturbances. There were a number of short, more or less plotless, accounts of a variety of these: lumps of hail as big as baseballs, a flash flood that rained small fish, a bolt of lightning that poached eggs in the henhouse. One story gave an account of a hailstorm that taught an important moral lesson.

One "Hail" of a Payback

People remembered a particular year in the 1930s as a troublesome one, even for farmers who made bumper crops. The weather was tricky and unpredictable. A small area of the county would get much-needed rain while a section no more than a couple of miles away would remain blighted by drought. Cutworms or weevils would strike one farmer's crops; the crops of a nearby farmer would seem to be unmolested by the pests. So, although some farmers had an anxious time of it and did not do well, others were more prosperous than usual. One of the lucky farmers was a big landholder. When his cotton opened, his fields were a sight to behold. From a distance, one would have sworn that these fields were deep in snow.

As was their custom, the small farmers hurried to gather their own crops so they could hire out to the big farmers to make extra money. But when they reported to the prosperous farmer for work, he had an unpleasant surprise for them. His cotton, he told them, was "easy picking," and he was willing to pay only half the going rate for every pound picked.

Although the small farmers needed money, they rebelled at the more fortunate man's unfairness. When they told him they would not work unless he paid them a fair wage, he responded, "Get out of here then. I don't need you. I'll send for a truckload of migrant workers, and they'll work for what I'm willing to pay."

Sending for the migrants took a couple of days. On the night before they were supposed to arrive, there was a bad electrical storm with high winds and hail. Some areas were much harder hit than others—and one of the hardest hit was the big farmer. When he went out to his fields the next morning, he discovered that the hailstorm had stripped the cotton from the stalks and pounded it into the ground.

Such stories demonstrated the helplessness of human beings in dealing with the forces of nature. Telling them may have helped my parents acknowledge and confront their worst fears as they sat waiting for their fate to be decided by the volatile Texas elements. Certainly, it was clear to most farmers, my parents included, that nature did not always mete out justice, rewarding the good and punishing the evil. "The sun shines on sinners as well as on saints," they knew, and a hard-working, righteous farmer could lose everything he owned to blight and drought. Still, my parents had a tendency to give their weather stories a moral tack. The churchlike context provided by storm-cellar protocol may have influenced them to give their narratives a moral bent. Also, there may have been similarities to the Ward-Wolf (or maternal) storytelling mode, since my mother participated in storm-cellar storytelling.

I do not recall how much storytelling was done during the first, tense minutes of our stay in the cellar on that memorable May afternoon. My father often told jokes, riddles, or bits of favorite stories in order to reassure us and relieve tension—ignoring his own uneasiness and alarm for our sakes.

Time passed as we hunkered there expectantly—one never knew how much time because minutes drag in the dark isolation of the cellar. Then solid whacks against the tin on the cellar door riveted our attention.

"Hail," my father pronounced.

"Well, you said we would have hail," my mother reminded him, "when you saw how green the sky was."

"Then I'm afraid we'll get the twister, too," he admitted. He would, perhaps, have added some hopeful comment except that the hail against the cellar door drowned out his voice.

Without warning, the raining and hailing ceased. One second the hail was pounding against the tin-paneled door—and the next we were sitting in an eerie, stifling silence. We could hardly catch our breaths.

"The eye!" my mother whispered.

"We are right in the middle of it!" my father exclaimed softly.

"It'll blow poor old Uncle Sam away!" wailed my brother.

We strained to hear, listening for any sound that might be a clue to what was happening outside. Our breathing was shallow, difficult, as if the supply of oxygen had been shut off.

"There!" my mother reassured us. "I heard the sound of his fiddle. Just barely. He's still out there on the porch." Even after that May storm was long past, my mother maintained that she'd heard the fiddle, although we doubted that she really could have with the cellar door shut. But believing she heard the old man comforted us all at the time.

Again without warning, the silence was interrupted by rain on the tin of the cellar door—hard, driving rain with perhaps intermittent hailstones. The crisis was past (whatever it might have been), and the damage was done (whatever it might prove to be). We resigned ourselves to waiting out the rest of the storm.

No doubt, convinced as we were that we had spent some harrowing moments in the very eye of a tornado, we were especially keyed up and impatient for a break in the storm so we could climb out of the cellar, make certain our old uncle was unharmed, and repair the damage. I can't be certain how much storytelling was done during this tense wait. Normally, during such times of waiting, my father told stories. He enjoyed humorous yarns about family members, particularly incidents involving his own father. My brother recalls hearing my father tell this story.

Apprehending the Smokehouse Burglar

Then I'll tell you the story about Grandpa and the guy that was stealing meat out of his smokehouse there during the Depression. They had a fella that lived across the pasture from Grandpa, and they were poor and up against it. So at nighttime, why this guy was slipping into Grandpa's smokehouse and getting the meat. To feed his kids. Well, you know, that seemed like the sensible thing to do.

But Grandpa didn't like a stealer, though, so he got ready, and he fixed up a shotgun shell that was filled with fat meat, and he packed it in that shotgun shell. And so, sure enough, the poor old guy—I won't call his name—but he decided he'd come over again and steal some meat. So he had got in the smokehouse, and Grandpa heard him—so he got the shotgun and went out in that direction. The guy had already got his little chunk of meat or whatever it was, you know, and he started out across there—and he'd just got to the fence and was fixing to go through the gate, and Grandpa cut down on him. Shot him right between the shoulder blades with that hunk of hot meat because, of course, the gun had heated the meat.

And it was hot grease, you know, and it hit the fella between the shoulders, and the guy thought for sure as the world he was dead! He could see this hole that was obviously knocked in his back, you know.

And he was lying on the ground there, praying and crying and everything. Grandpa went out to him, and he said, "Now, look," he said. "If you need food for your family, you come over here and ask me for it, because I'll give it to you. But," he said, "don't ever come back here stealing meat again." And sure enough, the fella never did come back to steal the meat.[1]

There were several stories about Grandpa Winniford's problems with various county agricultural agents. Grandpa was a stubborn, ornery little man with a strong distaste for "big government," and my father found his escapades humorous and, probably, somewhat heroic. My brother tells of an incident involving Grandpa and some county agents in much the same manner that my father told such tales to us down in the storm cellar.

Bluffing the County Agents

You know, my grandpa always said that if we started letting the government get involved in farming, they'd eventually be telling us how many acres of everything we could grow. And sure enough, during the Depression, well they started this business of cutting down on the number of acres of this crop and that which they'd allow you to plant, and they also decided that in order to relieve the conditions of the Depression, the thing to do was to exterminate some of the cattle.

Now Grandpa already had what I guess you'd call a biased opinion about the government boys, anyway. So he decided they were up to no good, no matter how you looked at it. So he misinterpreted some of the things that were being said and just got the part about "cutting down on the number of cattle so the value of the cows would go up." He thought that the government was going to come out and just shoot his cows. Well, they were actually going to pay him, something like five dollars or ten, and it was going to be on a voluntary basis that you allowed them to exterminate some of your cattle.

Well, poor old Grandpa, he was kind of an ornery little devil. He was about a hundred and forty pounds, but he backed most of it up, if he needed to, with a shotgun. So, he was not to be messed with.

Well, the government boys drove up one morning out there, and they started telling Grandpa what they were going to do, what they were there for, and that they were going to alleviate this unfortunate surplus of cattle that existed. Well, Grandpa already had his mind made up what it was all about, so he said, "Well, you boys wait here just a second," and he stepped back in the house and brought out his gun, and he said, "All right," and he said, "It's not going to go very far. Now then, you all can start killing cows." But he said, "It's not going to go very far because every time a cow goes down, a man goes down." Well, these government boys decided that the best thing to do was to leave. They had encountered a person there that obviously didn't understand their motives.[2]

Other family members were the subjects of humorous tales that were often told while our family sat in the storm cellar. As mentioned previously, I have never really thought of my Grandmother Winniford as a storyteller. Unlike the Winnifords, who were enthusiastic about their ancestors and current kin, my grandmother was extremely reticent in revealing information about her own family. Apparently, though, she had sometimes talked about certain memorable incidents. My brother recalls my father telling the story of Great-uncle Luther's rather questionable activities, and he offers this retelling.

Uncle Luther Turns Horse Thief

You know, they say that any time you start looking back into your family history or running a family tree, you're going to find some outlaws. I think that I found my portion of outlaws among all these people—but one in particular was a guy they called Uncle Luther Lantroupe. Now it *might* be that I have the wrong first name, but he was a Lantroupe and Luther was one of them. These people were half Irish and half Indian—had dark hair, and they could very well and very easily mix in with the Indian people.

But Uncle Luther had a lot of skills. He was quite the artist, and so he used his artistic abilities. And from what I understand (now this was a story related to me when I was a very young person) but from what I can understand, Uncle Luther (now he was not my first uncle; he was way on back there in the ancestry, but they just spoke of him as that) used his artistic skills to produce Confederate money, or whatever be the case, and he was doing quite well.

But, of course, your sins will find you out—so, finally, he came to that situation where they closed in on him, and he knew that he was going to get caught, and he knew that he was facing some troubles. So he simply chooses two of the best horses in that part of the country—and, of course, at that time horse thieving was rewarded by allowing you to make very taut a rope between your neck and a tree limb. Old Uncle Luther decided the best thing for him to do was to depart the scenery.

And so he takes these two of the *best horses* out of the community and goes more or less Indian style from this standpoint: he led one horse and rode the other. And they found one of the horses just turned loose, you know, up between where he lived and the Oklahoma Territory—it was not a state then—and he rode one horse until it was tired and worn out, and then he had the other horse that hadn't been carrying a load. So, therefore, he could continue on his journey, and they made much better time than people who might be trying to follow him.

Well, he got himself into the Oklahoma Territory and dissolved himself among the Indians up there and lived there for a long time. Everybody back home thought, well, somebody has caught up with him and killed him finally, and so they never heard anything from him. It was a long time before anybody ever heard from him. Finally, he *did* send a letter down, and he told everybody—he sent a letter to my grandmother, and he told her that everything was fine, that he was up there and was in good health and nothing to be worried about. That was our Uncle Luther—yes, that was the horse thief in the family![3]

On occasions when our family was not sitting directly under the eye of a Texas tornado, both parents used good-humored ingenuity to keep my brother and me from growing impatient and restless. There were games that could be played in the cramped conditions of the cellar: "Feed the Crow" and "Take It Off or Knock It Off" were favorites. It was primarily down in the cellar that my brother and I learned our multiplication tables before we started first grade. We had spelling bees, and my parents drilled us on state capitals. We also had long discussions about what it meant to be alive and what it would mean to die.

Memory is fallible. But I suspect that no games were played, no jokes or riddles told, no songs sung late that May afternoon while we waited for the wind and rain to let up enough that my father could lift the cellar door and permit us to emerge and survey the damage. We considered the possibility that Great-uncle Sam might have been killed or hurt badly, a circumstance that my father said we would accept with grace because "Sam had a right to decide how he wanted to meet his Maker." My parents discussed worriedly the various crops that might be substituted for cotton, which could not be replanted that late in the year. They felt certain the hail had riddled the new stands of cotton and corn. My mother resigned herself to the probable loss of the entire flock of young turkeys, and she doubted that the brood hens would lay much more so near to summer. The outlook seemed bleak.

As soon as the winds had subsided enough that my father could be certain the storm had passed, he undid the chain that held the door and climbed up the steps, slowly pushing the door against the rain. "You all stay where you are, and let me check on things first," he told us.

"Oh, no, we're right behind you," my mother insisted. The three of us crowded close against him as he shoved the door open.

There was still a steady downpour, and big, fibrous-looking chunks of hail still fell occasionally, but it all glistened and sparkled in the evening sunshine. Our initial surprise and elation at the sight of sunlight was short-lived. Debris was everywhere: riddled leaves and branches, shingles off rooftops, broken pieces of lumber, and unaccountable things that had never belonged to us like a half-unwound roll of chicken wire and a length of twisted metal gutter from someone's roof. The devastation was so momentarily overwhelming that the details hardly registered. We saw the strangely sagging back porch, the uprooted tree, and the tilted smokehouse pulling the attached clothesline wires taut to the verge of snapping.

There was, however, instant reassurance regarding our chief

concern. The minute we stepped outside the cellar, we heard the sound of the fiddle. Great-uncle Sam had safely weathered the storm.

"Sam, are you still sitting on that porch?" my father yelled.

The fiddling ceased abruptly. "John Horace? Well, it's a good thing! I was beginning to think I'd have to come dig you folks out!"

But it was not a time for levity.

"The barn's gone!" my father gasped. The barn was so completely demolished that, amid all the other confusion, we did not at first notice its absence. My mother and I were concerned with the turkeys, and we groaned when we noted the coops (or brooders) lodged against a far fence line.

The next hour was a frantic, nightmarish one. My father and brother rushed down to the barnyard where the barn had once stood. Several newborn calves were pinned under the roof of the shed where they had been shut away for safety's sake. While the calves' mothers bawled and ran about hysterically, trying to break through the barnyard fence, my father and brother struggled to free the calves. They credited an amazing burst of adrenaline with their ability to lift the roof aside over the area where most of the calves had shoved together in their fright.

For our part, my mother and I had invested a great deal of time, energy, and high hopes in the fledgling flock of turkeys. We ran down past the barnyard to the area from which their shelters had been carried off by the twister. Turkeys were scattered everywhere. When young turkeys get cold and wet, they go into shock and become stiff and comatose very much as if rigor mortis has set in. It was therefore like seeing the ground strewn with a couple of hundred dead turkeys. But my mother and I hoped some of them might revive given proper care, so we located big buckets, filled them with the "carcasses," and hurried back to the house. While I spread comatose turkeys on the floor around the cookstove and the front-room heater, my mother built fires in both appliances. Then we ran back and forth with our buckets, gathering up and delivering additional loads.

For the four of us, it was a strangely rigorous, wordless time. In the gathering twilight, my father set out across the fields to determine how much damage had been done to the crops. Forget about milking, he said. He had turned the miraculously unharmed calves out to their frantic mamas. Even Great-uncle Sam was considerably subdued. Eventually, he sidled up to my mother and me as we worked with the traumatized turkey flock and suggested timidly, "You know, you might want to check the chimneys. If they're blown down, you could set the whole house on fire." We did check. They were down. But as my mother said, it was too late to worry about that now. The fires were going, and some of the turkeys were beginning to stretch and come back to life.

As darkness settled in, one of my aunts arrived. From a distance, the farm place where she lived with my grandmother (widowed then) and another aunt had appeared to escape the storm unscathed. But my aunt had horror stories of her own to tell. "I was putting that old Rhode Island red and her chickens in their coop—rushing, you know, trying to get them into shelter—and all of a sudden the wind picked that coop up right before my eyes and just left that hen and her chickens sitting there, right out in the open. I did the best I could to shoo her under the back porch—and then I tried to get to the cellar. Mama and Lucille were out there too by that time, and we'd get nearly to the cellar door, and the wind would spin us like tops and push us clear around the corner where the chimney is. Finally, we caught hold of that little bois d'arc tree and made our way from there to the cellar. We were all scratched and bruised and mighty scared."

We marveled that my grandmother's house and barns, not even a quarter of a mile away, had not been severely damaged although they seemed directly in the path of the twister that had demolished much of ours. "That's how a cyclone does," my father commented, "Sort of bounces along, jumping over some things and hitting others. There's no accounting for them logically."

A neighbor man pulled into the drive in his pickup. He had seen that the twister had hit our place and had come to check on us. The storm had leveled one of his hay barns. Immediately, he and my father began planning how they could help each other rebuild: which lumberyard would let them have building materials on credit, which neighbor boys might do a few days' work cheap. The neighbor was amused by the account of Great-uncle Sam's "riding the whole thing out" on the front porch. "Well, Nero fiddled while Rome burned," the neighbor laughed, "and Sam fiddled while that twister blew his farm to smithereens!"

Sam, the neighbor reminded us, had a reputation for becoming oblivious to his surroundings when he was giving a performance—of any kind. He recounted an incident from my great-uncle's youth.

Great-Uncle Sam Quotes Whittier

Uncle Sam and some of his buddies were playing a gig at a Christmas dance. A pretty girl there caught Sam's roving eye. She was impressed by his fiddling and was coyly receptive to his advances. But Great-uncle Sam wanted to be admired for his brains, as well; he was proud of his intellectual abilities.

Someone noticed that a light snow had started falling. People gathered at the windows to look out, excited at the prospect of the first snow that winter. Well, Great-uncle Sam could recite John Greenleaf Whittier's "Snowbound" in its entirety. Inspired by the snowfall, he began declaiming the poem in his sonorous, emotional style, certain that this feat of memory would win the heart of the pretty girl.

An appreciative audience gathered, and Sam warmed to his performance, forgetting all else except the poet's fine words and the anticipation of applause. The applause was forthcoming, but when Sam finished the last line and looked around, he discovered that the girl was gone. She had become bored and left with another young man.

Great-uncle Sam accepted this ribbing good-naturedly. He was willing to acknowledge that he'd had some character defects, especially if they were assigned to his remote, youthful past. He had, in fact, himself related this anecdote to me, chuckling at the ridiculous figure he must have cut at that winter dance. Yet I knew that the old man's judgment that I was "bright and sensible and not a bit like most silly girls" was based primarily on the fact that I was generally a willing and enthusiastic audience to his recitations.

Once my aunt and the neighbor had gone their ways, our family gathered in the lamplight to recoup our energy and our fortitude. My parents did not dwell on their losses but instead assessed what they had left. My father's walk over the fields had been reassuring. The hail had followed pretty much in the path of the tornado, so most of the cotton and corn had been spared. A small field of sorghum had been flattened, but young hay had been known to revive and "spring back up." Thus, even that field might not be a total loss. Falling lumber had struck one of the calves along the spine; the animal was up and walking around, however, so it would likely survive. The chickens were all fine, and an encouraging number of the turkeys were reviving. They were, indeed, sprinting round and round through the house calling for their mothers, their spidery little feet scratching against the strips of fallen wallpaper as they ran.

There was a certain wild insanity about the scene: the herd of scampering, chortling turkeys; the sagging strips of wallpaper; the memory of the rubble outside in the blackness of night; and Great-uncle Sam's repetitious sawing away at "Turkey in the Straw" on his fiddle. The old man's defiant performance was his idea of an ongoing joke, for he chuckled occasionally as he played. Yet we drew together in a kind of strange serenity, catching our breath after the crisis and summoning strength for whatever lay ahead. Not wishing to tempt fate unnecessarily by renewing fires in the two stoves (knowing now that the chimneys were down), my mother had buried new potatoes in the hot ashes to bake. We ate them that night for supper, after peeling away the crusty skins, with butter and cornbread left over from the noontime meal and glasses of lukewarm buttermilk. As we ate, my father spoke softly, telling one of his favorite stories.

Sweet Potatoes and Switches

When he was a little boy, his father's mother, Great-grandma Sarah, was a source of great comfort and delight to him. At every opportunity, he and his younger brother slipped off to visit her at the original part-log, part-frame dwelling that had once stood where the house we lived in was standing now.

Both his mother (my Grandmother Winniford) and Great-grandma Sarah were strong-willed women who apparently "locked horns" on occasion. Grandmother Winniford was convinced that Great-grandma Sarah spoiled her grandsons shamefully, in a way she would never have thought of spoiling her own three sons. So the younger woman tried vainly to curtail her little boys' visits to their grandmother.

One fall morning, my father and uncle slipped off down through the dried-up cornfield to spend some time with their grandmother. She had just finished baking some large sweet potatoes, and she fixed one for each boy, garnishing the potatoes with butter and brown sugar and wrapping them in a clean dishcloth. Just as the boys were beginning to devour these special treats, Grandmother Winniford appeared with willow switch in hand. She ordered the boys home, and as they ran ahead of her back through the cornfield she followed, applying the switch each time she caught up with them. My father ran especially fast, not only to escape the stinging switch but to have time to eat the soft, warm potato before he was forced to relinquish it.

My father was fond of this story, and he told it in a gentle, tender way, relishing the memory of his aged grandmother's love and the taste of the treat she had given him. Whether we were consciously aware of the connection between the pleasures of a hastily eaten sweet potato and those experiences that our family shared after the storm, over time and many such tellings unconscious connections were made. Hardships had always been a part of life, as the numerous family stories certainly demonstrated. But even in the midst of something bad—even with a willow switch fanning one's rear—it was possible to grab a moment of joy and remember it forever.

For the paternal side of my family, an ever-accumulating history or saga served as a framework within which current happenings took on meaning and fell into perspective. Confronted with life's vicissitudes, we persevered because that was what the family had done through generations of similar triumphs and trials. Storm-cellar lore seemed especially geared to themes of acceptance, renewed determination, and perseverance. At formal gatherings—Christmas, Thanksgiving, and birthdays of older relatives—where stories about the exploits of ancestors in the Revolution or the gold rush or the Civil War were told and debated, my father generally deferred to my grandfather, great-uncles, and even some of his older cousins. But our storm cellar was his own domain. In my memories of my father as a master storyteller in the Winniford-Alexander mode, I most often visualize him in the storm-cellar setting, hunched in that close, dark space, surrounded by my mother, brother, and me, telling tales and singing songs to keep us entertained and comforted until the inclement Texas weather relented and let us emerge and return to our warm beds.

Chapter Five

Place Permanent and Place Portable

WINNIFORD-ALEXANDER AND WARD-WOLF FAMILY LEGENDS

The Hopkins County Genealogical Society is housed in a small white frame building (obviously once a dwelling) on a narrow side street about two blocks from the old courthouse in Sulphur Springs. On a clear, cold January morning my brother, my niece, and I visit the facility. I have completed more than a week of my schedule of interviews, tapings, and fieldwork expeditions—and James and Shannon have shared most of these experiences. Our attempts to "separate fact from fiction," as my brother puts it, to sort details, to align our perceptions of past events, and to accommodate the troublesome differences in versions of the tales we recall have prompted all three of us to look for answers in some concrete data. Probably of the three of us, my niece is most certain about what she expects to find in the archives of the Genealogical Society. She is researching her family tree, pure and simple. Although we each have a different agenda, my brother and I hope that the archives can reveal something about the stories told on both sides of our family while we were growing up. It is not clear to us what, exactly, we might find or how such findings might reconcile our sometimes disparate experiences with our family's lore.

We are ushered into a rather cramped, book-lined room and left to our own devices. The little archivist is pleasant but reserved, and she does not warm either to my enthusiastic account of my folklore fieldwork or to my niece's heartfelt expression of her determination to learn more about her ancestors. Because the room is small, how-

The old Hopkins County courthouse

ever, the archivist is privy to our conversation as we puzzle over where to begin our search for records that might corroborate some of the familiar family stories. When we mention a couple of great-uncles by name, the archivist suddenly becomes animated and friendly.

"Why, you two are great-great-grandchildren of Urbane Alexander, then!" she exclaims, addressing my brother and me, and the ice is magically broken.

My brother and I have both known that an Alexander great-great-grandfather doubtless figures in the family tree, but if either of us had ever been told this gentleman's given name, we had forgotten. It is therefore a surprise to be so quickly and easily assigned to his progeny. Urbane's primary claim to fame, so far as we are able to determine, is the fact that sometime before 1845 he left Illinois with his still steadily increasing family, moved to Texas, obtained a Texas land grant, and became one of the first settlers in the Black Jack Grove-Cumby community.

Great-great-grandpa Urbane's role as first settler is sufficient to establish our "rootedness" in the region in the opinion of the archivist. It is clear that she no longer regards us as snoopy strangers but as "homefolks" with a legitimate claim on the old records and documents that might enrich our knowledge of our ancestry. Consequently, she supplies several fruitful leads regarding our research and offers to make copies of significant discoveries.

It is easy to forget, after a lengthy absence from the Cumby-Hopkins County area, just how important such a sense of rootedness was to people living there forty or fifty years ago—and how important it still is, apparently, in some sectors of present northeast Texas society. Belonging to one of the families who first settled that part of the country established members' rights to that *place* in a fundamental, almost organic way that will never be possible again. No one ever has the same unquestionable right to *be* there as have the first settlers. Probably another generation will pass before Alexander and Winniford land will cease entirely to be Alexander and Winniford land, although most of it has already changed hands two or three times and would be unrecognizable to Great-great-grandpa Urbane Alexander or Great-grandpa George Winniford. The right to place involved the right to a sort of independence and self-sufficiency that permitted no interference either from outside individuals or from government. The privilege of arriving at a lifestyle and of determining the rules that would govern that way of life resided in the power structures (the lines of authority within each family and the significance of that family to the community) of these families of original settlers in a manner too subtle and pervasive for latecomers—or outsiders—to successfully comprehend or appropriate.

Already, I have decided that many of the family stories, or family legends, if indeed they are (especially those originating from the paternal Winnifords and Alexanders), served as a means of perpetuating this sense of the right to place: place as it applied to the land, place as it applied to the community and the country at large, place as it applied to history. In asserting his (or sometimes her) right to place, an individual automatically laid claim to all the positive traits of character that were recognized as important in the family's value system. These included strength of body and will; independence; "nerve" (as opposed to courage); fortitude in the face of danger, sorrow, and loss; persistence; and what passed for common sense.

The family stories that were told and retold centered around family members who had (or in a few instances, had not) asserted their right to place in an especially edifying manner and against great odds. These stories seemed to telescope into the past through generations of Winnifords and Alexanders who had participated in this continuing tradition. Because there have never been very many Winnifords (there are presently only sixty-three Winniford households in the continental United States), the perception of ancestry and tradition was, perhaps, more focused for them than for the more numerous and more widely dispersed Alexanders. Although historical data might be fuzzy and entire generations inadvertently skipped over, the Winnifords traced their lineage through Great-grandpa George, who fought in the Civil War, all the way back to a David Winniford, who fought in the American Revolution. His wife, Judith Robertson, was a descendent of Robert I, called "the Bruce," of Scotland.

Despite the grand design implied by stories of the past, asserting or defending the right to place in the present—certainly the present of forty or fifty years ago, the time frame with which I am familiar—could translate into attitudes and behavior considerably less grand and often less admirable. If you were a Winniford and you met someone walking along a narrow sidewalk, you were never the one who stepped aside. Consequently, if you were a Winniford kid, you fought a lot in school and had a reputation for arrogance and foul temper. Significantly, the cemetery became the final, material representation—a metaphor of sorts—of how successfully each individual had established his or her right to place. It mattered where each person was allotted burial in the family plot. The family patriarch occupied a central position and was granted the tallest, most impressive monument in that particular plot, always the one that bore the family surname or patronym prominently inscribed. Other family members were buried on either side of this personage or behind him, in descending rank, as it were. This ordering reflected how well each individual had measured up in the opinion of that patriarch or of other members of the family. There was much jockeying for position—or, once again, literally for place—among the living, for no one wanted his or her grave and marker to reflect alienation, family disapproval, or extreme poverty and failure. The Winnifords and Alexanders were not the only ones who applied this formula for correct family interment, as a visit to the Cumby city cemetery or even (though to a much lesser extent) to Long Cemetery will demonstrate. This was fairly common practice.

What has occasioned my visit to the Genealogical Society archives this January morning is my assumption that in their storytelling, the various branches of my family have at least touched base with authentic, verifiable facts of family history. A part of my intention is, indeed, to separate fact from fiction. Once my brother, niece, and I discover where to look, these verifiable facts quickly emerge. For instance, the original land grants are in place, along with continuing records of their division and sale; Great-grandpa George's name appears in an alphabetical list of recruits for Company K, Thirtieth Texas Cavalry, C.S.A., and a Winniford and two Alexander kinsmen appear on similar lists; and there are records of marriages and deaths, with at least half of any given family's offspring dying in infancy or early childhood from diseases such as typhoid fever, "cholory infection," and "dypthery." Older family members generally died of ailments such as "congestion," Bright's disease, and "dropsy."

Basically, our findings support my perceptions of the Winniford-Alexander background and the stories that developed from their experiences. Both groups came to Texas from Illinois, North Carolina, and Virginia (where they had probably not been very prosperous or successful) with the idea of acquiring large tracts of Texas land and setting themselves up in their new surroundings in a social and economic situation patterned after that in the Deep South. The notable exception was that they did not seem inclined to own slaves. The stories that these settlers told supported their claim to such a lifestyle based on family character strengths and on a heritage that reached all the way back to the American Revolution. What they insisted upon was their place, their permanence, and their existence as distinctive strands of humanity whose intrinsic worth had been forged through their participation in meaningful historical events. For them, as for many of the original settlers of Black Jack Grove-Cumby, ownership of land was absolutely essential to this notion of family importance and to each individual's perception of self. On one's own land, one enjoyed autonomy, freedom, personal dignity, and control over everything except "God and nature." Better to starve on one's own land than to eat well off someone else's table.

Although the records and documents in the Genealogical Society's archives generally support my view of the Winniford-Alexander background, the kinds of stories they told about themselves, and how they meant those stories to be received and to operate within the family system, this morning's work in the archives produces some major revelations regarding the maternal side of the family, the Wards and Wolfs. Both my brother and I have always assumed that our mother's and father's families were very much alike. True, relations between the two families were always strained, at best, but we have thought that their differences were superficial and exaggerated, probably because of personal jealousies and piques. Our research leads us to the surprising conclusion that we have been very much mistaken.

Documented facts about the Wards and Wolfs tend, in the first place, to be elusive and perplexing. What we note initially is that there had obviously been a long-term close association between these two groups of people even before our grandfather, James Ward, married our grandmother, Minnie D. Wolf. Then what emerges as we examine census rolls and records of marriages and deaths is a pronounced pattern of migrations back and forth between Texas and Oklahoma on the part of various family units within the broader kinship groups. Furthermore, these family units change frequently in composition, with children dropping off the census roll and then turning up again. These changes correspond loosely, we decide, to treks back and forth between Texas and Oklahoma. Individuals with the Wolf surname will appear on the census roll living with a family whose head of household bears the surname Ward—or the reverse may be true.

The Wards and Wolfs did not acquire land grants. They tended, apparently, not to purchase land at all, and if they did, they bought small tracts and sold out within a few years. Rootedness and permanence were obviously not priorities with them. In fact, there is a marked indecisiveness about them concerning where they wanted to be and the role they expected to play within any community. The reason for this indecisiveness should occur rather readily to my brother and me, but we are slow to grasp the implications of these frequent migrations. "Why did they all keep going back to Oklahoma?" my brother wonders. My niece startles us with the simple, obvious answer: "Because they were Indians! You have always talked about how both your grandparents had Indian blood—enough to be on the Indian rolls under the Dawes Commission."

As children, my brother and I romanticized our Indian heritage, encouraged by our mother, but we never considered the possibility that this fraction of mostly Cherokee blood might have influenced the beliefs, values, and lifestyle of our mother's family in any major way. But as we examine the records and documents in the archives of the Genealogical Society this morning (and as we pursue our research in other facilities), we realize that the Wards and Wolfs were quite probably families making a troubled, uncertain transition from Indian life to existence within a dominant white society. Intermarriage with whites had given both families Texas connections, and family members who could "pass for white" were attracted by the opportunities that joining the dominant culture made possible.

Succeeding in such a transition meant maintaining a stolid silence about the specifics of their backgrounds and ancestry and about their exact blood relationships to each other. Indians had trouble purchasing land and entering into other contracts, finding employment, and participating in the life of a community. Thus, renouncing their origins, except in the most generalized terms, was essential to functioning economically and socially in rural northeast Texas. (It was acceptable to have an "Indian princess" in one's ancestral background, if she were well-shrouded in the mists of time. Common, everyday Indian grandpas with real names and exact locations could, on the other hand, be detrimental to social and economic advancement.) At the same time, the pull of tribal life, or at least life near the tribe, was strong, and both individuals and entire family units vacillated between striving to make a new life as members of the dominant white society and returning to Oklahoma or Arkansas, where they may have felt more comfortable and secure.

In *A History of Hopkins County, Texas,* Gladys St. Clair notes that in the first half of the nineteenth century, the Cherokees began to crowd across the Red River from Arkansas, believing that all territory north of the watershed of the Red River belonged to the United States. Chief Bowles of the western Cherokees, tired of being harassed by American settlers and of the delay of any settlement, sought the jurisdiction of Mexico by coming to East Texas. As St. Clair states, "They were united with other refugee Indians, forming a confederacy known as the 'Cherokee and their Associated Bands.' About four thousand Indians settled between the Trinity and the Red River from 1837 to 1839."[1] At one time, the author goes on, there were about two hundred Indian families living on Sulphur Prairie. It was probably true, as St. Clair insists, that the Cherokees were a menace to early settlers. But these troubled conditions nonetheless help account for the opportunities for intermarriage between Indians and whites. The confusion on the part of crossbreeds such as the Wards and Wolfs apparently stemmed from doubt as to where they had a right to be and in which culture they could best survive.

Very probably the Dawes Severalty Act, passed by the U.S. Congress in 1887, contributed to the bewilderment of people who were wavering in their racial and cultural alliances. Sponsored by Senator Henry Laurens Dawes, this act stipulated that American Indians give up their tribal lands in return for individual land grants and was intended to promote the integration of Indians into the homesteading way of life. The Cherokees, in particular, were reluctant to cooperate with the Dawes Commission because they guessed, correctly, that allotments of Indian lands in severalty would result in the dissolution of tribal governments. Nevertheless, the commission proceeded with the work of enrolling members of the Five Tribes. By 1902 it reported the receipt of nearly fifty thousand applications of Cherokees, Shawnees, Delawares (by blood and intermarriage), and freedmen for entry on the Cherokee rolls. Indians who were duly enrolled selected an allotment of 110 acres of "average land" from the tribal domain.[2] In some cases there were additional benefits, resulting from the distribution of monies acquired through the sale of vast tracts of Indian lands.

Thus, there was strong economic incentive for getting one's name on the Indian rolls. Not surprisingly, Cherokee enrolling centers—like those of all Five Tribes—were jammed with white applicants who claimed that they were of Cherokee descent. Weeding out white impostors became a frustrating task for the enrolling agents, for the Five Tribes were "bleaching out" and the appearance of mixed bloods often belied their Indian heritage. It was estimated that 300,000 persons, instead of the 100,000 Indians known to be entitled to enrollment, showed up at the centers before the rolls of the Five Tribes were closed.[3]

Recalling accounts that our grandparents had at least twice seriously debated whether they should attempt to get on the Indian rolls, my brother, niece, and I decide to examine records of cases brought before the Indian Affairs Commission to determine whether members of the Ward and Wolf families commonly applied for government assistance on the basis of their Indian blood. There are indeed a number of such cases, but the perhaps deliberate vagueness on the part of family members regarding exact kinship makes it difficult to be certain whether these cases actually involve members of our particular family. It seems reasonable to assume that some of them do. (My brother and I dismiss the possibility that our kinfolk might have been guilty of making fraudulent claims, partly because of both families' frequent references to their Indian heritage and, too, because their troubled migrations suggest to us a real and ongoing problem with place and lifestyle.)

One such case in point is #8194-7190, in which a James Ward of Bonham (probably a second cousin of my grandfather) on August 24, 1908, presented the following "Miscellaneous Testimony": "I claim my Indian descent through my father; my mother is a white woman. My father claimed through his father, Thomas Ward. . . . Don't know how much Indian he claimed, but he was descended from the Cherokee tribe. Don't know that he lived with the Indians as a member of the tribe. . . . My father was recognized as a white man in the community. Don't know whether my father or his father were ever on any rolls, but suppose they were. . . . I think my father made applications to the Dawes Commission, but I did not. Don't know what the result of the application was, but I never got anything."[4]

The sketchiness of James Ward's testimony—when exactness would likely have been more beneficial in making a successful claim—is typical of the manner in which Wards and Wolfs spoke of their past and of relationships with each other. (Granted, this testimony may have been rendered sketchier by the court recorder, if it was given orally, and by the speaker's problems with the English language.) Either they were very noncommunicative even with close family members about matters of personal business, or they exercised great care in implicating other family members (or even more-distant relatives) in the particular course of action they had decided to take. A Ward or Wolf who had succeeded in the dominant white society could be hurt by any public reminder of kinship to a relative whose name appeared on the Indian rolls. Thus, the blurring of identities, places, and time frames seems to me to emphasize the transitory nature of the Ward-Wolf situation at this time when some family members were blending into the dominant society while others were returning to their original culture, at least economically and legally.

During a visit to Long Cemetery on a previous excursion, I was surprised to note a detail that had escaped my notice on other visits. In a small family plot, measuring at best 30' by 30', the name *Wolf* is inscribed on various markers using three different spellings: "Wolf," "Wolfe," and "Woolf." Yet these were siblings and children of siblings. Identity was, apparently, fairly plastic, and each individual was permitted to shape his own—to whatever mold worked best for him in his particular circumstances. (I use the masculine pronoun advisedly, because I think the persons involved in this particular process were primarily men.)

All these foregoing possibilities considered, it does become obvious—somewhat belatedly for my brother and me—that the paternal Winniford-Alexander branch of the family and the maternal Ward-Wolf branch represent very different (in fact, highly contrasting) sociological developments. The Winnifords and Alexanders self-consciously stressed family history and tradition and interpreted that history and tradition through the region's and the nation's past. They expected their background and traditions to continue to function meaningfully in the present and future. These families valued permanence and order, independence and hard work.

The Wards and Wolfs, on the other hand, were in the process of renouncing their origins; they lacked a clear sense of identity; they lacked any real commitment to place. They were not ready to settle into any permanent arrangement, even in professional or community involvement. On the census rolls, from 1870 to 1900, heads of household in Ward and Wolf families are usually listed as farmers. They must have farmed only minimally, however, both because their land holdings were small or nonexistent and because their actual reputations were made doing other things. The men were well-known horse traders and trainers, auctioneers, self-taught veterinarians, blacksmiths, and well diggers. Any real farming was probably done by the women and children. Essentially, the men made their living at trades that gave them mobility and that did not tie them to the land.

It is interesting that in the end, the more transitory life of the Wards and Wolfs contributed to the social and economic success of their children and grandchildren. When advanced technology—and poor farming practices—pushed the Winnifords and Alexanders off their land, many of them did not fare well. Certainly, their "dream of empire" was finished. The already mobile and survival-oriented Wards and Wolfs, however, moved easily on to places like Dallas and either went into business or entered professions such as law and law enforcement (the families are represented by numerous sheriffs, deputies, and constables, probably because they had always carried guns and enjoyed fighting). They thereby accomplished, at last, the transition into a rapidly changing social and economic system in which they were very likely just about as comfortable as anyone else.

When I first began examining my family's folklore, I noted distinct differences in the types of stories I was dealing with. An early theory was that these differences could be explained primarily along gender lines: female storytellers and male storytellers had dissimilar interests and agendas, and the stories they produced reflected these gender affinities. I still think sex differences in tellers and listeners were important in shaping the narrative content and style of the tales that were told by both branches of my family. It has been revealing, for instance, to note similarities between my family's storytelling and Karen Baldwin's description of storytelling on the maternal side of her family, where the contrasting storytelling modes of male and female members struck a sort of narrative balance, resulting in a collaborative "family story."[5]

Female storytellers in both branches of my family produced material that is more subversive than the narratives recounted by males, employing coding strategies such as those discussed by Joan N. Radner and Susan S. Lanser as well as by Sandra Gilbert and Susan Gubar.[6] The older women in my family—certainly Grandmother Ward—used tactics generally associated with nineteenth-century women writers. Judith Lowder Newton, for instance, in her introduction to *Women, Power, and Subversion: Social Strategies in British Fiction*, 1778–1860, mentions strategies that I am aware my grandmother resorted to—notably the subversion of traditional power relations and the insistence upon and sometimes substitution of the power of women's energy, potential, and capabilities for the kind of power manifested through masculine control and dominance.[7] Such narrative strategies are explored in the chapter 7 retelling of a number of Long Cemetery legends.

Nevertheless, with gender differences duly noted and acknowledged, the basic division in the tales from my childhood reflects exactly the two branches of the family. The Winniford-Alexander branch tells stories about family members, sometimes humorous anecdotes and sometimes longer accounts of significant adventures or accomplishments, that accrete to form a family history or saga. The Wolf-Ward branch, on the other hand, veers toward stories that are often not specifically about family members and that give evidence of or credence to the presence of the supernatural in everyday lives of simple people. In view of the almost diametrically opposed social and economic interests and tendencies in the paternal and maternal branches of my family, it would seem only natural that the Wards and Wolfs would develop a very different sort of lore from that of the Alexanders and Winnifords. This lore sprang from subtly or even strikingly disparate family interrelationships and contacts with the culture at large, as well as probably dissimilar perceptions of nature and divinity. Such material sometimes served for them purposes radically different from those served by the Winniford-Alexander family history. Tales told in the Winniford-Alexander mode take their meaning from and are limited interpretatively to a specific place and specific people living in a permanent location; they are rarely religious or moralizing in nature. Stories in the Ward-Wolf mode pose truths and suggest moral lessons that have broad application in any location. In other words, they are portable.

This distinguishing characteristic of the Ward-Wolf stories, their "portability," is a feature that I come to understand only gradually as I trace the puzzling history of these people back through the old records. I know that stories told in this mode made an indelible impression on me when I was growing up, as did the setting and occasions that I associate with most of the tellings: cemetery working days at Long Cemetery, the burial place of my mother's people. These are stories that cannot usually be checked for "accuracy" or "truth" against records or documents. They are generalized and inexact regarding place, time frame, and (to some extent) people involved. It always somewhat troubled me that, in connection with the Long Cemetery stories, the cast of characters was larger than the stage. Lost graves notwithstanding, there were more bodies than the little cemetery has space to accommodate. It seems likely that some of the stories are geographically displaced; that is, they are based on incidents that befell Ward-Wolf family members during their wanderings and their stays in other areas but told as if these things had happened in the immediate (or Black Jack Grove-Cumby) locale.

A story that demonstrates many of the foregoing characteristics (and one that has inspired much family debate because of the problems it raises regarding truth and accuracy) is the story of Little Mose. My Grandmother Ward was often called on to recount this story on graveyard working days, and she could be counted on to further embellish it during long Sunday afternoon visits at her home in Cumby.

Little Mose

Around the turn of the century, brush arbor meetings were popular in rural northeast Texas. On hot summer nights, people would gather under a brush arbor, lighted either by a bonfire or by hanging lanterns. They would pray and sing and listen to a sermon by a spirited, fiery evangelist. Often, especially on Sundays, the religious services were preceded by a covered-dish supper spread on tables either under or near the arbor.

On a particular summer Sunday evening, the people of the community were gathered at such an occasion. As they prepared to sit down to the covered-dish meal, they were joined by a strange woman who told them that she had traveled some distance that day by foot and that she was tired, thirsty, and hungry. She offered to help serve the meal and clean up afterward in exchange for food, drink, and a chance to rest before she went on her way. The women in charge of meal preparation agreed.

After the stranger had helped with the meal as promised, eaten, and rested for awhile, she bade the group goodbye and headed for a wooded area along the creek. By that time, the sun had gone down and the evening was growing dark. She was a large, raw-boned woman dressed in loose, shapeless clothing. Several of the people commented that she looked as if she might be pregnant.

The next morning, some of the neighborhood men, my Great-grandfather Ira Ward among them, had occasion to ride into the wooded area down by the creek. As they rode along, they became aware of a commotion among a bunch of wild hogs, and they decided to investigate. In a little clearing, the men came upon the hogs gathered in a noisy, excited circle around a still-squirming newborn boy. They were amazed that the hogs had not attacked and eaten the child, but the little boy was unharmed. Nor was this the only supernatural phenomenon connected with the baby's birth and abandonment. Thereafter, grass never grew in the circle in which the infant had been found.

Great-grandfather Ward had nine daughters but no son, and he longed for a little boy, so he decided to take the orphan child into his home. Word of this unusual event spread. A couple of days later, a group of people from a nearby community arrived in a wagon, carrying the corpse of a vagrant woman who had died in their community from complications following childbirth. They assumed she was the mother of the abandoned child and had decided that she should be buried in the community that had adopted him.

For a time, all went well for Little Mose, as he was appropriately called. But then my great-grandmother had an unexpected late-life baby, the long-awaited boy (my grandfather). (Actually, census records show that two of the nine girls were born after my grandfather.) Great-grandfather Ira would brook no competition with the actual son of his own loins, so he turned the adopted son out of his house. According to my grandfather's sisters, Little Mose anticipated this fate. The little boy stood crying in a corner of the room, watching as my great-grandmother cuddled her newborn son. Meanwhile, his joyous foster sisters were excitedly ringing the dinner bell to call their father in from the fields and running across the furrows to meet him and tell him the glad news.

Little Mose's life came to an only-to-be-expected tragic ending. Passed from one foster family to another, he grew up to be a wild young man given to thievery and fighting. Eventually, he made the fatal mistake of attempting to force his attentions on a young lady in the community, and her angry brothers shot and killed him. He was buried in Long Cemetery beside the woman whom everyone believed to be his mother.

My grandmother and aunt used to designate two mounds in a far corner of the cemetery, under a twisted little bois d'arc tree and marked by bois d'arc posts. Now mounds, posts, and tree are all gone, and no entry in the list of those buried in Long Cemetery, contained in Tuck and Young's *Cemetery Inscriptions,* seems to correspond to either of these sad figures.[8] It is thus difficult to know how factual my grandmother's account of their deaths and burials may be. (Of course, the bois d'arc posts were not exactly "inscribed," so the graves could have simply been "lost" with the passage of time and new practices in graveyard upkeep.)

For many years, my grandmother's version of this story went unchallenged, despite its lapses in logic. Then, a few years ago, Wolf kinfolk from Oklahoma reported that they had heard stories of an old man named Moses Wolf who had moved to Oklahoma and had eventually died there. He had claimed to be the abandoned child found in the woods. Furthermore, page 161 of the September 29, 1870, census for Hopkins County, Miller Grove, lists a Moses Wolf, a male twenty-five years old, with a wife named Hettie and two sons, Henry and Burton, ages three and two.[9]

There is, of course, no evidence that this young farmer is the same person as the Moses in my grandmother's story—although he certainly may be. His age at the time of the 1870 census would be more in keeping with the actual dates of other events in her story (my grandfather's birth, for example) than her "around the turn of the century" reference, which she used much like "once upon a time," simply to set the narrative in motion. Based on this more recent evidence, my brother, James Winniford, tells the following version of the Little Moses story.

Little Moses II

Another one of the kinfolks was Moses Wolf. He was known as Mo. Actually, he was no blood relationship to us because Mo had a very strange beginning.

The story is told that one day a woman came by, wanting to do some work in order to have food, because she was very hungry and she was in trouble. And the family consented to allow this woman to come in, and after she had cleaned herself up real good, she helped in the kitchen and helped with some cooking and with washing and things of that sort. They gave her food and lodging there for a day or so.

They realized at the time that she was pregnant. It seems as though when she had gotten food and had gotten some rest and so forth, she more or less disappeared, and they didn't know where she had gone. But the men were out working in the field the next day, and they heard a baby crying, so they started searching, and they found this baby wrapped up in a blanket over against a big old oak tree. So they took this baby. They didn't know where its mother was, but they figured that the baby belonged to this woman that had worked for them.

Naturally, they took the baby and brought it back to the house—it was a little boy—and they went through a lot of trouble trying to figure out how to feed the baby. They didn't even have a baby bottle. They tell about how they took a piece of cotton cloth and fixed up a kind of sponge; then they freshly milked a cow and filled this spongelike thing with milk and more or less squeezed the milk into the baby's mouth and fed the baby that way. It was quite an ordeal. Of course, there were times when they thought they'd lose him, but they managed to raise the child to be full grown. They named him Moses because of his origins. As we look back through the old family records, we see the record of Moses Wolf. They gave him his name, Wolf, and he lived with them and grew up and carried the family name and so forth. They raised this one child that had his origin in such a strange way.[10]

My brother is a storyteller in the Winniford-Alexander mode. In his version, the Little Moses story becomes a family legend on a par with accounts of Winniford and Alexander exploits. It accomplishes much the same purpose as the Winniford-Alexander legends, demonstrating the decency and strength of the family group and their ability to deal with a difficult situation successfully. In my brother's account, the entire series of events involving Little Moses or Little Mo is a private family matter in which the community is not involved. By omitting completely any involvement of Great-grandfather Ira Ward, my brother exonerates this ancestor of behavior that by present-day standards would be considered cruel and socially incorrect. He depicts the Wolfs as good-hearted, generous people. Despite good intentions, the Wolf family is taken advantage of by a woman of questionable morals. Nevertheless, they do not hesitate to take on the responsibility of raising her abandoned child (and they may, in fact, have done this) in spite of the real hardships involved.

I do not recall that my grandmother included details about feeding the orphaned infant in her story of Little Mose. Such details, however, were often discussed by people in both branches of my family in connection with premature, undersized, or orphaned infants and multiple births. That my brother appropriates these details in his story of Little Moses or Little Mo strengthens the impact of the story, graphically suggesting the difficulties involved in raising an orphaned child and the patience and generosity that such a commitment entailed. All of this makes the family's success in rearing the child to manhood more impressive. Granting this probably bastard child the privilege of bearing the family name is, of course, their greatest gift and demonstrates, beyond doubt, that they "did the right thing" by him. The young man's name on the census rolls seems to be proof of this final magnanimity.

Although supernatural elements are focal points in my grandmother's version of the story, my brother omits completely any reference to the wild hogs, their inexplicable gentleness toward the baby, and the magic circle in which grass never grew again. As both a preacher (of a faith that discounts the miraculous in the post-Biblical era) and a scientist, he considers these elements invalid and so dismisses them as not applicable to the story as he is telling it. He is, after all, relating the story as a factual account that he is attempting to make as accurate as possible.

I have no objection to believing my brother's happier version of the Little Moses story, in which family members behave admirably, the child is nurtured kindly, and he lives to a ripe old age. I will admit that some concrete evidence seems to support his version. But I think my grandmother's story is a lot more exciting. Her story involves complex human conflict, contains moments of real pathos, and raises intriguing social and moral issues. For her, the story becomes, among other things, a belief legend. As is evident from other tales she told, my Grandmother Ward strove to find concrete evidence of a hereafter and of the existence of a divine power that not only took note of human affairs but became involved in their unfolding and resolution.

Her story opens with a religious function in which the entire community participates, so the far-reaching religious and moral implications of the events that follow are inescapable. The woman stained by sin is placed in contrast with good, righteous people gathered to praise their God and to hone themselves to moral and spiritual perfection. It is no accident that the sinful woman is a stranger, an outsider, because it seemed unthinkable that someone in the close little community group (most of whom were probably kin) could be guilty of the immoral act she has apparently already committed or of the even greater sin that she will perpetrate in abandoning her child. The supernatural elements (the hogs that do not behave characteristically and the magic circle where no grass grew) were important to my grandmother and to many of her listeners as concrete evidence that a divine power was as cognizant and as disapproving of the strange woman's unnatural acts as were people in the community. In view of these explicit signs of divine intervention, my grandmother could hardly afford to supply a happy ending. The wages of sin, after all, is death—and that was the moral of her story.

Certain aspects of my grandmother's story, however, are impossible to explain unless one accepts them as simply factual. Probably the most gripping part of her tale was her description of the morning my grandfather (her husband) was born and of the orphan child's sorrowful realization that his place in the Ward family had been usurped by the newborn son. My grandmother was a Wolf, and if the abandoned child was actually raised to manhood by one of the Wolf families, she should have known. Why, then, would she have included this section of the story that implicates her in-laws in the child's tragic fate? Even granting that people of his time would have sympathized with Great-grandpa Ira's putting his own son first, he comes off as a heartless villain—and my grandmother does not mitigate the destructiveness of his selfishness by permitting things to work out happily for the child. She does not, for instance, say that Mose was given to a Wolf family (which might have been what actually happened) and reared to productive manhood. Just how subversive is her account?

It might be interesting to know whether she told the story in the same way before she was widowed or before she reached an age where she was beyond reprisal. On the other hand, hers may be the accurate version. Certainly, her "characters" seem in some respects more human than the consistently good, well-meaning Wolfs of my brother's story. I do think the story can be differentiated along gender lines; in this, as in other stories told by female storytellers, an accurate recounting of events is not a primary concern. Grandmother Ward took subtle jabs at the arrogance and prejudice of patriarchy, at the community's concept of mothering, and at the socioreligious system of reward and punishment. Her story also expounds a not-so-subtle warning against sexual promiscuity: both Little Mose and his mother wind up dead because (at least by implication) of overactive hormones.

The Winniford-Alexander family legends do not pose the same problems of authenticity as does the Little Moses story from the Ward-Wolf repertoire. Unlike the Wards and Wolfs, who seemed to exert considerable effort to remain nearly anonymous and to reveal as little about themselves as possible, the Winnifords and Alexanders were frankly proud of their past. Their stories were generally open and above-board in being claims to strength of character and, as I have suggested before, the right to *place:* land, position, an acknowledged role in history. Most of these stories originated from real events, and the essential truth of the event is usually preserved without much distortion or subversion. There are, indeed, exaggerations, embellishments, and appropriations as well as omissions and truncations. But when these occur, it is usually easy to see what the storyteller hoped to accomplish through these changes in his or her raw materials. Three or four of the most popular Winniford-Alexander family legends cannot be substantiated by records and documents—in a couple of cases for obvious reasons—and one does wonder if these stories were invented outright and, if so, from what motivation. But overall, the paternal side of my family was very compliant about sharing their legacy of family tales and very direct about what they expected this sharing to accomplish. They happily contributed to newspapers and personal histories, offering views of the past as they saw it (and to some extent as they invented it).

The Winnifords and Alexanders were, however, sometimes victims of misconceptions. The David Winniford who had fought in the Revolution had always been a dim but legendary figure, much revered by each succeeding generation of family members. He had been a patriot, of course, but more than that, he had been wealthy and "refined." Further—and this was crucial to the family image of him—he had been successful and prosperous without depending on slave labor to operate his considerable holdings. Texas Winnifords, at least those around Cumby, soundly rejected the idea of using slave labor, primarily on the grounds that they were following a family tradition: if David Winniford, their most illustrious ancestor, had prospered without using slaves, why should *they* turn to the questionable practice?

Alas for these idealistic Winnifords, however! A female cousin decided to apply for membership in the DAR, and in the process of suitably documenting the family patriot she turned up some disturbing information. To begin with, there was an appraisement of the estate of David's father, George Winniford (spelled Winneford), signed on December 20, 1757, by Wm. Hopson, Wm. Clarke, and Christopher Robinson, listing George's earthly possessions. At the very end of a list that includes such items as "18 head of Cattle," "Eleven old Hoes," and "a Percel of Puter," the document designates "one Negro man and one Negro woman."[11] George's holdings were surprisingly modest, but the real shocker was the two black slaves with which his list of possessions ended.

Additional documents did not improve this disturbing scenario.

David Winniford (spelled Wineford on his deed) did acquire property, 182 acres granted to him "by Patent under the Seal of the Colony and Dominion of Virginia" in 1735, but he sold this property to a John Mayo for "the sum of eighty Pounds Currant Money" in 1762.[12] By the time David made out his will in 1771, his estate was even more modest than his father's—except that he owned three black slaves to his father's two. The slaves are the first properties that David Winniford disposes of in his will, bequeathing them to his three grandsons. He requests that his neighbor Jacob McGehee take the slaves into his possession until the grandsons come of age, but he is equally concerned about the safekeeping of an iron pot and copper kettle, which he bequeathed to the two younger boys: "It is likewise my request of my neighbor Jacob McGehee to take care of the pott and kettle given my grandsons David and Charles till they come of age."[13] David Winniford was, in fact, wounded in the battle of Brandywine, was on the field at the battle of Valley Forge, and was present at the surrender of Cornwallis. On the basis of his military services, my cousin was accepted into the DAR, amid widespread family disenchantment resulting from her somewhat ill-advised search through old records.

In the generations that followed the American Revolution, Winnifords continued to take part sporadically in historical movements and events, and family legends developed from these ambitious undertakings. One story that was often told by women in the Winniford family concerned a young Winniford man who had traveled west in the gold rush. This tale had as its controlling theme the potential destructiveness of romantic love. It was often used by the older women as an example of the tragedies that could befall an individual, male or female, who got too emotionally involved with the opposite sex and took rejection too seriously. The story represents the feminine mode of storytelling in that the narrators were much less interested in facts and in accuracy of details than they were in how effectively the story worked to modify young people's social and sexual behavior.

The Rejected Lover

Back in the 1840s, there was a young Winniford man who made the mistake of falling in love with the wrong girl. He was a good-looking boy, but he was shy and hadn't made his mark in the world yet. He was a poor boy, even if he did have promise. He fell head over heels in love with a pretty, flighty girl who had been spoiled all her life by her father and brothers. She was used to getting everything she asked for, so she didn't know the meaning of hard work or of having to pinch and save.

For awhile the two courted each other, and the boy was sure that some day they would get married. He just needed some time to get some money together and prepare to settle down. But the girl was giddy and easily influenced, and her father and brothers convinced her that her young Winniford suitor was not ambitious and would never amount to anything. So when a well-to-do man with land and a house started paying his attentions, she spurned the young Winniford lad and was soon engaged to her more affluent admirer.

The young Winniford man was heartbroken—and very bitter. He knew he had been rejected because he was poor, and this hurt his pride. He had heard about the gold in California, and he made up his mind that he would join the gold rush, find gold, and come back to Texas a rich man. He would show them all.

He selected one of the family's best horses, loaded up with rations, and finally got in with a group of men—absolute strangers to him—who were headed for California. Everything went well for a time, and the men had many exciting adventures. But somewhere just beyond the great American desert, most of the men came down with yellow fever. The young Winniford man was sicker than the rest, and when the others recovered enough to travel, they loaded up and just rode off, leaving him there to die.

Fortunately for this young man, a small wagon train soon passed that way, and these people took him into one of their wagons and nursed him back to health. The wagon train was headed for Oregon, so the young man went on out there with them. He never did get back to Texas. He had failed to get rich in the gold rush, and besides he had found him an Oregon wife and started a family. He is the reason why there are Winniford kinfolk in Oregon.

Actually, three Winniford brothers made the trip to California together during the gold rush. One of those brothers, W. J. Winniford, wrote a detailed account of their adventures that was published in the *Lancaster Herald,* beginning on Friday, November 12, 1909, and running in twelve installments through Friday, January 28, 1910. W. J. Winniford describes how he and his brothers, Norve and David, Norve's pregnant wife, and two friends, Arch Lavender and Will Morgan, set out to travel by oxen-pulled wagons through the rough western terrain and across the desert into California to seek their fortunes in gold. W. J.'s detailed, often lively, account contains the stuff of at least a dozen family legends. It seems a shame, therefore, that this grand Winniford undertaking was, so far as I know, represented among existing family legends only by the story just recounted: a comparatively dull, very generalized narrative in which the three brothers, with their distinctive characters and fates, are melded into one nameless "young Winniford man" whose main problem is a broken heart.

Spurned love gets practically no attention in W. J. Winniford's serialized "In Search of Gold." In the first paragraph of his Friday, November 26 entry, W. J. does comment: "I had no wife, but I did have brothers and sisters and sweethearts. I was then nineteen years old and in my first wonders. I might have known the girls did not care anything for me, for girls had sense in those days as well as they have now. I was a poor boy without anything to support a wife on, and no wonder I found some of them married and the others about to be when I returned. Back to the subject; I am getting tedious."[14] W. J. does here express some rather good-humored bitterness about his poverty and girls' practicality, but his disillusionment comes when he returns home and does not motivate his daring venture. Too, it is hard to work up much pity for W. J., who talks of girls in the plural; he seems more like a swinger than a melancholy rejected lover. If the female storytellers based their tales on W. J's serializations, they read a great deal into this humorous passage.

The intriguing thing about W. J. Winniford's "In Search of Gold" is that he is guilty of some inadvertent—or could it be deliberate?—fictionalizing. In his installment of Friday, November 19, W. J. Winniford describes the sad events that occurred during the winter of 1850 when the group was camped a few miles outside San Diego, still six hundred miles from the gold mines.

> David moved in with Norve for he was getting weaker all the time. On Christmas, Norve's birthday, David died without a struggle. He simply went to sleep; imagine our sorrow. There were some U.S. Soldiers camped there because there was a spring and they buried him without any coffin, at the foot of the hill. The open Sea was just over the hill some two hundred yards away. There were but a few at that burying. Well, just three weeks from that day Norve's wife died. They buried her in a box with her baby on her breast. No one but Ames' wife and her sister were there and they did all they could for her. "Poor Malindy!" It was a beautiful baby; Norve showed it to me. Alas! How many have lost their lives in search of gold.[15]

W. J. Winniford's manly sorrow at these multiple losses seems honest enough, and certainly the details of his brother's death and burial appear the result of close observation. Later developments, however, indicate that something must be seriously askew about W. J's account of these misfortunes. In an article in the *Dallas Morning News* for January 19, 1986, A. C. Greene and Ella Winniford Taylor provide the following revelation: "Despite W. J.'s detailed account of David's demise, it was proved many years later that he had lived on for many years in Oregon. In 1952, a David Winniford IV appeared at the old Winniford homestead at Lancaster. He related that his great-grandfather David had been left for dead on the California desert and that a wagon train had found the dying man 'with a clammy fever' and nursed him back to health. Norvell and W. J's brother had never written to let his Texas family know he was alive—possibly because he felt he had been deserted."[16]

Greene and Taylor go on to explain that W. J's older brother, Norvell Winniford, married two more times. During the Civil War he was associated as a gunrunner with William Marsh Rice of Houston, and in 1867, he was appointed Reconstruction sheriff of Dallas County and served two years. He died in 1885.

The unfortunate David is, of course, the model for the lone young Winniford man of the family legend, and it is perhaps possible that David did set out on this nearly fatal venture with a broken heart. In that case, the events of the trip certainly heaped insult upon injury. It is noteworthy that the storytellers protect the family's good name, for their nameless adventurer travels with strangers, not with two brothers, and their desertion of him does not reflect on Winniford integrity.

Aside from the somewhat disappointing Revolutionary War hero, David Winniford, the most truly legendary figure in the Winniford-Alexander ancestry was a woman, Great-aunt Becky Alexander. And Great-grandma Sarah Alexander Winniford ran her a close second. The two were sisters, daughters of the old first settler, Urbane Alexander, and Mary Ann Drennan Alexander. I have described the Winniford-Alexander family legends as generally centering around some individual's asserting his or her right to *place:* the right to the land and to the independence, autonomy, and personal freedom that ownership of land ensured. It also meant the right to make one's mark, or to exert one's influence—both in a local sense, within the community, and in a broader, more historical sense. Probably no two people—at least within these two family groups—ever asserted the right to place with more authority, greater determination, more strength of character, and against greater odds than did these two women. Although Great-aunt Becky was the more colorful character, both women were widely known and respected.

Most early histories of Hopkins County at least mention Great Aunt Becky—Rebecca Jane Alexander. In *Pioneers of Hopkins County, Texas,* volume 2, Sylvia M. Kibart and Rita M. Adams, eds., assess Great-aunt Becky's difficult circumstances, even before the Civil War.

> Rebecca's father died 20 December 1853, and her mother died 4 June 1854. . . . Keeping the family together fell to her. She is listed as a seamstress on the 1860 Hopkins County census, living with her brother, John S. [Alexander] Thomas Carroll [the youngest brother] is also living in the same household. She was 24 years old. She had a little money and some land and a home her parents had established when the family moved from Illinois. Becky, as she was called, kept the usual livestock; cows for butter and milk and chickens for eggs. Whatever she could sell in town provided a small bit of cash that she could hold for taxes or seed for her crops.[17]

Great-aunt Becky's responsibilities increased when the war began and most of the able-bodied men left to join in the fighting. As the oldest child in the family, Becky was called upon to handle business matters that did not normally fall to women at that time. According to some accounts, for instance, a problem arose about the legality of one of the Alexander land grants, and Becky had to go to the state capital in Austin to settle the matter. Accompanied by a younger brother—most probably the youngest, Thomas Carroll—Becky traveled on horseback from Hopkins County to Austin, a round trip requiring several days of hard riding through country that was fraught with danger from Indians, outlaws, and renegade soldiers. Great-aunt Becky acquired a reputation for being strong willed and fearless.

The most widely circulated story about Great-aunt Becky did not, however, have to do with any of her daring exploits. It is for her poignant, tragic love story that she is best remembered. Cousin Mamie Robertson, in an interview in Cumby not many months before her death, told the story very much as I had often heard it told when I was a child. (Cousin Mamie seemed to believe that Aunt Becky's lover belonged to a local family, members of which still reside in Cumby, and she used that family name in her account. Records show that she was incorrect in this detail, so I have substituted the name "Doe" where the name of the local family was used.)

Great-Aunt Becky's Beau

Yes, I do know the story about Aunt Becky's beau that went off to the Civil War. You know, it's a beautiful story, how much Aunt Becky loved that boy and how faithful she was to him her entire life. But that's not the part that ever gets told; they tell the gruesome part. So I don't know much about how she met this boy or how long they'd been seeing each other when the Civil War broke out. He was a Doe. I guess he was kin to the Does that are here now, but I don't see them keeping his grave.

Someone—and it was probably Uncle Sam because he was always agitating—said that Aunt Becky flew in and got engaged so she could have a man to send off to war like Grandma Sarah. Those sisters were close, and maybe they competed some, too. But from all counts, Becky was too headstrong and independent to get engaged to marry just because Grandma Sarah was married and Grandpa George was leaving her and going off to war.

The two women stayed on the farms and kept things going and took care of Sarah's two little boys—that was Sam and my daddy, who was Norve—and I think that first they got word that Grandpa George had been wounded and then word came that the Doe boy had been killed.

The Doe boy's daddy was getting up in years—I think that was his baby boy—so he was determined that he would go get the body and bring it home. He traveled into the Deep South mainly by train, I think, but he brought the body back most of the way by wagon.

The old man got to the grove of blackjack trees that used to stand about a half-mile outside of town and pulled in there. Someone brought Becky word that he was there, and she got on her horse and rode out to meet him; she took a jar of cold cistern water. And then they came on in through town and went directly to the cemetery. Men were already there, getting the grave dug in a hurry.

They said the smell was so bad it was just overpowering at first, till you got used to it; it just about knocked you over. They said that Becky talked about how strange it was, riding along beside that wagon and knowing the smell was this boy she loved; but also she said it was comforting, in a way she couldn't explain, because it meant that she was close to him again and he was home.

Becky and the boy's mother just flat demanded that the box be opened. They'd both had these bad nightmares that the old man was hauling home the wrong body and that the boy was really in a prison up north and no one knew, so they wouldn't back down. They identified the body by the hair—it was bright red, I guess; some of the Does have red hair—and by the shape of the fingers. The mother fainted, but Becky wasn't the kind to faint. She jumped all over some of the men who came to look because they started gagging and vomiting. She thought you ought to show proper respect no matter how bad it was—and maybe her high temper kept them all from caving in.

So I think a preacher said a few words, and they got the burying done quick. And the old father didn't live long after that ordeal. But, you know, even if she did see the body, I've always thought that maybe Aunt Becky still believed that nightmare she'd had and kept expecting that boy might turn up again alive. For she never showed any interest in anyone else and never married.[18]

Certain storytellers gave other reasons for Great-aunt Becky's lifelong celibacy, the most popular being that Becky was so traumatized by the sheer horror of the whole experience that she never again wanted to take the chances involved in forming a deep emotional attachment to a man. But no matter what explanation was given for Becky's faithfulness to her dead lover, the gruesome details of his return and burial remained a consistent and essential part of the story.

One of the puzzles that I hope to solve this morning in the archives of the Hopkins County Genealogical Society is the matter of the Civil War lover's exact identity. Various storytellers, when they gave Becky's lover a name at all, assigned him various surnames. This confusion of names is odd, because some of these storytellers claimed to know where the young man's grave is located and so should have seen the inscription. In the biography of Rebecca Jane Alexander included in *Pioneers of Hopkins County, Texas,* Kibart and Adams refer to him as C. C. Mount. I want to investigate this possibility. June E. Tuck's *Civil War Shadows in Hopkins County, Texas,* provides the following information about "Mount, C. C., 2nd Lieut.": "b. February 11, 1830, d. March 9, 1862. Killed in battle at Elkhorn, Arkansas, March 7, 1862, and body brought back and buried in Cumby Cemetery after the war. Cemetery stone reads March 9, 1862, but other records show March 7, 1962 [*sic*]. Enlisted at Black Jack Grove (Cumby) Texas, July 5, 1861, Co. K. 9th Texas Cavalry."[19]

What startles me, other than the obviously misprinted "1962," is the statement that Mount's body was brought back and buried in Cumby Cemetery after the war. If this information is correct, then the gruesome account of the aged father's return to Texas with the reeking body of his son and the morbid details about viewing the bloated corpse and rushing through its burial are imaginative embellishments. Granting that the decomposition of the human body is inconsistent and that, even by war's end, Lieutenant Mount was most likely not a nice, clean sack of bones, nevertheless the return and interment of the remains of a young man who had been dead for a considerable time would have been a much less morbid and dramatic event than that described by Cousin Mamie and most of the other storytellers. Further, a trip into Arkansas would not, for most Texans, qualify as a trip into the "Deep South." Such embellishments could reflect any of a number of motives: an emotional need to stress the carnage of the war, and perhaps a need, also, to give that carnage immediacy, to "bring it home" and give it more impact and meaning than it could have on some distant battlefield. There may also have been a need, from a narrative standpoint, to provide Great-aunt Becky with another opportunity to show courage and composure in dealing with the most horrific experience that could possibly confront a young woman in love.

Most stories and anecdotes about Great-aunt Becky represent her as "bigger than life" and reinforce her heroic qualities. Most storytellers or supposed historians could not quite avoid getting emotionally involved in their subject when that subject was Great-aunt Becky. Even Kibart and Adams cannot resist the temptation to romanticize a bit as they bring their biographical sketch of Rebecca Jane Alexander to sentimental closure. "She is buried in Cumby Cemetery in Hopkins County within sixty feet of the one she had plighted her troth to in those happy, carefree days of her girlhood. One can only speculate what her life would have been had she had the chance to marry Mr. Mount. If Mr. Mount's last conscious thoughts were of the black-haired girl he left behind on the Texas prairie, would it have been a comfort to him to know Aunt Becky would forever remain true to the man she never ceased to love?"[20]

On March 14, 1860, Aunt Becky's younger sister, Sarah Alexander (my great-grandmother), had married George C. Winniford. By the time Great-grandpa George joined Company K, Third Texas Cavalry, C.S.A., in 1861 the couple already had one of the three sons they would produce; a second son was born during the war years and a third—my grandfather—was born five months after the young Confederate veteran succumbed to war-related illnesses. Like Great-aunt Becky, Great-grandma Sarah was left with a farm to manage—and she had the added responsibility of motherhood. She and Great-aunt Becky often pooled their resources, not only material but mental and emotional. Both women were dedicated to keeping the family together and to preserving the legacy of Winniford-Alexander lands for the younger brothers and infant sons that they expected to grow to manhood and carry on both family names. One of the most interesting and controversial of the Winniford-Alexander family legends concerns an encounter between the two lone women and a couple of renegade soldiers who turned up one day determined to take their best horses.

The Embattled Sisters and the Renegades

A well just outside the barnyard of the old Winniford homeplace seemed a mysterious edifice to me during my childhood. Because it was shaded by a clump of chinaberry trees and caught water that drained off the steep roof of the big barn, this well was always full, even during the periodic droughts that plagued northeast Texas. The water was always sparkling clear and cold—a real temptation to children playing hide-and-seek in the haylofts. But my brother and cousins and I were warned *never* to drink water from this well. The water, we were told, was fit only for cattle and was strictly off-limits to human beings. Not until we appeared convincingly mature and stable were we "kids" told the family legend that explained the well's strange contamination.

During the Civil War, Great-grandma Sarah and Great-aunt Becky were left to tend their farms without the help of the menfolk. The two women pooled their resources, and Great-aunt Becky was particularly solicitous of Great-grandma Sarah because she had the burden of bringing up two small sons in the absence of their father.

One day in late summer, Great-aunt Becky and Great-grandma Sarah were together in the kitchen at the Winniford homeplace, doing some canning and putting up some jams and jellies. My brother, James Winniford, tells the rest of the story.

> The story is told that two renegade soldiers came—now whether they were Northerners or Southerners, I don't know—but two renegade soldiers came to the old farmhouse there and were going to take horses to travel on. And Aunt Becky knew they were renegades, and she knew they were not to be dealt with.
>
> But they had two old worn-out horses that they were going to leave, and that would be what Becky and the others would have to use as their wagon horses or buggy horses or plow horses. These horses were in bad shape. The renegades were going to go in the barn and take two fresh horses from the barn. Maybe they were going to take more than two. I don't know.
>
> Well, Becky told them to go ahead and go to the barn and get the horses. But while they were going in to get the horses, she darted in the house and got a rifle, and when they came out, she killed both of them. From all accounts, she took these soldiers down and buried them in a

> ditch, and, of course, they being renegades, they were never heard of again. But whether this be good or bad, that was Becky! You didn't mess with Aunt Becky.[21]

My brother attributes this shooting exclusively to Great-aunt Becky. In the story as I recall it, both women participated. Great-aunt Becky was the one who went out on the front porch, talked with the two renegades, and finally directed them to go to the barn to fetch fresh horses. But when she rushed back into the house, both she and Great-grandma Sarah grabbed guns and loaded them. The women were good shots, but they knew that this was one time when they could not afford to miss their targets. They made a quick decision as to which renegade each of them would shoot. When the men emerged from the barn, the two women slipped discreetly out onto the back porch, partly concealed by the vines and shrubbery. Each took careful aim and brought her assigned quarry down with one shot.

The fact that my brother gives the entire credit for killing the renegades to Great-aunt Becky may stem, in part, from a reluctance to admit that our great-grandmother was capable of murder, even when hard-pressed. More likely, his version of the story reflects his intense admiration for Great-aunt Becky and an unwillingness to share her glory with anyone, even Great-grandma Sarah. Having the women dispose of the renegades' corpses by putting them in a ditch (which would eliminate a lot of digging) probably seems to him a practical solution, but it ruins this version as an explanation for the well's mysterious contamination. Also, it seems to me that the ditch burial would have struck the two women as a very temporary and, therefore, unworkable way of hiding potentially damning evidence. With the first gully-washer, the bodies would have flushed out and started floating toward the creek.

Therefore, I lean toward accounts that describe how Great-aunt Becky and Great-grandma Sarah, finding it difficult to use the spade and shovel in the drought-hardened ground, settled finally for a soft area next to the barnyard well (an area that could conveniently have been further softened by drawing water and pouring it on the spot). The sisters dug a good-sized excavation there, deposited the two bodies against the bricked-in side of the well, and covered them up.

Naturally, they did not then consider the water suitable for drinking.

The renegade story is, of course, one of the Winniford-Alexander family legends for which there is no authority in records of any kind. This story was handled as a carefully kept family secret, at least until my own generation, and any evidence of its authenticity was no doubt destroyed soon after the incident occurred. There does seem to be a factual series of events in connection with horses that did involve the Northern army. Kibart and Adams give the following information:

> Becky raised horses and a few colts and finally moved into raising as many horses as the acreage and crops would support. . . . Toward the end of the Civil War, a federal officer who was in the Quartermaster Corps and who was a purchasing officer, contracted with Becky to purchase all the horses she could afford to sell. . . . The horses were duly picked up with payment to follow. In the course of ending of the war, all papers and records of transactions were apparently lost.
>
> Countless efforts on Becky's part failed to obtain payment for the horses. . . . She did not take this loss with a charitable attitude. Some felt it made her attitude toward Yankees harsher than it might otherwise have been. This treatment, along with losing Mr. Mount in the war, brought about a most disparaging remark when she later learned of the death of Abraham Lincoln.[22]

Whether there is any connection between this presumed historically accurate account and the dark family secret that the legend represents is another mystery. I do know that several years ago, I (with some hesitation) told the renegade legend to a group of acquaintances in Beaumont, and a woman in the group was absolutely incensed. The incident I described had happened to a relative of *hers,* she informed me indignantly, and my family had stolen her story! One must assume either that the story had widespread currency and was appropriated by more than one family—or that there are lots of moldy skeletons huddled in uneasy rest against the bricked walls of old wells.

It seems significant to me that the family's Civil War legends have women protagonists, even though Great-grandpa George and several Winniford and Alexander cousins fought in the war. Despite the family's pride in Grandpa George's service in the Company K cavalry division, there are no stories of his courageous actions as a soldier. A very general picture of his war experiences can be pieced together from what is known about the Texas Third Cavalry and the battles in which its various companies participated. In both the Union and the Confederacy, cavalrymen were an elite minority, surrounded by an aura of glamour and prestige, and they played only an ancillary role in the four years of fighting. Because men in the Texas Third provided their own horses and equipment, they were often drawn from the more prosperous elements of society. Texas cavalrymen were the first to volunteer from their various localities early in the war, so their enthusiasm, morale, and tenacity were probably higher than that of later recruits. Overall, men in the Texas Third Cavalry enjoyed relatively good fortune: they were spared participation in the most costly of the war's battles, so casualties were correspondingly less severe; on horses they enjoyed more freedom of movement, greater respect from the civilian population, and wider access to the scarce necessities of life; they were Texans, so their homes were relatively untouched by the ravages of war. They were thus atypical of Civil War soldiers.[23]

The Winnifords and Alexanders raised horses, which meant that acquiring suitable mounts and equipment posed no problem for Great-grandpa George and his Winniford and Alexander kinsmen and their friend, C. C. Mount (Great-aunt Becky's fiancé). Very likely, they went off to war like most Texans, as Douglas Hale puts it in his study of the Texas Third, "in a jubilant, light-hearted mood, 'rarin' for a fight.'"[24] Young men, all in their twenties and early thirties, they were under the delusion that the cause was just and necessary, that the conflict would be short and innocuous, that courage and determination would be keys to victory, and that the Confederacy would prevail. The Winnifords and Alexanders had just arrived in Texas, and they were motivated by a desire to protect the independent, autonomous lifestyle that they had moved to Texas to find from the encroachments of the federal government. They wanted to keep Union troops and fighting off their lands.

The issue of slavery was not a primary concern of my great-grandfather and his immediate kinsmen because they, like a majority of Texans at the time, did not own slaves. They probably disliked having abolitionist views forced on them, and, consequently, were willing enough to serve under company commanders, *all* of whom were indeed landed slave owners, including Robert H. Cumby (after whom the little town of Black Jack Grove was eventually named) and D. Y. Gaines, captain of Company K, in which Great-grandpa George and C. C. Mount were both enlisted.

The realities of war may have come as a shock for my young great-grandfather. Aside from some minor skirmishes, his first real experience with fighting was at the Battle of Pea Ridge, a battle marked by delays, confusion, and frustration for cavalrymen in the Texas Third and that ended in the retreat of the Confederate forces. Great-grandpa George's friend C. C. Mount was killed in that battle. Fought near Elkhorn, Arkansas, during the first week of March, 1862, the Battle of Pea Ridge marked the successful conclusion of a long campaign waged by Union Brig. General Samuel R. Curtis to push Confederate forces out of Missouri and preserve that state for the Union. After Pea Ridge, the fighting moved east of the Mississippi River—and it may well have been in the area around Corinth, Mississippi, where another battle began on May 8, 1862, that Great-grandpa George contracted the "fever" that cut his life short a few years later; Corinth gained an unhappy reputation as a breeding place for disease and pestilence during the war. Whether Great-grandpa George was actually wounded and the date of his return from the war are details that remain rather vague. The fact that a second son was born to George and Sarah before war's end would indicate that he did not complete the four-year "tour of duty." Nevertheless, Great-grandpa George was one of the Civil War's fatalities because he never recovered from the ailments contracted during his service in the Texas Third and died at age thirty-five, leaving a widow and two small sons and a third on the way.

Judging from the only existing portrait of him, Great-grandpa George looked more like a poet than either a farmer or a fighting man. In this portrait, he is a young man with a thin, sensitive face with clear, oddly tranquil pale eyes under brows drawn sternly together beneath a high forehead. His hair is fair, roached back and reaching to his shoulders. He is wearing a full-sleeved homespun smock, and his hands are long and slender, the hands of a musician—for he, like all three of his sons, was a gifted fiddler.

In my early teens, I developed a crush on this dimly romantic ancestor. With supreme insensitivity to my great-grandmother's long years of hardship, I wondered how the handsome man in the portrait could possibly have loved the grim little woman, whose nose and chin and brow I, alas, inherited. Great-grandpa George, who died when he was thirty-five, was probably still in his twenties when his portrait was taken. Great-grandma Sarah was well into her seventies when her portrait was made—and still wearing her widow's weeds.

While the cooperative little archivist at the Hopkins County Genealogical Society runs off copies of the records and documents that we have located, my brother and I sort out pocket change to pay for this service. We share a degree of satisfaction in having gathered bits and pieces of substantial evidence about the histories of both branches of our family. Yet pleased as I am with our small successes, I have doubts and reservations. The neat stack of copies represents a kind of truth, and I am aware that it is a kind of truth that is important to my brother. In my mind's eye, I balance the dead black-and-white finality of the stack of copies against the vivid, vital memories of my grandfather—or even Cousin Mamie—telling the stories about Great-aunt Becky and Great-grandma Sarah or of my Grandmother Ward telling the story of Little Moses, or Little Mose as she called him, on graveyard working day. I cherish the living memories, although they are elusive and perishable. I wonder what effect the stack of copied documents will have on the way the old stories are told from this point forward: what adjustments will be made, what additions, what omissions. Which truths will be preserved and which dismissed, perhaps to be lost forever?

Chapter Six

Two Graveyards

CULTURAL METAPHORS FOR THE HERE AND THE HEREAFTER

When our work in the archives of the Hopkins County Genealogical Society is finished, we set out for Cumby. We are now on a determined quest to locate the graves of a number of ancestors and their connections for whom we have acquired specific names and dates and the assurance that they are buried in the old Cumby cemetery. Once again we travel down Highway 67 and, just outside Cumby, are routed up around a loop and overpass, then down an asphalt-topped street into what was once downtown Cumby. The highway sign designating "Cumby Cemetery" is prominent, as if the cemetery were a tourist attraction—or that, at least, is the thought that first comes to me as we approach it. Actually, the sign probably is noticeable because it is the only one of its kind along the truncated stretch of road. The cemetery is the only point of interest requiring such designation.

As we ease down the narrow street leading to the cemetery, my first impression is that it is like other rural and small-town burial grounds: a flat square of land, surrounded by a fence with an iron entrance gate under a wrought-iron arch bearing the words "Cumby Cemetery." The graves are crowded close together in neat rows, very geometric, rigid, and unimaginative, with the predictable east-west orientation. As it turns out, however, as many of the graves face west as east. My grandparents are buried toward the front of the cemetery in a Winniford family plot, right on the main lane that cuts

Cumby Cemetery, front entrance

through the middle of the cemetery and not too far from the entrance gate. I did, of course, attend their funerals. But I come to realize that I am very unfamiliar with this cemetery; we have not wandered about here when we were children as we did in the Long Cemetery where my mother's folks are buried. This front section is all I know, so it is hard for me to imagine that mysterious Civil War and pre–Civil War graves can exist here.

We drive through the gate and down the lane for a short distance and park beside the Winniford plot. My grandparents' graves are much as I remembered them. But there is a large, relatively new marker, a huge rectangular thing meant to accommodate two graves. Across the top is the family name, "Winniford," and under that in equally large letters the word "sisters." On either side, over the area where each grave should be, are the names "Lynna" and "Lucille"—aunts of mine who between them went through several husbands but who ultimately faced old age alone. Aunt Lucille sold her share of the family land and chose material security and solitude. Aunt Lynna, who remained faithful to the land and stayed on in the old homeplace after everyone else was gone, is already buried in her allotted place.

My niece, Shannon, comments thoughtfully, "I guess they came back into the fold."

"Yes," I agree. "Blood is thicker than water—and most human arrangements, too, I suppose."

"So," Shannon pursues the matter, "I guess your marker will have 'Winniford' across the top?"

"Or maybe across the bottom," I agree. "I have in mind something graceful and monolithic. I'm not really into heavy granite slabs."

"You need to be careful about selecting something too tall and skinny," Shannon cautions, with a touch of grim humor. "It will just crumble and break off. Do you get this feeling of deja vu?"

"I get this feeling that this is a dangerous time and place to venture into anything too abstract and philosophical. I am borderline depressed already." But I can't resist adding, "You needn't be afraid that you're foredoomed, you know. You don't have to make their mistakes. Or my mistakes. We are not caught in some inescapable pattern. I am not at all like my aunts; my pattern is different from theirs."

Shannon shrugs and then hugs herself with a sort of shiver. "But when they bury you under your 'Winniford' marker, will it *look* like a different pattern? Or won't it seem like the same thing, all over again? I have sometimes thought," she adds, "that I might just keep my name, even when I do marry. Just keep the 'Winniford.'"

"That could save you a lot of inconvenience," I tell her, only half in jest. "Probably a good idea."

At my brother's prodding, we move on down the lane. The wind is penetratingly cold. The sky has been perfectly clear and a hard, vivid blue, but now it is becoming overcast with clouds that look like dirty, lumpy ginned cotton. The lane rises to a gentle incline and then suddenly dips down. It is like entering another dimension. The old part of the cemetery spreads out before us in graceful, sloping little hills and valleys with big trees, shrubs and small evergreens, and attractive monuments covered with moss and lichen.

The topography here, together with the trees and other vegetation that grow on it, is startlingly different from that of the seedy, cramped little town or any of the countryside around it. Obviously, the early settlers in Cumby set aside their choicest landscape for their graveyard. And in this part of the cemetery, there is no crowding. There are wide stretches of ground where there are no graves at all. There is no particular directional orientation, either; certain graves,

A section of the old Cumby Cemetery, 1997

especially isolated, single graves, are placed at an angle, usually in relation to some tree or grove of trees. Clusters of graves, on little knolls or near a distinctive tree, suggest a family group, and many of these are curbed and fenced.

It occurs to me that the first settlers around Cumby may have been influenced by the rural cemetery movement of the early nineteenth century, as discussed by Stanley French in his essay "The Cemetery As Cultural Institution: The Establishment of Mount Auburn and the 'Rural Cemetery' Movement." A basic concept of this movement was, after all, to set graves and memorials amid beautiful foliage in rustic surroundings. Mount Auburn, for instance, the famous parklike Boston cemetery, covered seventy-two acres. "The land," writes French, "was a pleasant, heavily wooded tract with a variegated topography of many little hills, valleys and streams."[1] This descriptive passage could just as easily be applied to the area of the original Cumby Cemetery. This old portion of the cemetery has other characteristics of the rural cemetery movement mentioned by French, such as iron fences around family plots and the obvious attempt to create a sense of history and aesthetic ambiance.

The three of us take off in different directions, strolling along the slopes of hills and under trees while we examine inscriptions on weather-beaten monuments and call out to each other when we make some interesting discovery. We have doubted that we will be able to locate the grave of C. C. Mount, Great-aunt Becky's lover—so we are astonished when this is the first grave that we find. Shannon comes upon the grave and yells to my brother, James, and me, "Come look! Here it is! Here is C. C. Mount's grave!" And here it is indeed, still protected by exceedingly rusty but mostly intact iron fencing and hidden behind a large shrub. It is clearly the original marker of C. C. Mount, Company K, Ninth Cavalry, C.S.A., with the dates of his birth and death. It is a strangely triumphant moment. The marker, safe within its ruined little fence, is an affirmation of past in present.

The Kibart and Adams biography, *Pioneers of Hopkins County, Texas,* states that Great-aunt Becky is buried only sixty feet from the grave of her lover, so we study the possibilities within that radius. Across a shallow ravine is a cluster of graves, which seems the most likely place, so we scramble down the sloping bank and up the other side. "It's an Alexander plot!" my brother comments. The most imposing monument on the plot is one that appears relatively new and stands shoulder high, towering over more modest gravestones. "That's old Cousin Billy's tombstone," my brother laughs, in amused recognition. Cousin Billy's marker is a family joke. He erected this impressive monument to himself and his wife several years before either of them died, a huge marble slab inscribed from top to bottom with their numerous worldly accomplishments—and then they both died in California and were not brought back to Cumby for burial. The marble slab marks an empty space. There is a story, told jokingly by amused but somewhat disgruntled kinfolk, that the ghost of proud, self-centered old Billy sometimes drifts in from California and lingers near the monument that boasts of his life's work.

There are some small, gray markers, very old, with illegible inscriptions. Next to them is a long, low slab inscribed with the names "Urbane Alexander" and "Mary Ann Drennan." We are standing at the oldest grave in the cemetery, although I doubt that the marker is the original because the inscriptions are so clear. Here is the first settler, the great-great-grandfather whose identity has been established for us just this morning in the archives of the Hopkins County Genealogical Society. Looking down at this ancestor's grave and then at Cousin Billy's rather obscene monument, I figure that if any ghost haunts this particular spot, it is old Urbane, indignant that an upstart, citified grandson has usurped his place as patriarch by erecting a monument that makes his seem mean and inferior by comparison.

"Here is a Winniford grave!" Shannon announces. She is examining one of three Civil War markers: thin, rectangular tablets with curved tops that look fragile but have held up rather well to more than a century of Texas weather. This Confederate soldier is Great-grandpa George.

Logically, Great-grandma Sarah and probably Great-aunt Becky, too, should be buried somewhere in the immediate area, but we see no markers that might belong to them. We are puzzled and at a loss as to where to search next. Then I wander over to read the grandiose inscriptions on Cousin Billy's monument. When I happen to glance down, I notice that propped carelessly against the base of the monument are two small, chipped headstones: Miss R. J. Alexander and Sarah Alexander Winniford! I feel a little tingle of shock run through me, and Shannon, coming up behind me, takes my hand and holds it.

The three of us kick around among the fallen leaves and matted dead grass, and, finally, in a space behind Great-grandpa George's marker, we locate the small foot stones that still designate both women's graves. They grew old together, so it seems right that the two sisters should be buried side by side. "They should have attended to their own stones," Shannon remarks, "like Lucille and Lynna did."

"Perhaps our aunts learned well from their mistake," I answer.

We place the headstones where we estimate they should have been and snap pictures of the graves as we had planned. But the whole thing seems a sham, empty and unsatisfying. Sons and grandsons and nephews relinquished the land tract by tract and retreated into mediocre schemes, but Great-aunt Becky and Great-grandma Sarah held firm during the worst of times. Their significance in family history, their roles as heroines in family legends seemed proven beyond doubt and, thus, intractable. I expected that in that final metaphor for place, the family burial plot, they would be solidly ensconced. To see them casually displaced and to be forced to regard their worth as eternally negotiable poses a disturbing dilemma here in the cold northeast Texas winter sundown.

The visit to the Cumby city cemetery proves fascinating and stirs an emotional response in me that is unexpected, simply because I have few memories of this place where the paternal side of my family is buried. My vivid memories are of Long Cemetery, but I must confess that my solitary visits to that familiar little graveyard where my mother's people are buried often leave me strangely distanced and unmoved. Cumby Cemetery is, at least superficially, more interesting. It is considerably larger than Long Cemetery; there is the surprise topography, the trees, the shrubs, the curbs and fences; and in Cumby Cemetery the graves are all marked with gravestones in a diversity of styles, with inscriptions that are frequently detailed enough to tantalize the imagination. The Cumby Cemetery makes a *visual* statement that has an impact even if one is just strolling through its grounds.

Long Cemetery, on the other hand, is a nearly meaningless little piece of earth unless a group of people are visiting there—for Long Cemetery has depended (and may still depend) on an oral tradition for its meaning. When I was a child, a cluster of weathered bois d'arc posts could become emotion-charged as my grandmother explained to me that they marked the graves of a particular family's children and described when and how each child had died. The uninscribed cement cylinders that now mark such graves, where the grave has not been lost completely, tell no stories. My memories of Long Cemetery are of occasions such as funerals and graveyard working days when people came and lingered and intermingled. The emotions they displayed, the beliefs they expressed, and the customs they observed gave meaning to their burial ground.

I am unfamiliar with the Cumby Cemetery because my family rarely went there. The paternal side of my family did not socialize in the cemetery, nor did their burial place have strong religious implications for them. I am sure they must have hoed and weeded their family plots before perpetual-care arrangements were made, but they did not make this a social event. For the maternal side of my family, however, Long Cemetery was a gathering place, a place where they renewed human contacts and tested and renewed their faith. Funerals and cemetery workings provided opportunities for both social and spiritual interaction. The two cemeteries, thus, work as metaphors for the subtle cultural differences that distinguish the paternal and maternal sides of my family.

Long Cemetery is located about four miles south of Cumby on a narrow, winding farm road. During my childhood, it was a sometimes treacherous sandy dirt road but is now occasionally blacktopped. Long Cemetery resembles the new and now "front" portion of the Cumby Cemetery, except that the monuments and markers tend to be smaller and less elaborate. There are also many "uninscribed" graves once marked by bois d'arc posts but now represented by unobtrusive cement cylinders. A half-century ago, both of these burial grounds could have been classified as southern folk cemeteries.

There are a number of interesting studies of the burial practices peculiar to these typically rural and small-town graveyards that were scattered throughout the southern part of the United States. For instance, William Lynwood Montell cites some intriguing folk beliefs and burial customs in *Ghosts along the Cumberland: Deathlore in the Kentucky Foothills* (1975). More useful to me in my understanding of the similarities and contrasts between the Cumby and Long cemeteries are Terry G. Jordan's *Texas Graveyards: A Cultural Legacy* (1982) and D. Gregory Jeane's "The Upland South Folk Cemetery Complex: Some Suggestions of Origin," an essay included in Richard Meyer's *Cemeteries and Gravemarkers: Voices of American Culture* (1989). Also especially thought-provoking is Anita Pitchford's "The Material Culture of the Traditional East Texas Graveyard," published in *Southern Folklore Quarterly* in 1978. These studies establish several characteristics that were applicable both to Long Cemetery and to the newer, front section of the Cumby city cemetery a half-century ago.

The southern folk cemetery was, first of all, usually located on high terrain. Anita Pitchford speculates that the reason for such a location may be that it offers better drainage, but she considers it much more likely that the purpose is ethereal, "involving a nearness to heaven."[2] Such graveyards were fenced, with an arched iron gateway at the entrance. It is theorized that the arched gateway has European origins in the *lichgate,* or "corpse gate," where the corpse was stationed to await the arrival of the clergy before burial. Jordan, Jeane, and Pitchford all call attention to the prevailing tendency for graves to be arranged on an east-west axis, with the feet pointing toward the east. As Pitchford comments, "This direction for grave placement is rather firmly fixed in folk tradition in the southern United States and Britain." She also notes that Christ was expected to arrive from the east at Resurrection.[3]

Certain types of vegetation were common in folk cemeteries—Pitchford mentions juniper, arborvitae, and evergreens like pine and magnolia—and inscriptions on gravestones are terse and unsentimental. Probably the most distinctive characteristics of the folk graveyards of half a century ago (traits that have disappeared with perpetual-care arrangements) were scraped grounds and mounded graves. Jordan and Jeane disagree about the origins of these customs. Noting that "rarely does one encounter scraping outside the Gulf and South Atlantic coastal plains, the stronghold of rural blacks," Jordan points to an African origin.[4] Jeane, however, argues that it is to Europe that one must look for the basic cemetery traditions that diffused with the settlers who fanned out across the southern frontier. He is convinced that it does not make sense "that the region's dominant culture would eschew most aspects of black culture for two centuries, but openly and wholly accept African burial traditions over time-honored European ones."[5] I am inclined to think that practical considerations instead of time-honored traditions influenced people around Cumby to scrape their burial grounds and mound their graves before the arrival of the riding lawn mower.

In her study of East Texas graveyards, Anita Pitchford notes her discovery that all but one of the twenty-seven graveyards she examined are located on high terrain. Long Cemetery would be another exception to the high-terrain rule, as would the Cumby city cemetery, since it dips down from the new front entrance toward the variegated terrain of the old section. Long Cemetery occupies a flat, level square of what must have been cleared pasture land, but there is excellent drainage toward the farm road to the west. I have never visited the cemetery when water was standing anywhere, and I suspect this feature was important to those who started burying their dead there. Everyone dreaded the thought of a "watery grave." Even so, it was likely the attractiveness of the locations, especially the large trees that could serve as landmarks, that inspired early settlers to select both sites for burial grounds.

There is a poignant story about the first burial in Long Cemetery. The following is a reconstruction based on a number of recountings by both males and females.

The First Burial

In the first half of the nineteenth century, just before the Civil War, a small wagon train of settlers traveled through the area around what was then Black Jack Grove. Several people in the train, mostly children, were ill with scarlet fever, so the travelers skirted the town to avoid contagion. These desperate people camped out in the country a few miles south of the business district.

A young man who had already recovered from the illness was sent into town to ask for supplies and to try to find a doctor. Women in town went from house to house and collected a load of supplies, but no doctor was available. The local midwife was afraid to go because two babies were expected any day, and she feared she would transmit the disease to mother and child during delivery. Finally, an

Long Cemetery, front entrance

old horse doctor agreed to take the medicine he had and go do what he could for the suffering people.

His kind efforts were helpful, but he was unable to save one little girl, a beautiful blonde child who looked like an angel. The young mother was overcome with grief at the loss of her only offspring, and she refused to relinquish the corpse for burial. They would wait, she insisted, until they reached their destination to bury the child; she could not bear to bury her "along the trail." The travelers were faced with a dilemma. They were not yet ready to move on, and they faced a long trip—and the child's corpse was not, of course, embalmed.

One of the early settlers named Long heard about this tragedy and took pity on the distraught mother and the rest of the train. He went to the mother and told her that he had a nice piece of ground already cleared, next to a beautiful grove of big oak trees. He promised that he would set that piece of ground aside for a real cemetery, which would be fenced and kept cleared. She could always find the grave of her child if she came back because the oak trees would serve as a landmark. The young mother responded to Long's concern and generosity, and the child was finally buried on the land he donated.

Whether or not this story is true, the location for the cemetery was probably selected, in large part, because of the grove of oak trees. When I was a child, the grove was fully intact and clearly visible from some distance so that it could serve as a distinctive landmark. This may have been especially important since the burial place was not on a hill or slope that stood out from the surrounding woods and pastures. Now only three of the trees remain.

Like other southern folk cemeteries, Long Cemetery, at present and as it was several decades ago, has an enclosing fence and a metal gate. A similar fence and gate form an entrance to the front or new section of the Cumby city cemetery, as well. In neither case would the gate qualify as ornate, but both gates are arched and bear the place name, "Long Cemetery" or "Cumby Cemetery." If such gates were indeed styled after the European *lichgate,* apparently people around Cumby were unaware that it might serve this presumed original function: I have never attended a funeral in either cemetery where the body was stationed at the gate. During my childhood, however, the gate at Long Cemetery, at least, was a distinct boundary regarding human conduct. Outside the gate, behavior might be relatively casual, but once one entered the gate, one was expected to be quiet, meditative, and respectful.

Neither Long Cemetery nor the front section of Cumby Cemetery contains the types of vegetation common to folk cemeteries. Both areas are, in fact, remarkably bare. The old section of Cumby Cemetery does contain a variety of evergreen trees and shrubs like juniper and arborvitae. There are also some true cedars: big, ancient trees that were probably, like the large oaks and elms, part of the indigenous growth. Some of the other decorative trees and shrubs represent later settings. As discussed previously, however, that section of Cumby Cemetery does not much resemble a folk graveyard. Evergreens, magnolias, and other shrubs have never grown in Long Cemetery. This is probably because the people who bury their dead there have always relied entirely on indigenous vegetation—the grove of oak trees at the entrance, primarily. Even now, people do not plant flowers or shrubs in their cemetery plots, so the cemetery has none of the decorative plants that Pitchford also mentions, such as crepe myrtle, spirea (bridal wreath), iris, and roses.[6]

During my childhood, there were, besides the oak trees out front, a number of bois d'arc trees scattered throughout Long Cemetery that provided welcome shade as well as posts for marking graves when no store-bought marker was available. Fred Tarpley comments that "in Northeast Texas . . . some farmers avoid plowing near groves of bois d'arc trees. According to tradition, bois d'arc trees were often placed as living fences encircling now forgotten graveyards."[7] It is debatable whether the bois d'arc trees that used to offer spots of shade throughout Long Cemetery had been planted or had merely been preserved; there seemed to be no intention of using them for a fence line. The interesting thing is that not a single one of the bois d'arc trees remains standing; the graveyard is bare and unshaded. Some years ago, when a committee was appointed to oversee the upkeep of the cemetery, some of the old-timers offered a whimsical if somewhat superstitious explanation, which eighty-three-year-old Aunt Minnie Martin Foster puts into words.

The Bois d'Arc Trees and the Cement Markers

For many years, a number of pretty, well-shaped bois d'arc trees were scattered throughout Long Cemetery. They gave shade in spring and summer and kept the graveyard from looking so bare and dismal. And they came in handy for poor people who couldn't afford store-bought markers for the graves of their loved ones.

But then some folks decided that the graveyard wasn't being kept up right and that we needed to be more organized about it, so they appointed a committee to tend to things. And the first thing you know, the committee decided those bois d'arc posts on graves weren't good enough, and so they ordered a bunch of little cement markers. And they took the bois d'arc posts up and built a fire and burned them—and put the cement markers in their place.

Then it was the strangest thing. All the bois d'arc trees started dying off. One by one, they'd just stand there and the leaves would shrivel and fall off and the trees would die—till they all looked like skeletons standing there. Now they're all gone.

And it started happening when they took those bois d'arc posts up and burned them. There's no way of knowing why, but it's the truth.[8]

The foregoing is a belief legend: it depicts human beings encountering the supernatural in everyday life. The implied homeopathic or sympathetic magic—that is, magic based on the association of ideas by similarity—is never insisted upon.[9] Instead, storytellers rely on the strange coincidence of timing to establish the point that there must be some connection between the removal and burning of the bois d'arc grave markers and the death of the trees. This story is concerned not so much with the supernatural, however, as with Nature responding to the human condition in extraordinary or "unnatural" ways. Probably the storytellers were not entirely comfortable with the changes made by the cemetery committee, and they felt that their uneasiness was, perhaps, validated by the trees' seemingly negative response to new values and procedures. (When I suggested to my aunt that perhaps the committee had deliberately killed the trees so that they could be cleared away, she was horrified: "Oh, I wouldn't think so! That would have been a desecration, sure enough.")

Another less magical but probably no more scientifically acceptable explanation was also offered for the death of all the bois d'arc trees. Probably, some folks suggested, the people who first began using Long Cemetery for burials cleared away all the female bois d'arc trees, leaving just the males. Female trees bear the apples, and bois d'arc apples are always large, plentiful, and full of foul-smelling "milk." They also break apart and create a terrible mess. No one would want them in a cemetery. According to this theory, the male bois d'arc trees were very likely cross-pollinated with female trees scattered around in the nearby woods and pastures. With the increased emphasis on dairying, some believe, many female trees in the vicinity have been destroyed. With cross-pollination thus impossible, the males in the cemetery sickened and died. This theory suggests a plot for a truly tender story that would rival *Romeo and Juliet,* and it certainly emphasizes the frustrations of life in northeast Texas, where even the trees have problems with relationships. No one we talked to, however, was positive that male bois d'arc trees die when they are not cross-pollinated.

Besides the bois d'arc trees that earlier provided shade within the cemetery proper, a giant old black mulberry tree once stood just inside the arched gateway. Given the size and age of the tree at the time when I recall seeing it, the mulberry tree must have been a part of the indigenous vegetation that was preserved by the original users of the cemetery. The tree bore its fruit in season—long, juicy, purplish berries that were a temptation to hungry children impatient for picnic cakes and pies. This tree, however, was the subject of a fearful little legend that mothers always told to discourage their offspring from stuffing themselves on the tree's bountiful, ripe fruit. I can remember at least a couple of times when my mother stood under the tree's fruit-laden branches and told the story to my brother and me and some skeptical city cousins. When talking with children, my mother used a gentle, persuasive reasonableness. My brother and I collaborated in re-creating my mother's "voice" for this story because I feel it loses much of its impact if it is not told in the first person.

The Deadly Mulberry Tree

Mulberries look mighty good when they are big and soft and juicy and falling off the tree—but you have to be careful about eating them, even when they come off a tree growing in someone's yard or orchard. The berries are always full of tiny, tiny bugs, so you have to soak them for a long time in cold water until all the insects float away and can be skimmed off. Then you sprinkle the clean berries with sugar and serve them with heavy cream—and that can be fine eating. Mulberries just need special preparation.

But you wouldn't want to eat mulberries off this tree in the cemetery no matter how clean you'd washed them. This is not your ordinary mulberry tree. Many, many years ago, somebody—probably Indians that used to live around here—told the first white people in these parts that they couldn't eat berries off this tree, especially since they were burying folks near it. The berries would be poison, and anyone eating them would get sick and maybe die.

Well, I'm sure that, even then, there were folks who didn't quite believe the warning—but no one was willing to take any chances.

Time went on, and no one really knew whether the tree grew poison fruit. Then this old man bought some land close to here and brought in a bunch of cattle. Obviously, he didn't know much about the cattle business because he didn't take care of his cows as he should—didn't feed them right and didn't keep up his fences. So his cattle kept breaking out and getting on other people's property. I don't know how many times they pushed through the gate and got into the cemetery and trampled graves and knocked over tombstones. People who had their dead buried here tried to get him to fix his fences and keep his cows up, but he was lazy, I guess, and just plain didn't care.

But his cows got out one time too many. They broke into the cemetery when the mulberries were ripe and the ground under the trees was just covered with berries. The poor cows hadn't been fed right, anyway, and they were hungry—so they stood around in the shade eating those berries. The next day the old man finally went looking for his cows, and he found them all lying dead under the mulberry tree. I'd imagine he was mad as hops, but he had brought it all on himself.

After that, everyone knew for sure that the mulberries off this cemetery tree can't be eaten.

❧ The main purpose of this story as I recall my mother and sometimes other women telling it was, of course, to prevent children from soiling their hands and their Sunday-best clothes by gathering berries or getting upset stomachs from eating too many of them. The story does, however, contain interesting elements. Although there is at least a hint that the tree's reputation for poison berries may have pre-dated the cemetery (my mother always included some reference to warnings by Indians, but others did not), the story nevertheless reflects the Long Cemetery folk group's very real—though never explicitly stated—belief in contagious magic.

There was a strong conviction, evidenced through behavior rather than words, that the ground within the cemetery was contaminated through its contact with death. Nothing that grew inside the cemetery would have been eaten by these people. One did not even *take* food into the cemetery and eat it, out of much the same feeling of revulsion that would make one hesitate to take food into a public restroom and eat it there. Furthermore, there is the object lesson implied by the old cattleman's loss of his livestock, for he possessed several character defects significant to my family and others in their community. He is lazy, he does not take care of his livestock, and he does not respect other people's property—in particular, the space set aside for burying their dead.

I do remember that at one graveyard working, someone's visiting relative—a hefty kid who whined continuously for sweets—slipped around and ate some of the mulberries. By mid-afternoon, he was wailing with stomach gripe, and one of the women offered to come to his rescue with a dose of baking soda and water. "It's no use!" he told his mother, wailing louder. "I'm dying. I ate some of those mulberries, so it's for sure I'm dying!" His family was forced to cut their graveyard working short and haul the sick boy home, although he did, of course, recover—a fact everyone attributed to sheer good luck and the earnest prayers of the entire gathering. No one seemed inclined to note the amazing variety and quantity of other delicacies with which the child had stuffed himself. Or if they did, they chose not to enlighten the kids who believed the story.

My early impression of Long Cemetery was that it was probably the bleakest, ugliest, loneliest place on earth if one imagined it once all the visitors were gone. The starkness of the little square of land was a result of the fact that the grounds were scraped and the graves kept mounded. These features would certainly have distinguished it as a southern rural folk cemetery. At present, probably to facilitate the kind of care now judged to be appropriate for the cemetery, graves (except those that are very new) are flat, and grass covers the entire cemetery—not only the graves but the spaces between them. Except for the upright markers, then, the area has the appearance of a perpetual-care or lawn cemetery and, thus, of being somewhat "modernized."

At the time of the graveyard workings during my youth, all weeds and grass were kept carefully hoed away, and the entire area was scraped clean so that it was a wide expanse of bare ground with no vegetation at all. Also, all graves were mounded, and the restoring of mounds constituted an important part of the work required on graveyard working days. An attempt was made to maintain the mounds in an approximation of the way they must have appeared immediately after the grave was filled: graves for adult males were mounded slightly wider and several inches longer than those for adult females, and the mounds on children's graves corresponded in length to the height the child might have been at his or her death. People searching for a particular child's grave among a group of uninscribed markers (and children's graves were often marked with posts or fieldstone) often used the length of the mound as a means of arriving at a tentative identification.

Apparently, people generally trusted that the maintenance of the mounds had been continual and accurate from the time of burial. During her exploration of twenty-seven East Texas cemeteries, all located in Cass County, Anita Pitchford noted that "scraped earth" graves and family plots were fairly common. She comments, however, that entire cemeteries barren of grass are not usually found in Cass County. She mentions that "a few" of the graves are mounded.[10] Of course, by the late 1970s, when Pitchford was doing her research, Long Cemetery would also have shown signs of the shift toward a more contemporary, perpetual-care or lawn-type cemetery, with grass in some areas and a tendency to smooth the mounds away to make mowing possible.

People who buried their dead in both the Long and the Cumby city cemeteries probably resorted to scraping more from practical considerations than concern for tradition. Keeping the grounds clear of weeds and brush was no easy matter before the advent of the power mower. Scraping was a sure-fire way of keeping unwanted vegetation under control. Long Cemetery was a small, flat area that a group of industrious people could scrape in its entirety. Cumby Cemetery was much larger, with uneven terrain, so keeping the entire area scraped doubtless posed an impossible task. I do recall that when I was a child, some areas were kept scraped and some of the graves were mounded. I think this practice applied primarily to the new front section of the cemetery; I doubt that there was ever any consistent effort to maintain the old section of the graveyard in this manner.

Grave orientation is another feature that would identify Long Cemetery as a folk graveyard. This was especially true of the cemetery several decades ago, before it entered what Jeane would term its "transition" phase. Graves are arranged on an east-west axis, with the feet pointing east. The people who buried their dead in Long Cemetery several decades ago would have agreed with Pitchford as to the reason for such placement: on Resurrection Morn, Christ was expected to launch his Second Coming from the east. Thus the dead were positioned so that, upon rising, they would be facing east.

Long Cemetery patrons felt some anxiety about matters other than the inconvenience of having to turn around in order to meet the advancing Christ. Rising from the dead, meeting Christ face to face, and the impending Judgment Day added up to a great deal of trauma, and few believed they had the courage to get through such an awesome ordeal alone. As people pondered grave placement in their family plots, there was always considerable discussion about who would be buried alongside whom. An especially timid and retiring daughter might be permitted a grave next to her mother, whose strength would comfort her when the trumpet sounded—while a more independent, self-confident daughter might have to settle (albeit hesitantly) for a space two or three graves over. "Just remember to grab Bessie's other hand," one woman advised a daughter who complained because her sister was the one who would rise standing next to the mother, "and we will all greet our Maker holding hands as one."

Misgivings about the dilemma of the risen soul did not seem to influence decisions about grave placement in Cumby Cemetery very much, at least among the people I recall discussing the matter. Someone was more likely to say, "Uncle Norve always wanted to be buried on that little knoll. We were afraid the knoll was too close to the ravine, but he was stubborn. Nothing else would have pleased him." Affection for some tree or grove or swell in the ground certainly seems to account for grave placement, in many instances, in the old part of the cemetery. The east-west orientation toward the front of the graveyard strikes one as having more to do with orderliness, keeping graves "lined up" properly, and conserving space than it does with getting the deceased in position to meet his or her deity at some future date. This is especially true in view of the fact that many of the graves face west.

The division into family plots is another feature of the folk cemetery noted by Jordan, Jeane, and Pitchford. It is in this characteristic, along with a couple of others they designate—the use of grave decorations and grave houses, grave sheds, false crypts, and aboveground burials—that the two cemeteries under discussion differ most drastically from a visual standpoint. In both cemeteries there is a tendency to divide into family plots. Such divisions are much more obvious, however, in the Cumby city cemetery, where plots are clearly defined by curbing or fencing, where every grave is marked, and where markers and monuments may be large, ornate, and distinctive in styling.

One becomes immediately aware of an intent to represent the status and importance of the family within the community (both of the living and the dead) and of the status, role, and importance of each deceased member within the family. In some plots, an imposing monument, perhaps near the center, pays tribute to the entire family, while male members are buried under somewhat less imposing monuments around it. In other plots, the "founding father" of the clan is granted the largest, most ornate monument, and other family males are buried alongside or in back of this ancestor in some sort of descending order. Women either share the headstones of their husbands, or they are granted much smaller, more delicate-looking headstones of their own. Children have even smaller markers. In some interesting cases, an especially imposing male headstone may curve around to enclose the grave of a wife or a child buried alongside, giving the visual impression that the "dependent" is still in the protective embrace of the male. Further, though the Cumby Cemetery is not characterized by grave houses or grave sheds, there are above-ground graves, mainly in the old section of the cemetery. Most of these have been vandalized.

The fact that the living create a visual metaphor—or a concrete, symbolic representation—for family prestige, permanence, and individual worth means that Cumby Cemetery pronounces judgments that the visitor can sort out without the assistance of a "tour guide." Deeply conscious of these "eternal pronouncements," Cousin Billy Alexander was motivated to assure his place and prominence in the family plot before he died, while he still had some control (or so he thought) over where they would dig his grave and what they would carve on his gravestone. Prompted by the same motivation, certain of his kinfolk were resentful of his high-handed use of money and influence in preempting them regarding order and prominence in the traditional burial place.

Once the deceased had been assigned to their appropriate place and decently buried, however, the paternal side of my family did not seem to feel a sentimental attachment to the graveyard, nor was it a site of social and spiritual renewal. (I am uncertain about other families who buried in Cumby Cemetery, but I note few outward manifestations of emotional attachment or social or religious activity connected with the graveyard itself.) Occasionally, visiting out-of-town relatives might inspire a tour of the family plots. Even at funerals, however, people did not linger long on the grounds after interment. If family and friends got together, it would be at someone's home.

In Long Cemetery, on the other hand, there was scant variation in the size, material, design, symbolism, or style of markers and curbing. Family plots there—contrary to Pitchford's findings in Cass County cemeteries—revealed little about the background and social standing of the families represented, beyond the obvious fact that all were poor. Even markers placed in the cemetery during the last decade tend to be decidedly modest. In keeping with Pitchford's findings in Cass County cemeteries, inscribed epitaphs in Long Cemetery are usually terse and uninformative.[11] One can examine a marker where mother and child are buried together, both dying on the day of the child's birth, or a group of markers for youthful siblings who died within a few days of each other and deduce that tragedy surrounded those deaths. Rarely, however, is any sad sentiment expressed in the inscription itself.

The cemetery contains no grave houses or grave sheds, nor are there above-ground burials or false crypts. Grave decorations are minimal to nonexistent: even in its present "transitional" to "modern" stage, the graveyard is rarely graced by the plastic flowers that so bountifully adorn many modern cemeteries. The absence of grave houses and grave sheds probably reflects the relative poverty of the people who buried their dead in Long Cemetery when such structures were in vogue.

Most of these people, however, would have been unwilling to erect these shelters even had they been more prosperous—for philosophical and religious instead of economic reasons. All of them took the "dust to dust" concept very seriously. Before almost every funeral there was heated debate about the "rightness" of metal coffins, for instance. The prevailing attitude was that those who requested such interment—for themselves or for a relative—were at heart attempting to evade human destiny and achieve some sort of physical immortality that was contrary to God's plan. Many of them saw and even tried to verbalize some inexact analogy between the corpse and a seed that, when planted, "rose again" or was "resurrected." But if it was shut away from earth and air, it dried out and never grew. The demands of their land, of tilling, planting, and harvesting, were never far from the minds of these hard-working people.

The absence of grave decorations is more difficult to explain. Markers are generally small and either gothic, tablet, or block in style, according to Richard V. Francaviglia's basic classifications.[12] Elaborate carvings are rare indeed, although three or four children's graves have the familiar angels or lambs carved into the stone. No objects were placed on the graves, with the one exception of a little girl's grave on which her parents had placed her favorite toys. An uneasy legend (to be discussed in a later chapter) justified the presence of those items in the cemetery. The paucity of plastic floral memorials at present may be explained by noting that many of the graves date back to the nineteenth century, and there are no living relatives who are active in their upkeep.

It is difficult to determine how significant Long Cemetery is in the lives of those who currently bury their dead there. To them I am now basically an outsider, tolerated good-humoredly because a wide swatch through the cemetery "belongs" to my brother and me: it contains at least a battalion of our deceased relatives. Thus, I am very aware of only being able to observe, inadequately, from the fringes. Through the 1970s and into the early 1980s, an elderly Cumby woman, Nettie Romans, sent out letters to the far-flung kin of deceased buried in Long Cemetery, inviting them to the summer graveyard working day and encouraging them to give financial support to cemetery upkeep. Such notices seem to be a thing of the past.

When asked about the cemetery's current meaning and function, people generally gave evasive answers. "My mother has kinfolk buried there," one woman told me. "But she wanted to be buried alongside my father, with his folks in Greenville. So I don't go there. It's way out in the country, you know." "I go there sometimes with my grandmother," a man told me. "It's where she wants to be buried." I suspect that scattered remnants of the old folk group account for most new burials in Long Cemetery and that when these remnants are depleted, the cemetery will have limited use thereafter. With the modern tendency to regard death in what is perceived as a "healthy," pragmatic, or distanced way, most people would probably not indulge themselves in strong emotional responses to burial places even if they felt them—and they would not likely confess such feelings to me.

I can be more certain about how the cemetery functioned in the lives of people several decades ago when, as an alert and imaginative child growing up, I moved among them as an insider, listened to them talk, and watched their actions.

Francaviglia points out that "cemeteries serve both functional and emotional purposes. They provide for disposal of corpses and, far more important, provide a place where the living can communicate with the dead." Because of this duality in purpose, Francaviglia concludes that cemeteries are thus "both sacred and profane. . . . The cemetery, both as a place and as a landscape, has spiritual and mystical overtones."[13] It is important to realize that for the Long Cemetery folk group of several decades ago, death had a significant impact on those left living, given that place and their circumstances. Isolated by bad roads, poor transportation, and the demands that fields, livestock, and running a household made on their time, people had access to few human relationships. A person's concept of self in relation to others and a person's sense of his or her own identity were limited to a mere handful of people who came within their circumscribed range of activities. When one of these people died, survivors lost part of their sense of self. The equally circumscribed society offered no opportunity for reclaiming it.

E. B. Fleming's valedictory to his wife at the conclusion of his volume *Early History of Hopkins County, Texas,* expresses two of the major concerns that prevailed among people in this area and among the Long Cemetery group in particular: the feeling of permanent deprivation in the loss of a close family member and the corresponding need to believe in a resurrection and reunion that would alleviate the loss. "Grim death has visited our home and removed from earth our dear companion. . . . We will never see her sweet and innocent face again until the morning of eternity breaks open the gates of death and turns the black night of grief and sorrow into everlasting pleasure and never ending sunshine. . . . Farewell, until we meet again on yonder pearly shore, beyond death's chilling flood."[14]

Despite his flowery flourishes with words, Fleming sets up a contrast that was deeply and honestly felt by many people of this time, between the "black night of grief and sorrow" of the death of a loved one and the "everlasting pleasure and . . . sunshine" of a hereafter in which reunion can occur. Already facing the east, some essence of the dead person waited in the grave for the "gates of death" to "break open." Visits to the loved one's grave were a source of reaffirmation, a tangible contact with the part of the person's identity that had vanished with their death. The preoccupation with graves, the sense of a presence in them, and the emphasis on some kind of reunion between those dead and those left alive (all of which characterized the folk group's perception of the meaning of death and burial) were not, therefore, altogether morbid and sentimental.

That the Long Cemetery folk group tended their graveyard very much as they tended their land did not make the graveyard a less sacred place or their efforts there less reverential. What had developed among these people was a religion of the land that quite engulfed any of the abstract doctrines of religious sects to which they aligned themselves. To them, nature and God were indistinguishable. They wrestled with their divinity day in and day out, flinching at his anger, squaring their shoulders at his indifference, and mouthing chapped-lipped thanks for his meager blessings. For them, "good" was determined by what they perceived as enabling them to survive; "evil" was that which appeared to "go against nature." It was this particular kind of faith, this religion of the land, that—so far as these people were concerned—determined the rituals, burial procedures, and graveyard decorum at Long Cemetery.

I have used the designations "place permanent" and "place portable" in an attempt to suggest the contrast between the two sides of my family—in lifestyle, outlook, and values. Cumby Cemetery was and is the formal burial place of a segment of Cumby society that included and seems still to include local business people, professionals, landed farmers, and dairymen. This segment of the community, to which the paternal side of my family once belonged, perceived themselves as established, stable, ongoing. Even today they use their cemetery to make a statement about the structure of their society, the relative prominence of their families within that society, and the meaning of each person's life in relation to family and the community at large. Though humble, perhaps, compared to other city cemeteries, Cumby Cemetery is a landmark, a showplace, that must be arranged and maintained appropriately and with care and decorum. I think, however, that those who bury their dead there have never done much "living" in and through their burial ground.

Especially before and during the time when I was growing up, Long Cemetery, on the other hand, was probably the most permanent place that existed for people to whom place was, for the most part, "portable." No matter how many times they sold out, left, and then came back again, no matter how far-flung their wanderings, these people had a right to gather at Long Cemetery because they had buried their dead there. To Long Cemetery they brought their "portable" yearnings, beliefs, values, hard experiences, anguished lessons learned, and joys found and treasured. They mingled together seeking spiritual renewal, affirmation, hope, and a sense of comfort and security in the here and the hereafter.

Just as the two cemeteries serve as metaphors through which I can examine the contrasts between the two branches of my family, so too, I have discovered, the two graveyards offer metaphoric or symbolic insights about gender. These insights are valuable in understanding the narrators of many of the stories that are important to me. Most of the tales told by the paternal side of my family were told by men—men sitting before their glowing hearths, or talking boisterously while outside killing hogs or quietly down in storm cellars. They were men who thought (some of them misguidedly) that they had achieved "place permanent."

Most of the storytellers on the maternal side of my family were women, and they recognized that sometimes place has to be very portable and that the only things that one can truly possess are those she carries in her head and heart. There were female storytellers on the paternal side of my family, too, but I was not so deeply moved by them, and their stories often seemed very similar to those told by their men. But the metaphoric message evident in both cemeteries is that the female storytellers in both branches of my family had one thing in common: being women in rural northeast Texas.

The merely token headstones that had marked the graves of the legendary Great-aunt Becky and of Great-grandma Sarah in the old Cumby city cemetery should not have been cause for surprise, nor should the fact that some family member or graveyard worker had casually propped the dislodged stones against the monument erected in memory of one of the Alexander dominant males. (That the stones may have been deliberately dislodged to facilitate mowing is a nagging possibility that remains disturbing.) I had been away from this area and these people for many years—and time and space have the effect, eventually, of distancing a person from realities that were once so familiar as to be taken for granted.

In his collection of essays on Texas, Larry McMurtry comments: "Years ago someone pointed out that Texas is hell on women and horses. He was wrong about horses, for most horses are considered to be valuable, and are treated well. He was absolutely right about women, though: the country was simply hell on them, and remained so until fairly recently."[15] McMurtry referred in his essay primarily to West Texas, but the blackland prairie around Cumby that the first settlers broke and tilled in order to raise cotton and corn made equally stringent demands on people trying to survive on its soil and in its climate.

Nothing came easy. During a period in history when "women's

work" was not valued in the culture at large, my great-grandmothers, my grandmothers, and even my mother were attempting to do that work in an environment especially hostile to their efforts. Out of custom and as a result of religious teachings, most women were, in fact, guilty of complicity in the perversion of the female principle. They expected that the father or husband would be the unquestioned head of the household and accepted that their own interests and welfare—their very identities—would be subsumed under that masculine authority. The family plot in the old Cumby Cemetery served as a means of maintaining the memory and life of this aspect of the "dead past," or of their social heritage. As W. Lloyd Warner points out, the graveyard has tended to reflect the basic recognition of the superior and inferior statuses of males and females in our society. Males are given larger and more prominent headstones and greater ritual recognition at their funerals.

Interestingly, Warner does suggest that although men are given more formal recognition, women are more fully recognized informally.[16] Perhaps the family legends in which Great-aunt Becky and Great-grandma Sarah are heroines constitute such informal recognition. The Winnifords and Alexanders who buried Great-aunt Becky and Great-grandma Sarah were probably aware of the significance of these two women within their specific families: as chief functionaries rather than mere appendages. But these surviving kinfolk were unable or unwilling to escape from the larger cultural metaphor as it applied to placement and designation in the graveyard. Succeeding generations have been unwilling to disturb the arrangement even if they have thought corrections might be in order.

The inequalities in the social, economic, intellectual, and even spiritual possibilities for men and women doubtless permeated life in the community in which I grew up—yet I think that my childhood failure to be entirely aware of these injustices was not entirely because I accepted them without question. Although a patriarchal system was certainly well in place, in both my families there were decided differences between principle and practice. In the paternal and maternal branches of my family, there were long stretches of time during almost every generation when the family functioned as a matriarchy: a woman was the head of household.

Great-great-grandpa Urbane Alexander died at age forty-one

after a fall from a wagon. Although his wife did not long outlive him, the responsibility for the farm and family fell, of course, to Great-aunt Becky. After he came home sick and wounded from the Civil War, Great-grandpa George Winniford lived at least a couple of years longer than the stories about him seem to imply. But he was dead by age thirty-five, and the land and his three young sons were taken over by the indomitable Great-grandma Sarah. From all accounts, her authority was rarely questioned even after those sons were grown, married, and had broods of their own. My grandfather, Robert Lee Winniford, was a virtual invalid during the last twenty years of his life, and the farm was run by my grandmother and two of her strong-willed daughters. My mother was only ten years old when Grandfather Ward died, and Grandma Minnie Wolf Ward exerted a tyrannical control over their offspring that extended years beyond the hot, moonlit summer night when she died. *Her* mother and siblings had been brought to Texas by the pioneer-spirited Great-great-grandma Elder, widowed somewhere up in the Oklahoma Territory. My own father was ill for almost as long as I can remember and died relatively young, so my mother learned to be aggressive and resourceful.

When the menfolk—usually inadvertently—vacated their "power positions," the women stepped in and filled the vacancies thus created. As a rule of thumb, widowed mothers did not remarry, in order to turn all holdings over to children (especially sons) intact. A couple of my aunts habitually married drifters who then found themselves working as "hired hands" on the farm, hated it, and eventually drifted on their sundry ways. But these two ladies never got around to reproducing, and their high-handed treatment of the men in question meant that these alliances did not hamper them much or endanger their inheritances.

The upshot of all this was that the activities of the women in my family, on both the maternal and paternal sides, did not seem seriously restricted. Winniford women handled the livestock, engaged in horse and cattle trading and selling, did the hiring and firing, participated in rodeos, worked out deals with the bank, bought their own vehicles and farm equipment, hauled their own cotton to the gins, and baled their own hay. Division of labor along gender lines was more social than actual. A son might be assigned a figurehead position at the Christmas dinner table that acknowledged his potential dominant maleness, but his true authority might be as shaky and ineffectual as his carving of the country ham. Both sides of the family preached the precepts of patriarchy, but in practice women often filled roles that were culturally designated as masculine.

These conditions possibly set the two sides of my family apart from their communities, where women were generally restricted to the domestic sphere. Because they lived in town and the responsibilities imposed by the land were not there for them to assume, the women in the Ward-Wolf side of the family (my mother's immediate family, at least) were more like their female neighbors in their activities than the Winniford-Alexander women were like theirs. Perhaps as a consequence, the Winniford-Alexander women were not, for the most part, great storytellers; their lives were physically active and demanding as well as mentally challenging. When they told stories, they tended—like the men—to stress bits of family history. Although they took more liberties with names, dates, and other details than did the male storytellers, only a few of their stories seem blatantly subversive.

In many respects, there was more interaction between storytellers of both sexes among the Winnifords and Alexanders than among the Wards and Wolfs. Like the men, the Winniford-Alexander women took advantage of a number of storytelling situations that were not connected with domesticity. They recounted stories, recited proverbs, told jokes, and sang songs, for instance, in the cotton patch, in the storm cellar, or while riding the fence lines. On such occasions, both males and females might be present and participating.

The Ward-Wolf women, on the other hand, almost always told their stories in a domestic context. Their stories emanate from thoughts, feelings, longings, and resentments unavoidably repressed by the isolation of their circumstances and their resulting inaction and lack of contact with the world outside their household. My Grandmother Ward and my unmarried aunts enjoyed considerably more leisure than most women of their time and station—and their imaginations were obviously prone to exploring dark and forbidden regions.

In "Woman to Woman: Fieldwork and the Private Sphere," Margaret R. Yocom discusses the importance of a storyteller's setting in determining the nature of the story and the way it is told. The men in Yocom's family told their tales in what she calls the "public sphere." The women in her family, on the other hand, did their storytelling in what she terms the "private sphere." She makes the point that "this sphere of theirs may be indoors or outdoors, in any room or on any lawn; the location does not matter to their storytelling as much as the privacy that those locations afford."[17]

Yocom goes on to note that this privacy may come from natural isolation or from a created detachment as when, for instance, amid a flock of relatives, several women turn and face one another. Often storytelling in the private sphere includes the sharing of work, "in all those areas that feel not merely a woman's touch but also her dominant influence and control." Stories told within the private storytelling sphere (Yocom is specifically interested in personal narratives) have little competitive edge to them, as do most men's narratives told in the public sphere, nor do they exist primarily to entertain: "Exemplum-like . . . women's personal narratives provide support as they teach other women what is possible for them."[18] It seems important to note that Yocom is concerned with situations in which adult women are telling stories to each other, with the youngest listeners being, perhaps, teenage girls. When stories are told with smaller children present, such personal narratives may have broader application.

The storytelling in the Ward-Wolf private sphere almost always excluded men (as Yocom indicates is frequently the case). This may have been partly because my Uncle Bernice, who was the only male living in their home, was a "loner." However, I often thought, even as a child, that Uncle Bernice's need for privacy was a powerful fiction perpetuated by the females from probably selfish and maybe even sinister motives. I invaded his privacy with stubborn persistence—to the clamorous horror of my grandmother and aunts and sometimes my mother—and I found him wonderfully communicative and entertaining.

He told me all his amazing experiences that, according to his womenfolk, were "so horrible he couldn't stand talking about them," as well as the grisly details that, they presumed, had been obliterated from his shell-shocked brain: the horrors of trench warfare in World

War I, the day an exploding shell blew off his finger, the long hours of lying still while they took shrapnel from his back and legs, his struggle to remember who he was and where he came from as he lay in an army hospital with missing dog tags, the glorious days and nights of his courtship of a beautiful French girl, and his secret sorrow that he could not bring her to the states (for he claimed he had married her and she had borne his child). All this was heady stuff for an unsophisticated farm kid—but I was a precocious reader, so I listened with a fairly sympathetic and unstartled ear. And I understood that I would never acknowledge having heard the things he told me—not in that time and that place.

Uncle Bernice was six foot six and looked like an Indian warrior. He played the mandolin, sang old love songs pleasantly off-key, and did funny little watercolors of birds and flowers. In view of his whimsical gentleness, it always puzzled me that people—his womenfolk included—gave him a wide berth. But I know that he could be intimidating. If some man seemed about to get out of line, Uncle Bernice's jaws would knot up and he would look down at the fellow and say quietly, "You don't want to cross me!" And no one ever did. He was always building and carving me some exquisite special piece of doll furniture (long after I had passed the age of playing with dolls, a circumstance that no one mentioned to him). During bad Texas winters he kept me abundantly supplied with store-bought lace handkerchiefs in lieu of Kleenex—because, he said, he wanted no niece of his wiping her nose on her sleeve. When I went off to college, he wrote to me almost daily, but each note read much like the one the day before. Yet he was a riveting storyteller, one who had been silenced except in *his* highly selective private sphere. The women excluded him and wove their web of legend around him and denied him an audience, which is part of their mystery and of his. I always thought of him as a prisoner, and I believed him when he said many times that he was still in the trenches.

But although the Ward-Wolf women excluded men from their storytelling (with a few notable exceptions), their domestic private sphere was open to children of both sexes. Sunday afternoon visits to the Ward home in Cumby were always gossip and storytelling sessions held out on what they called the "sleeping porch," a long room lined with windows. As the oldest female, my Grandmother Ward was an expert storyteller and the final authority when other women needed to get their stories straight.

Although when it came to avoiding unpleasant tasks my grandmother got a lot of mileage out of being "in delicate health," she gave an energetic performance. Usually she stood up while she spoke so that she could move freely about the room, swooping around, dancing, creeping up on people. She could mimic characters gasping their last breath, or strangling on their own blood, or screaming in terror. She could be a panther growling and hissing, ready to attack. She used her apron over her head to achieve a wide variety of disguises. And she knew Indian war whoops and chants and she could yodel—to all of which she added a special dimension with a tambourine made out of Coca Cola lids. When she began singing, slowly and ponderously, "Old Growlie is dead and laid in his grave, ummm humnh, laid in his grave . . .," all of the children present would grab each other and huddle together because they knew that scary business lay ahead. Their responsive squeals would be no less real and their fear no less delicious because the end of the song was familiar. Not infrequently, visiting teenage cousins or even the adult women would forget themselves and gasp or squeal at one of Grandma Ward's carefully contrived "surprise" endings—for her audience never knew where she might swoop, what sound she might make, or whom she might grasp in her talons when the horrific moment arrived.

But the other women, including my mother, were fine storytellers, too, relishing fascinating details, building the dramatic tension to a fever pitch, working their audience with uncanny skill. Because they manipulated their audience, I suspect that they were much less concerned with the accuracy of their account—even when they were supposedly narrating an actual event—than they were with getting the desired listener response. An inattentive audience called for embellishments, even for new twists in some "sacred" old plot.

My Aunt Dovie was a tall woman with that rare Ward phenomenon, flaming auburn hair, and my grandmother considered her a great beauty. According to the two of them, Aunt Dovie had ventured into a tragic marriage during her teenage years. My mother had never been aware of this union until it was suddenly announced on my aunt's fortieth birthday, and no records of or references to such a marriage have ever turned up. But Aunt Dovie was inclined toward secretive activities. From all outward appearances, she lived a quietly refined and reclusive life with my grandmother and Aunt Minnie, guarded from the outside world by my brooding, shell-shocked Uncle Bernice, who understood well that he would defend her honor at all costs.

But from time to time, my Aunt Dovie discreetly left town for clandestine engagements with men who were definitely not locals, and she always returned from these strictly hush-hush excursions with her finances and her wardrobe much improved. Everyone, at least in the immediate family, was vaguely aware of these goings-on, but no one ever dared utter a word for fear that my grandmother would be mortally upset. They all presumed she did not comprehend the nature of my aunt's arrangements.

Possibly, Aunt Dovie's double life revealed itself through her approach to storytelling, for she could be depended on to ferret out or invent either the most gruesome or most salacious details with which to "spice up" a perfectly innocent story. She would also yank a plot around a bit so that it suggested more than was originally intended. My mother was eternally saying, "Now Dovie, be careful of the children!" and Aunt Dovie would always laughingly respond, "Oh, Beryl, they're too young to catch my meaning!" We children always "caught Aunt Dovie's meaning"; even if there were words or whole phrases that seemed shrouded in mystery, her husky, teasing voice and the way she relished the words as if they were sticks of spearmint gum got her message across. We *knew*.

Ours was in some ways a dysfunctional family group. But none of us knew that we were dysfunctional, and so we all had a lot of fun—except for my father and Uncle Bernice, who did not like each other and who were relegated to the parlor or the front porch for an afternoon of carefully polite religious and political debate. What a relief it was for them when wars or floods or earthquakes happened and they could get out all the maps and have something to do with their hands.

Of course, having fun was not perceived by any of the Ward-Wolf womenfolk as being the primary outcome of their gossip and storytelling. As Yocom points out, many of these women's stories were exempla, demonstrating, especially for girl children, "what [was] possible for them." Or they were warnings against what this group considered socially and morally inappropriate behavior; ironically, their standards were rigidly ideal. My grandmother knew her scriptures, and even the most wildly entertaining horror story would, after the shuddering and squealing had ceased, be followed by a prim little sermon and a verse or so from the good book. Overall, her performance carried a double message. Aunt Dovie, for her part, was a past master at moralizing. Her face suddenly serious and her voice firm, she always provided two moral tacks: the first one for the adults who had "caught her meaning," and the second, a sweetly simple one for the children who she thought had not. This took real skill, and it is unfortunate that more of her gems were not recorded for posterity.

Recording Aunt Dovie's materials has been a nearly impossible task because I am unable to adequately re-collect and recollect them and have found no sharer who heard and remembered the stories or their ingenious moral tacks. This has been one of those "disastrous surprises" that sometimes happen when one is attempting to collect or re-collect. Several factors may explain why I have only sketchy memories of the contents of Aunt Dovie's storytelling. I think the main reason for my inability to recall the stories is that they were not retold, not repeated. Aunt Dovie rarely told the same story twice; my mother or grandmother would shush her as soon as they recognized that the story would be inappropriate. Certainly, my brother, cousins, and I were warned never to repeat the stories that my aunt told. To some extent, I think, we obediently dismissed her stories as "bad." Too, although as children we almost always caught the gist of the stories, many of the important details may indeed have been "over our heads." And I suspect Aunt Dovie was less concerned with a logical, memorable plot than with the manner of telling and getting the effect she desired.

Thus, I attempt to reconstruct only one of Aunt Dovie's stories in the next chapter. I am able to accomplish this feat because hearing this story alarmed me enough that I repeated it to female schoolmates and, hence, recall most of its details. Even though I cannot retell most of my aunt's stories, I nevertheless believe her presence was an important shaping influence on stories told by other women, especially my grandmother. Aunt Dovie never told stories at graveyard workings, but her active audience participation opened up lively possibilities that my grandmother might have missed had my aunt not been there to encourage her.

The private sphere of the sleeping porch or some other very similar enclosure was the only place where these women revealed themselves in quite this same way as storytellers—with the exception of graveyard working days. Under other circumstances at home, and certainly in public, my grandmother was a tiny, fragile-looking lady with lively blue eyes and shiny black hair (the only evidence of her Cherokee genes). She seemed gentle, reticent, and almost decorously proper and appeared shocked and embarrassed by other people's crudities, of which she was openly critical. Aunt Dovie was haughty, remote, and uncommunicative. My mother and Aunt Minnie were more gregarious than the other two women, but even they were careful and self-contained in public.

As a child I noted with humor that all the menfolk—including my grandmother's brothers and half-brothers, my mother's brothers, nephews, male cousins, and in-laws—staunchly shielded the women from the very sights, sounds, and subject matter that were the primary sources of interest and delight during Sunday afternoon story sessions. It seemed a wonderful secret to share with my grandmother, mother, aunts, and other women in the extended family. Obviously, those Sunday afternoons provided a sort of safety valve that permitted these women to release pent-up emotions, acknowledge forbidden thoughts and ideas, and indulge in behavior much freer than that which was socially prescribed.

Graveyard working days at Long Cemetery, where a number of the Wards and Wolfs have family plots, provided the only other storytelling situation in which (so far as I am aware) the Ward-Wolf female storytellers performed. Storytelling at a graveyard working may, of course, be perceived as a removal from the private sphere of the home into a decidedly public sphere out in the open air, surrounded by a relatively large crowd of people. Actually, for the Ward-Wolf women storytellers, graveyard workings served more as an extension of the private, domestic sphere, providing opportunities that the sleeping porch could not.

Women at graveyard workings, in the first place, took on the same type of domestic chores they customarily did in the home. They brought foods already prepared for the noon picnic under the trees, and other food preparations continued once they had arrived on the site. They swept under the big trees, set up tables in the shade (assisted by the older boys), and laid out the tables for the meal. At noon they served the meal and afterward cleaned up the area just as they did their own kitchens. In the graveyard, they performed the same sort of chores that they usually did in their yards and gardens—sweeping, raking, pulling up weeds, and dusting or washing off markers and monuments.

When the actual graveyard working began, people separated along gender lines. The men went off in groups to do the sort of work they, too, habitually performed: "heavier" tasks such as mending fences, filling in gullies and graves that had sunk during winter freezes and spring rains, repairing mounds, setting up or stabilizing monuments and markers that had settled or fallen, and hoeing areas where weeds persisted. The women, thus left to themselves as they were in their homes, could gather in small, intimate groups. These groups changed their constituency and rotated throughout the day so that one did not always have the same audience. The same tale might therefore be told more than once because the storyteller was provided with a new group of listeners.

Certainly, a different kind of behavior from that in the sleeping porch was in order. My grandmother's war whoops, yodeling, and vigorous rain dances would hardly have been acceptable—and how shocked and disconcerted most of the more distant kinswomen and neighbors would have been to discover she could do these things! Everyone observed proper graveyard protocol. But the cemetery working offered numerous, ready-made occasions for physical activity and for venting the emotions. Women always wept as they visited graves of departed loved ones, and they hugged and comforted each other. They held impromptu, highly emotional little "prayer meetings," praying aloud and virtually competing in the areas of rhetoric, facial expression, and overall emotional appeal. They passed babies around and took turns burping, bouncing, and singing to each other's offspring. The older women dipped snuff and invariably made a happy foray into the narrow wooded pasture to dig for redbud roots to make fresh brushes for dipping. And the sermon that followed the meal on the grounds was (if the preacher understood his role at all) loud and dramatic and gave another excuse for weeping and hugging and shouting "amen." At its conclusion, a bevy of reprobates, young and old, dutifully "rededicated their lives," inspiring more tears and hugs and moments of real or pretended ecstasy. Thus, graveyard workings offered both the intimacy and the emotional release that appealed to the Ward-Wolf women storytellers—and to other women of the wider community who shared their interests.

Chapter Seven

"Home Is Where You Bury"

LONG CEMETERY LEGENDS I

Graveyard working days were an important tradition among the Long Cemetery folk group in the past. They are still held occasionally, with special notices going out to far-flung relatives who may have an interest in the various family plots. At the graveyard workings that I attended as a child, the folk beliefs and peculiar customs of the group of people who gathered there were probably more in evidence than at any other time, including funerals.

Graveyard working day or decoration day—or "cleaning" or "homecoming," as the event is variously called—was one of the major features of all southern folk cemeteries and is still observed in those cemeteries that have not made a complete transition to a perpetual-care arrangement. At such "workings," falling on various weekends from April to August (often on the Saturday preceding the first Sunday in May), scraping, decorating graves, and other related chores are usually accomplished for the first time each year. In many places, two or three subsequent workings during the summer and autumn are customary.[1]

In a paper titled "'Decoration Day': Alabama's Day of the Dead," Joey Brackner describes a two-day affair. Most families visited the graveyard on the day before "Decoration Sunday" with hoes and shovels in order to scrape the ground and attend to other traditional aesthetics such as mounding the graves, making new plantings, or pruning old ones. He adds, "Typically, working on Saturday is followed by Sunday's 'dinner on the ground,' church singing and vis-

Long Cemetery, 1997

iting with friends and family. On Sunday, participants come dressed for church and engage in what amounts to a family and community reunion."[2] It is interesting that William Humphrey, who uses a Texas graveyard working to frame the action of the plot in *Home from the Hill*, describes a breakfast on the ground that sets the activities of his graveyard working day in motion. He includes similar descriptions of cemetery practices in *The Ordways* with perhaps even more emphasis on family tradition.

For the Long Cemetery group, a May graveyard working would have interfered with an important phase of their farming. April and May were the months when cotton was chopped and corn was thinned; May, in particular, was a busy month in gardens and truck patches. Long Cemetery graveyard workings were, therefore, usually held toward the end of June or the first part of July, after crops were laid by but before hay needed baling or ripened feed crops had to be gathered. People who attended the work days at Long Cemetery generally allotted only one day for the event—almost always a Saturday. They crammed into that day a dinner on the ground, a sermon, and renewing contacts with friends and out-of-town relatives, along with the required labor in the cemetery.

All this could be accomplished because, in the first place, Long Cemetery is small. Then, too, it is possible that some of the men visited the graveyard during the week before graveyard working day and completed heavy, dirty work or tasks that required special equipment such as chain saws, bushhogs, and so forth. Whole families and out-of-town visitors, however, only gathered at the cemetery on the one day set aside for both work and socializing. Concerning the custom of bringing food and serving it from long tables near the cemetery, Anita Pitchford theorizes that this association of eating with death may have forgotten origins in Old World ceremonial cannibalism.[3] The Long Cemetery folk would have been aghast at such a suggestion, for they thought that feeding all the industrious workers was a practical expedient. Besides, they *never* ate in the cemetery proper or allowed foodstuffs to be carried in and perhaps dropped on the grounds, for fear of attracting ants to the graves.

During my growing-up years, graveyard working day was one of the high points of summer, at least in my mother's immediate family. There would always be a flurry of correspondence with out-of-town relatives, followed by mounting excitement because certain kinfolk planned to attend, especially those whom no one had seen for a long time—or keen disappointment when favorite kinfolk wrote that they could not come that year.

My mother was the seamstress for her mother and sisters as well as for herself. Her old pedal-type Singer would rattle steadily all afternoon and into the night during the weeks before the graveyard working as she stitched up suitable outfits for the womenfolk and female children in the family. Selecting proper apparel for this one-day event was a tricky matter because it involved both physical labor and social activity. The occasion also included visitors (like big-city kinfolk from Dallas) whom they all wanted to impress favorably. Silks and other easily soiled and unwashable fabrics often used as Sunday church-going clothes were not suitable for work and outdoor eating and visiting. Thus my mother and the other women usually selected cool, thin summer fabrics such as dotted swiss, voile, pique, and batiste. The trick was to utilize these fabrics in garments that looked "dressy and stylish" but that could be washed and mended with ease.

Early on, before synthetic "wash and wear" fabrics came in

vogue, the prospect of wrinkles occasioned great anxiety. Little girls were urged to please not "wallow around and mash up" their skirts, at least until after the meal and the sermon. This warning ruled out most normal activities such as running, sitting down, or even leaning against a tree for support. I do not know whether my own aversion to skirts dates back to those hours of standing around in tight, new shoes smoothing my ruffled dotted swiss, or to that awful era a few years later when fashion demanded that girls wear at least a half-dozen crinoline petticoats.

There was much preoccupation with food during the weeks before graveyard workings. My mother would take note of three or four outstanding young fryers among her flock of chickens, and their eventual doom would be sealed. Or she would select a particularly fat young hen from which to boil off the broth for dumplings. Canning and jam and jelly making would have been already in progress, and jars from the most successful batches of these delicacies would be set aside for the anticipated feast. Certain anxieties cropped up in the absence of home freezers: would the speckled butter beans still be "making" by the end of June or would the drought ruin them? What a shame if Cousin Johnny from Dallas missed out on his beloved pot of butter beans and okra!

Green peas bloomed early, and the vines were usually bare by May. My mother therefore often put up enough of them in big gallon jars to ensure that she would have a pot of peas to put on the picnic table. Potato digging was a late April or early May undertaking, and every woman had her own secret recipe for potato salad. Tinting the potato salad pink with beet juice was considered the height of culinary artistry for a (thankfully) brief period of time, and all the women experimented with new potatoes and beet juice. The problem was how to keep the hard-boiled eggs (a necessary ingredient) from becoming so discolored that they discouraged even the healthiest appetites.

A couple of days before the graveyard working, baking began. My mother was famous for her coconut cream pies and her cornbread. Grandmother Ward baked angel biscuits, using yeast for rising, and she made a sugary tomato cobbler that was the high point of the meal for those who had developed a taste for it. Tomato cobbler requires carefully trained taste buds and a degree of courage and daring that many people lack. There was no cooking contest on graveyard working day, but all the women competed quite as earnestly as if there had been, cherishing compliments and flattery as if they were blue ribbons. Uncle Bernice was convinced that no outside meal was complete without large quantities of bologna, liverwurst, and cheese. "There'll be so much chicken we'll all wind up crowing with the cocks at sunup," he would argue. He always created a general commotion (and a mess in the trunk of the car) by icing down several pounds of these cold cuts, to the dismay of the womenfolk and the delight of most of the children.

I do not recall that it ever rained on graveyard working day. Those days were always clear, sunny, and swelteringly hot. Women brought whatever funeral-home fans they had accumulated—essential during the sermon—and everyone hoped for a breeze. My family always got to the cemetery early, primarily because Uncle Bernice hauled one load of family members there in his old Pontiac and then drove back to Cumby for another. Faced with such a mission, he was firm about getting an early start. Other people arrived in cars and pickups, and some of the old farmers who did not live very far away still drove horse-pulled wagons. After the pots and sacks and boxes of food had been unloaded, everyone stood around for awhile greeting other early arrivals and deciding which tasks needed immediate attention. The first hour or so of a graveyard working day was spent in informal socializing and "paying one's respects" by spending some quiet time at the graves of one's closest kin.

As we proceeded through the ritual of paying respects, the storytelling usually began. Entering the cemetery was a sober if not somber moment; all levity ceased as we passed under the arched iron gateway. Children were cautioned not to run and to keep their voices down. The volume of noise would increase as the day progressed and work began, but in the early hours the mood was respectful and meditative. Inevitably there was a warning not to step on graves as we moved through plots that were not curbed and graves marked only by posts. "Be careful where you step," my grandmother might warn. "There are a bunch of children buried along here. Graves so small you hardly notice, with nothing but those posts to show where they are. Poor little things. You don't want to step on them." Several of the sources in William Montell's *Ghosts along the Cumberland: Deathlore in the Kentucky Foothills* refer to superstitious beliefs concerning stepping on graves, generally stating that the person who does so will die.[4] I do not recall that we were ever issued such a warning. One avoided stepping on graves out of consideration for the occupant.

My grandmother always went to my grandfather's grave first, and she always wept although he had been dead for many years. My mother and my aunts generally accompanied her to the father's grave, and they all invariably relived impressions of the hot summer noonday when he had come in from the fields, asked for a drink of cool water, and died of a heart attack before my grandmother could even fetch it for him. The weeping and the memories were part of a pattern that became familiar to me through its repetition, highly ritualized and yet strangely sincere. Another part of the pattern was my grandmother's tragic complaint that two of her children, dead in infancy, were not buried beside their father: little Nathaniel and Aubrey had both died in Oklahoma during the family's migrations.

When my grandmother at last moved on in the direction of the Wolf family plots, the other women often stayed behind, probably to humor her. They knew that she enjoyed having my brother and me (and any visiting cousins that had tagged along) all to herself when she told the saddest and yet, in her view, the most inspirational of her stories. Even before she visited the graves of her parents, my grandmother would stop at the grave of Little Pearl, a beloved younger sister who had died tragically at the age of ten. Little Pearl was the heroine of my grandmother's favorite belief legend.

Little Pearl and the Pearly Gates

My grandmother belonged to a large family that had resulted from the deaths of spouses and the remarriages of surviving partners. She had Lynch stepbrothers, Lynch half-brothers, and Wolf brothers and sisters. The youngest of this extensive brood was Pearl, a child who in my grandmother's memory was a model of sweetness and beauty. Pearl was not dark like most of the Wolfs but instead "took after" the Elders: she had curls the color of "spun honey," blue eyes, cheeks that were a "pretty pink," and deep dimples. The little girl was the family's darling. Though admittedly spoiled, she was good-natured, generous, and—what was most important—spiritually inclined, having insisted on baptism during a camp meeting when she was only eight years old. Everyone loved Little Pearl, even her classmates at the country school just across a meadow from the Wolf farmhouse.

Tragedy struck during potato-digging time. One of my grandmother's older brothers was using a recalcitrant, wall-eyed young mule at the turning plow. As he went down each row of potato plants, plowing deep and turning up the moist soil with its crop of new potatoes, Great-grandma Lynch-Wolf and some of the younger children followed behind him with buckets, gathering up the potatoes. The children were engaged in a sort of contest to see who could find and snatch up the largest potatoes.

Little Pearl was a lively child who enjoyed such sport, and she was by nature somewhat aggressive and competitive. Normally, her older brothers and sisters would have left behind many of the largest potatoes in order that she could have the pleasure of "winning," but potato digging happened only once a year, and the children took this competition seriously. Pearl was further frustrated by their mother's demand that they all take time to gather up the small potatoes, too, before they moved on to more attractive ones ahead.

Suddenly the plow turned up the biggest potato anyone had seen that morning, and in the same instant it struck against a large underground rock and the mule balked. Spurred by excitement and frustration, Little Pearl darted ahead, forgetting the many warnings not to get too close to her father and the mule. In her excitement she stumbled just as she reached for the prized potato and pitched forward under the feet of the mule. The mule shied at this commotion, kicked backward, and delivered a solid blow to Little Pearl's head.

It was a terrible moment that no one in the family ever forgot. The little girl screamed and then lay still. The mule's shod hoof had all but scalped the child, and blood gushed from the terrible gash. The brother gathered his youngest sister up and rushed with her into the house.

For two days Little Pearl lingered, slipping in and out of consciousness. The family used what means they had to stanch the flow of blood, and they smoothed the scalp of "spun honey" curls back in place. A doctor of sorts was finally located, and he did what he could—but he offered little hope for the child's recovery. So the extended family gathered, expecting the worst.

In her lucid moments, Little Pearl apparently relished all the attention and the drama of the situation. She requested that various of her relatives kneel by her bed and pray with her, and at other times she insisted that they all join in singing favorite hymns. Word of the tragedy quickly spread, and people from the country all around paid visits to the dying child's bedside. During one of Little Pearl's times of full consciousness, some of her schoolmates came by to see her. Having caught on that she was expected to die, she insisted that her mother fetch several of her small treasures, which she distributed among her tearful friends and then fell unconscious.

Rousing again some time later, Little Pearl reconsidered her generous action and asked her mother whether her schoolmates would return the items in the event that she lived. "Little Pearl wanted to do what was right and good," my grandmother always excused her tenderly, "but, after all, she was just a child."

On the day of her death, Little Pearl's periods of consciousness grew shorter and farther apart. She was alert, however, when her teacher and several of her schoolmates walked across the meadow to visit her at noon. While her friends stood around her in awkward silence, openly weeping and uncertain what to say, the teacher at Pearl's request recited the Twenty-third Psalm. Suddenly, Little Pearl called out, "Mama, who is that at the gate?"

The mother rushed to the window to see what new visitor might be arriving, but she saw no one there. "There's no one at the gate," she answered.

"Oh, not *our* gate, Mama," the little girl exclaimed. "That gate up *there*! Don't you see? That shiny, shiny gate up there!" Everyone in the room understood that Little Pearl had glimpsed the pearly gates of heaven.

The little girl was soon unconscious, and she never revived again, dying peacefully in her sleep an hour or so later. As she had promised, the mother went out and rang the dinner bell so that the children in the school across the meadow would know that Pearl was gone.

As my grandmother told it, the story of Little Pearl was a belief legend in the special sense that it, like others she told, depicted ordinary people coming in contact with the supernatural in everyday life. For my grandmother, the story had possibilities as a "belief" legend in a much more private, personal way: she was certain that the story would strengthen the belief or faith of her listeners, that it might indeed convert the cynical. To her, Pearl's vision proved beyond any doubt the reality of a hereafter and the existence of at least one feature of heaven as it was represented through familiar biblical interpretations. More than once, preachers at the graveyard workings (most likely at my grandmother's insistence) used the story in much the same way she did.

It was evident to me that my grandmother's rendition was not an unchallenged version of Little Pearl's death, even when I was a child and most inclined to accept it without question. On at least a couple of occasions, at informal family gatherings when the story was mentioned, my grandmother's brothers teased her that Little Pearl had not been quite the "angel child" that she chose to remember. According to my great-uncles, Little Pearl had spent about as much of her conscious time "cussin' the mule" that had kicked her as she had singing hymns, and they were much less certain than my grandmother about the gist of Little Pearl's final utterances.

To the extent that she improvised Little Pearl's deathbed performance, Grandmother Ward echoed nineteenth-century attitudes about death, dying, and the hereafter. Especially during the first half of the nineteenth century, Americans had a proclivity for participating in the ritual of death, which centered more directly on the deathbed than on the grave. Family and most intimate friends would gather round the deathbed, first to offer solicitude, emotional comfort, and reassurance to the departing but also in the hope of receiving inspiration by witnessing a calm, clear-eyed death and perhaps hearing some profound utterance escape the dying lips of the loved one.[5] This ritual remained important to many of the people around Cumby well into the twentieth century. Failure to notify a relative or friend of an impending death in time for them to reach the deathbed for the loved one's last moments was a slight that could not be forgiven, nor could the failure of a close relative to join those gathered at the bed of the dying.

Grandmother Ward may have borrowed, also, from the consolation literature that was popular throughout the nineteenth century and to which she would probably have had access during her girlhood. As Ann Douglass states in "Heaven Our Home," "Consolation literature of all forms between 1830 and 1880 became ever more preoccupied not just with the last scenes and earthly resting places of the dead but with their celestial destination and doings."[6] My grandmother's story about her little sister's dying glimpse of heaven (or, at any rate, of its front door) covered all these bases niftily and defied cynical rebuttal. Whether Little Pearl died so gloriously up to "expectations" may be open to question, but she certainly does so in the legend that my grandmother wove about her.

Little Pearl's death and burial, and the significance of the memories of these events to my grandmother and other kinfolk as well, are revealing with regard to the folk group's beliefs and customs—both at the time of the girl's death and during the period when my grandmother told her stories. Little Pearl's marker is, in itself, revealing. In other contexts, the marker would not be imposing—but in Long Cemetery, where many children were buried with no markers at all except uninscribed fieldstone or bois d'arc posts, the marker of my grandmother's tragic sister strikes the observer as perhaps unusual. Little Pearl's marker is an obelisk mounted on a pedestal, a type of monument that, according to Richard Francaviglia, was common between 1890 and 1905.[7]

The Wolf family thus provided the girl with a tombstone that was much in vogue at the time of her death—1891. It was, furthermore, relatively expensive because of the ornate carving and the need for stone of sufficient quality to withstand such carving. The stone's superior quality is borne out by the fact that her marker has remained in better condition than nearby markers from the same period. Even given the fact that Little Pearl was a favorite with the family, one wonders that parents with so many mouths to feed and such limited means would consider such an expenditure.

There is a strong possibility that the unfortunate Wolf family succumbed to community pressure in the wake of their tragedy. Unusual circumstances surrounding a death may focus public attention upon a family and bring them at least temporary prominence and prestige; the funeral in such a case often becomes a focus of public attention and may attract an unusually large attendance.[8] After receiving many callers during Little Pearl's last days, the Wolf family probably anticipated a large funeral and continued interest in the child's grave once burial was completed. Anxious to fulfill what they perceived as the community's expectations in their response to the loss of their child (and probably needing to purge guilt feelings for not preventing the accident), the Wolfs were perhaps tempted into an extravagance they could ill afford.

My grandmother always led her listeners next to the graves of her parents. As female grandchildren approached puberty, they were told a story about Great-grandmother Lynch-Wolf intended, presumably, to inspire them to high moral standards and sexual restraint. This story was sometimes told out on the sleeping porch at the Ward house in town, where it generally stimulated much speculation and debate among pre-adolescents and adults alike. It might also, in the right group, be told on graveyard working days when the women were sure of privacy. My girl cousins and I were generally reminded of the story when we stood looking at our great-grandmother's tombstone. We would beg my grandmother to tell us the story then, but we could be sure of her refusal. Oh no, she would not even *think* of telling such a thing standing right there at her poor mother's grave! A dead lady's sex life was not a suitable subject for the cemetery, at least once one passed through the gate.

A grave that fascinated all children was a child's grave located some distance across the cemetery from the Ward and Wolf family plots. The grave belonged to a little girl (not related in any way to Wards and Wolfs), and her family had placed a number of her playthings on her mound just in front of her headstone. These weather-beaten, faded, rusty toys caught the imagination of most youngsters who visited the cemetery, and my brother and I always wanted at least a brief look at this unusual grave. The womenfolk, including my grandmother, were reluctant to allow us more than a quick walk-by. Since the dead child was not a relative, my grandmother did not wish to "intrude" on family—though, in fact, the child's parents had moved from the area and were rarely if ever present. Primarily, though, I think our interest in the toys embarrassed them. The truth is that we did not want to take the toys or even to touch them; we looked at them merely in an effort to grasp the meaning of their being there, to make some connection between toys and death. This grave had its own story.

A Child's Toys

A young couple moved to the Cumby area and bought a small farm, mostly to be near the young woman's aging grandparents, who had no one else close by. The couple fixed up the little farmhouse, put out shrubs, and mended fences. Everything seemed to be going well for them, and they lived happily with their two small daughters.

The second winter they were in their new home, however, was a harsh one. When their younger daughter died in a flu epidemic, the parents' grief was intense. Of course, they still had a living child, so they turned their attention to the remaining little daughter. For awhile, they sometimes let the older girl play with the dead child's toys—and the girl kept coming down with mysterious ailments.

Finally, the parents decided that perhaps the dead child yearned for her toys out in the lonely graveyard and that they might lose the other daughter, too, if the lost daughter were denied her special playthings. So they arranged these treasures on the girl's grave.

When the elderly grandparents both died, the couple sold their farm and moved away, for they had never been very happy living there after the death of their younger daughter. The older daughter, however, grew up to be a healthy, rosy-cheeked charmer, so apparently the parents' efforts to placate their dead child were successful.

At its simplest level, this story is told to justify the presence of grave decorations on a particular grave when they are rarely used on other graves in the cemetery. Whoever first told the story, or first devised the explanation, obviously considered parental sentimentality or a desire to make the grave more attractive insufficient reasons for leaving the toys there. This would suggest a stronger aversion to grave decorations than I ever heard verbalized by any member of the folk group and would open questions about the origins of such aversion. The story leaves a listener vaguely uneasy, as if some important element is missing: a well-meaning, industrious young couple comes into the community and seems to settle in successfully, but a stroke of misfortune ruins their chances for happiness. In the end, the grave with its rusty toys seems somehow abandoned. Often listeners did ask questions after this story was told, but there was uncertainty whether the couple actually left before or after the grandparents died, where they went, and whether they were happier elsewhere.

What is definitely implied, as is the case with several of the stories connected with Long Cemetery, is a willingness to accept the possibility of sympathetic, or specifically contagious, magic in the association of the dead child's toys with the living child's illnesses. James Frazer explains contagious magic as proceeding from the notion that things that have been in close contact or have been conjoined remain in a sympathetic relation even after they have been separated or dissevered.[9] This is, thus, not so much the story of a haunting as it is an expression of a willingness to believe that some force or influence could flow from the dead child to the living through the deceased's treasured toys.

Despite the variety of tasks and activities that required attention, graveyard working days usually proceeded at an orderly, leisurely pace. After the first hour or so of socializing, visiting graves, and, many times, offering comfort to individuals or families who were returning to the cemetery for the first time after having buried a loved one, the crowd broke apart along gender lines. The men went into the cemetery proper to begin making the necessary repairs, and the women gathered outside the arched gate under the oak trees. The women usually preferred to postpone their cemetery tasks such as sweeping and raking until afternoon because they wanted to stay as clean and fresh as possible until after they had prepared and served the midday meal. The men were less consistent in their work habits. Some preferred to do the heavy tasks in the "cool of the day" and arrived at the serving tables somewhat soiled and sweaty. Others did light yard work before the meal and sermon and then tackled filling gullies and mending fences in the afternoon, just before it was time to load up and go home, where they could change clothes and bathe.

For a time, there would be considerable activity under the shade of the oak trees as the women began to set things up for the "meal on the ground." Ladies who perceived themselves as in charge directed some of the older boys and athletically inclined girls in the task of arranging tables, a process that differed from year to year. Early on, broad boards were placed on sawhorses to serve as tables, and I remember an unfortunate accident or two when these materials were not stabilized and collapsed at a critical juncture before or during the meal. On other years, long tables had been hauled in for the event, greatly simplifying the serving arrangement. At present, a permanent shed or arbor has been built near the remaining trees, and it is equipped with tables and benches.

After the tables were in place, the women began to spread them with some sort of covering and then to set out the food. Most frequently, women brought whatever starched, ironed tablecloths they could spare from home. One year a lady insisted on bringing rolls of butcher's paper, but everyone was dissatisfied with the way the paper worked out because the wind kept whipping it about and upsetting smaller containers that had been placed on the tables.

As the less physical process of deciding where to place various pots and plates of food began, together with adding final touches to individual dishes, women tended to draw together in small, rather intimate groups. The orgy of talk, which so impressed me during my early years, got underway in earnest. There were decisions to be made, and these were argued vigorously. The meal was served family style, so each table had to be provided with a representative array of the foodstuffs brought. Each table must have fried chicken, dumplings, potato salad, a couple of pots of peas or beans, and bread.

There were inevitably some tricky moments: what to do with young Mrs. Cox's tasteless, watery snap beans? Which tables deserved the special dishes that everyone yearned to sample? No problem with Uncle Bernice's cold cuts—there was plenty for a platter on every table. But debating these issues opened the lines of free communication. Even women who had not seen each other for a considerable time or who were now different in background and experience—one still on the farm, another working a big-city job in Dallas—would relax, begin to laugh easily, and exchange bits of gossip and household advice.

Certain stories that I remember might be told during this time before the noon meal. Although the group under the trees was predominantly women, the older boys were still usually around, children were still excited and energetic and moved among the clusters of working women, and the men tended to wander in from their chores from time to time, drawn irresistibly by the tables of food and anticipation of the meal in preparation. The stories told at this time were often somewhat impersonal and dealt with subjects not limited entirely to women's interests. Sometimes men lingered long enough to join in the storytelling, usually in a peripheral way by adding details or by reminding the main storyteller of some other version of the events (or some problem with the logic of the whole thing). For women accepted and relished the magical, supernatural elements in certain stories, while men insisted on scientific, "down-to-earth" interpretations. The menfolk's familiarity with much of this material suggests that they may have told some of these stories among themselves, perhaps in a more prosaic, robust style. One of the stories that was often told concerned a man that most of the folk group claimed to have known years ago.

A Local Lazarus

Old Oscar often showed up at cemetery workings to hang around on the sidelines. People were civil to him, but no one lingered in his presence. Even his aging sister acted quite put-upon as she arranged for him to have food and a place to sit when the covered-dish lunch was served.

When he was a young man, Oscar went out one summer morning to cut oats. Around noon, one of his brothers noticed the team of horses and the reaper standing idle in the field. When the brother checked the matter out, he found Oscar lying unconscious on the ground. The brother got help and carried Oscar to the farmhouse, and there the family determined that Oscar, beyond all doubt, was dead. As a matter of fact, a constable and the local doctor/veterinarian also pronounced the young man dead, making Oscar's condition official.

Since it was summer and embalming had not yet caught on in that part of the country, the decision was made to bury Oscar as soon as a sister who lived some distance away could be notified and get there. A casket was brought from a nearby town, and Oscar was laid out in the parlor.

On the appointed day, friends and family gathered, awaiting the arrival of the sister. She came at last, accompanied by an outbreak of fresh grief at her arrival, and she and three other sisters gathered around Oscar's casket, wailing. Suddenly, Oscar opened his eyes and, in a state of total confusion, sat up.

His confusion was nothing compared to that of those around him, especially his sisters.

Oscar's funeral had to be postponed indefinitely, of course. However, the fact that he had rejoined the living did not occasion joyous celebration. His family felt uncomfortable when he was around, a feeling intensified by the fact that he was never "right in the head" after that. He became a drifter, disappearing for long periods of time but always returning and being shuffled about like a hot potato from one relative to another until he left again.

Ironically, Oscar outlived all of the brothers and sisters who had been ready to bury him.

Old Oscar's story develops a theme that still fascinated the folk group at Long Cemetery: the possibility of premature burial. Oscar, of course, escapes this dreaded fate. Nevertheless, he encounters family and community superstitions and prejudices that complicate his chances for a "happy ending." Oscar's family obviously interprets his recovery not scientifically or medically, as his coming out of a coma, but supernaturally, as his returning from the dead. They therefore regard him as alien or Other, and their behavior reveals their superstitious dread of him. In the mainstream American value systems (especially those of the present day), Oscar would probably attract understanding and sympathy because—not surprisingly—his brain was damaged by his ordeal. Instead, to his family his mental deficiencies were cause for embarrassment and alarm, as they would have been for many of the people in the Long Cemetery folk group even at the time of the graveyard workings I attended. Tolerant attitudes toward mental illness and mental deficiency were slow to develop among these hard-working farm folk—possibly, in part, because nonproductive persons posed such a problem for people who lacked time or means for caring for their needs.

All the people who attended graveyard workings at Long Cemetery during my childhood had been long accustomed to turning their deceased over to a funeral home for embalming. One of the primary reasons for the wide popularity of embalming was that it ensured that a corpse was indeed a corpse by the time the process was completed. Therefore, being buried alive was not a real threat to the Long Cemetery group.

The group's continued interest in premature burial harked back to the nineteenth century, as did many of their attitudes and customs. They were isolated and conservative, and old ideas lingered. The morbid preoccupation of people at this time with the prospect of being buried alive probably stems, according to Robert Habenstein and William Lamers, from an earlier period of the great plagues. In the confusion and haste of disposing of many corpses, the stricken were sometimes mistaken for the dead. In fact, even in classical antiquity there were customary acts performed by the bereaved that functioned as crude tests of death. In America, the nineteenth-century concern with premature burial was expressed in prose and poetry. But given that century's rather morbid participatory interest in dying, the deathbed, and ceremonial burial, it is not surprising that the burial receptacle received attention and that there was a corresponding increase in inventions designed to reveal to the living whether life still existed in the grave.[10]

The earliest of these caskets equipped with "life signals" was patented by Christian Eisenbrandt, of Baltimore, Maryland. It was so designed that by an arrangement of wires, pins, and a spring lid, the occupant could by the slightest movement of hand or head cause the coffin lid to spring up. This coffin, of course, had utility only before it was buried. Later devices were designed to operate even after the body was interred. Incorporating cords, springs, ladders, speaking tubes, electrical alarms, and even a device to release a flag from the foot of the grave, these creations offered some degree of reassurance to people who could afford them. Cost would have been prohibitive, and Habenstein and Lamers state that it is doubtful that any of these inventions, though patented, were ever marketed. Yet the very fact that inventors experimented with "life signals" indicates that the fear of being buried alive was widespread.[11]

Some sort of life signal might have been helpful to the young boy who figures in another premature burial story that was often told while people went about their tasks at graveyard workings.

Rushed Burial

My grandfather had nine sisters. One of these sisters had a little boy who was given to cataleptic seizures. On several occasions his parents thought that he had died—but after a few hours, he revived. A doctor (a specialist of sorts) in one of the larger neighboring towns warned the couple never to bury the boy without first contacting him and letting him check the child.

During one bad winter, the boy came down with the flu. He was very ill for several days, running a high fever. The father drove the wagon into Cumby and brought out the local doctor as well as another of the nine sisters, an opinionated and tyrannical old maid who came to help tend the house and the sick child.

The boy did not improve after the doctor's visit; in fact, his condition worsened until finally he apparently died. The sorrowful couple did not prepare the body for burial, however. The father went to fetch the specialist, and the mother continued to sit at the boy's bedside. As misfortune would have it, the father's trip was fruitless: the specialist had gone on a trip and was not expected to return for another two or three weeks.

In the interval, a couple of days had passed. The old maid sister began to insist that preparations be made for burial. It was uncivilized, she said, to leave the boy where he was. She argued that the body was already beginning to "stink." (Close, overly warm sickrooms often had a foul odor, especially when the patient was feverish.)

At last the father relented and drove back into town to purchase new pine lumber for the casket. He lined the pine box with black velvet, even padding and lining the lid. The mother, still unable to believe her child was actually dead, demanded that the boy be buried at the back of the orchard instead of miles away in the cemetery.

Satisfied, the old maid sister helped clean out the sickroom and left. The mother remained inconsolable. Day by day her doubts and anguish increased. She was certain they had buried the child alive. Finally, seeing no other way to relieve her mind, the father and two neighbor men opened the grave. When they lifted the lid to the casket, the child's body came up with it. Suffocating, and trying to claw his way out, the boy had tangled his fingers in the torn velvet.

Some years later, the family had to sell the farm and move. Fearing that she might be denied access to her child's grave behind the orchard, the mother insisted that her husband take up the body and move it, at last, to the cemetery. The man did so privately.

❧ There was, consequently, considerable debate about this grave. Had the father indeed moved his child's body, or was the grave actually empty? With only a pine box for protection all those years, would the remains have been intact enough to move? Might the child's remains have been scattered—part in the orchard and part in the cemetery—and, if so, how would the poor boy manage on Resurrection Morn? (This is one of several "fabled" graves that I have not been able to locate during recent trips to Cumby. I recall being shown a grave with a small marker, but I assume that it must now be indicated by one of the anonymous cement cylinders.)

Grandmother Ward could have her listeners' "hackles" rising in terror by the end of this story, even when she kept body movements and voice modulations at a minimum. I used to have recurring nightmares about lifting the lid of a coffin and having a body come up with the lid. Listeners sympathized with the mother and thought that the father did his best in view of the circumstances. They also believed, however, that if he had followed the wise old adage "let the dead stay buried," the couple could have avoided learning the truth—when it was too late to remedy things. There would then not have been so much guilt and blame and suspicion to live with for the rest of their lives.

Unanimously, listeners condemned the maiden aunt, whose high-handed, insensitive actions made her responsible for the tragedy. The character of the aunt is, in fact, stereotypical: she has the qualities that most people in this place and time associated with unattached but somewhat independent women. There was a general distrust of women who did not marry and have children: surely, such women must have serious character defects, or some man would have offered marriage (that a woman would choose a single life was unthinkable). The most commonly listed defects were bossiness, hard-headedness, lack of compassion, and a sharp tongue.

If after the two stories of premature burials the audience still clamored for tales that were scary and exciting, a tale about a grisly accident at the cotton gin would most likely be recounted. It was often told in spite of frowns and warnings from some of the women: "Don't tell that awful story right before we eat! You'll turn everyone's stomachs!" This story was definitely one that was narrated by storytellers of both sexes and in a number of contexts. I have heard my father tell the story, so it was familiar to members of both sides of my family (if only, perhaps, because my father heard it at a Ward-Wolf graveyard working and passed it on). But if the group was gathered under the oak trees and the women were mostly carrying the storytelling session, instead of launching into the story himself, a man would suggest to the female storyteller, "Why don't you tell them the one about the migrant's kid and the cotton gin?" My grandmother did not like to tell this story. She avoided the cotton patch and knew very little about cotton gins, so some other woman always told this gruesome tale.

Cotton Gin Calamity

An old farmer with a lot of land fell sick late in the spring, after he'd got all his crops planted and a few of them laid by. When he and the doctor saw that he wouldn't be getting up and around any time soon, he hired a migrant family to finish laying by his crops and harvest them when they came in.

The migrant worker had a wife, a couple of teenage sons, and a bunch of little kids. They moved into the old farmer's rent house and kept his farm up for him.

During cotton picking time in the fall, the migrant worker brought a load of cotton into town to the gin. His wife and all the little kids rode into town with him on top of the load. When he got to the gin, there was a long line ahead of him, so he had to wait a good while for his turn under the chute. While he waited, his restless kids played around the wagon and climbed up and down on the bale of cotton. One little boy, about two or three, crawled up in the cotton and went to sleep.

When at last his turn came, the migrant worker called to his kids to get away from the wagon and drove up under the chute. He was tired and was looking forward to heading for the feed store and having a cold soft drink.

No one even thought to look for the little boy until they heard a terrible scream. By then it was too late. The child had been sucked up through the chute and into the separator, where the cotton was being processed to remove the seeds. They shut down the cotton gin as fast as they could, but the boy was a mangled mess that couldn't really be separated from the blood-drenched cotton. And that's how they had to bury him—cotton and all. More than half a bale of cotton was buried with him, they said. And the whole bale was ruined.

On the surface, "Cotton Gin Calamity" may seem a simple horror tale—and that was possibly how it was received on graveyard working days. Audiences of men, women, and often children as well wanted to be entertained, and horror was a reaction they could all share and find exciting. In other contexts, however, horror was rarely the main thrust of the story's telling. Certain details that might be overlooked by someone not acquainted with farm practices at the time are significant in expressing the community's attitude toward migrant workers, who—not very incidentally—were poor whites. Hispanics and blacks would not have been hired even if they had ventured into the area. The hired man is guilty of a number of flagrant mistakes. No cotton farmer would allow children or anyone else to climb or play on the bale before ginning: cotton could be knocked out, and the ginned bale would weigh in short; a stone, a shoe, or a pocketknife might be dropped in the cotton and could set the bale on fire in the separator; trampling and matting the cotton down was believed to affect the staple or fiber length, and the sample might show poor quality.

In addition to knowing nothing about cotton farming, the migrant worker is a poor parent. A good father would have thought it too dangerous for his children to ride into town with him on the bale. Certainly he would not have permitted them to play around the gin; if he had, he would have rounded them up and checked the bale before pulling it under the chute. The reason given for the migrant worker's carelessness—that he was looking forward to lounging around the feed store and having a soft drink—completes the stereotype.

Migrants were suspected of slipping away from work, of loitering, and of indulging in frivolous pleasures. The point is made that the migrant is ignorant and irresponsible, with the result that his son is horribly killed. That the farmer also lost a bale of cotton was hardly a minor point for those telling the story. This tale was part of the graveyard lore, but it was also recounted on other occasions to discourage children who wanted to play on the cotton bale or ride the bale into town and visit the gin. The implication was that only a feckless migrant would allow such activities. Told in this context, the story was indeed "functional"—and it generally worked.

A scary story that children especially enjoyed concerned two little girls who encountered danger walking home along a lonely country road. The first part of this legend employs a popular motif or tradition in American family storytelling. As Mody C. Boatright says, "For a story placing a human being in jeopardy, the panther was the favored animal."[12] This legend follows the popular tradition closely, even to having the girls drop items of clothing while in flight. One must assume that if the legend is not pure invention, two skittish and insecure little girls—probably familiar with the panther stories—imagined they were being followed by such an animal and "walked through" the well-known legend.

A Protective Papa

One of the oldest graves in Long Cemetery belonged to a man who died in the prime of life, leaving a large family.

Late on an evening some months after his death, two of his young daughters (aged about ten and twelve) started home from a farmhouse where they had been helping with a woman who had recently given birth. When they were well out of sight of the farmhouse, they became aware that they were being followed by a large animal. The beast—which they discovered to their terror was a panther—was between them and the farmhouse, so they had no choice but to go on. They had been taught that to show fear and run would only cause the animal to attack sooner. Therefore, they proceeded calmly, meanwhile tearing off strips of their petticoats and leaving them in the path. The panther would pause to sniff the pieces of cloth and tear them up.

Try as they might, the girls could not gain on the panther, and they were running out of energy and petticoats. When they came in sight of the small plot of ground where their father was buried, just that concrete reminder of their father's loving protection was reassuring. Both girls ran weeping to his grave. The panther sprang after them, but at the entrance to the burial plot, it stopped short. For a time the beast circled the area, but it did not approach the girls closer, and finally it left.

What could this have been except the father's spirit protecting his children?

The mother, who had been expecting the girls, sent two of their older brothers to meet them, and the brothers found the girls at the grave—still frightened but safe.

What is important—and the part that visiting preachers always stressed when they used this story in their sermons—is the resolution of the story. The girls sought and found refuge at the grave of their beloved father. Here was a good man, the preachers would intone, strong and protective, kind and loving, whose powerful influence exerted itself even beyond the grave. To be such a man was, indeed, the ideal of most of the males that made up the folk group.

Families were organized along strongly patriarchal lines. The father was the head of the family; he was the bulwark against the storms of life; his were the words of wisdom that guided the rest of the family in right-thinking and right-doing. Both parents were generally revered. Mothers were catered to by older children. Sons continued to go to aging fathers for advice and, as far as was practical, often modeled their attitudes and lifestyles after the old patriarchs.

Girls usually had a strong sentimental attachment to their fathers—and not altogether without reason. To the extent that they understood what the term meant, these rough farmers were "gentlemen" around their women. They did not use foul language in the presence of females. They took on the dangerous tasks and the ones considered repulsive to the senses. In view of the crowded conditions in small, ill-arranged, poorly heated farmhouses, the men were modest about dress and bodily functions. Drawing the biblically suggested parallel or analogy between the ideal earthly father (represented by the dead man whose very essence protected his young daughters) and the Heavenly Father who would likewise guide and protect his children on earth made for a nearly "prefabricated" sermon that was certain to be well-received. It expounded an earthly and heavenly design that most of the people in the folk group believed in or wanted to believe in.

Nevertheless, the occasional use of this story in sermons given on graveyard working days seems oddly misleading on the part of preachers. Its use involves some logical and theological gymnastics that are perplexing—the same sort of gymnastics required in the folk group's sense of a presence in the graves of their dead or in the young couple's conviction that their dead child could harm their living child through her toys. There was a disparity—a moral blind space—between these people's stated theology (what they believed on a conscious, or self-conscious, level) and what their actions and reactions revealed that they actually felt and must have believed (at some more subconscious level).

The preachers were probably a varied and motley crew. I have often wondered where the townspeople located them and where they vanished after they eagerly gathered up sacks of leftover food and took off in their rattletrap coupes. Probably, however, none of them would have admitted to believing in ghosts, or hauntings, or good papas' spirits emerging from the grave to chase off panthers, or homeopathic, black, or any other type of magic. People in the folk group would have rejected such ideas, too, as decidedly "unscriptural."

But ministers, without acknowledging it, managed to accommodate an affinity for the supernatural that ran always just beneath the surface of their rather primitive instrumentalism. On these occasions theology was not approached very critically, anyway. Preachers at graveyard workings were mainly there to give a stirring performance, to "put on a good show." They needed to be loud and forceful, they needed to be able to keep their balance on the most rickety of platforms, and they needed to know when to wave their arms and pound their fists. Ministers had to keep the audience awake and also get audience response—some laughter, lots of tears, plenty of amens. Often they had to lead the singing. If they were good-looking and didn't perspire until their shirts stuck to their bodies, that was a definite plus. A fellow had to be versatile to be a graveyard preacher.

After the sermon, there was opportunity for the most intimate and often the most interesting storytelling among the women. Often restive during the sermon, the menfolk were eager to move about and stretch their muscles, so they always returned to their graveyard repairs with new vigor. The women were left to clear the area under the oak trees. The pace was definitely slowed. Children were tired and settled down to play quiet games together; smaller children took naps on pallets (or folded quilts) in the shade of the trees. So the women, relieved of some of their responsibilities, took their time clearing the meal debris away and gathered in small groups to talk.

My grandmother assumed a very different persona among these more distant kinswomen and friends in the community from the familiar one she used on the Wards' sleeping porch. Immediately noticeable was the absence of playfulness, of an element of nonsense, of *freedom* that was so much in evidence on the sleeping porch. In no way was she ever a clown under the oak trees in front of the cemetery. The other women deferred to her, for reasons that are a mystery to me. Many of the women were older than she was, so her age alone was not a factor. She did not have a commanding presence, at least in the usual sense; because she was small and dark-haired and had a lively step, she could have looked almost girlish had she not insisted on wearing dull, shapeless clothing. But she was intimidating. She was *that* in her own home, of course: surely poor Uncle Bernice and Aunt Dovie might not have been so confused and eccentric had she been less so.

At graveyard workings, everyone called her Aunt Minnie, and any group of women she joined reacted as if she were bestowing a special favor. Did they respect her because she was head of her own household? Did her somewhat wider travels make her seem more a woman of the world? Did her Cherokee blood promise a strange earthy wisdom and insight that the other women felt they lacked? She was nearly a recluse: was the novelty of seeing her sufficient to ensure her an eager reception? Maybe the women just enjoyed hearing her tell stories. She was an expert. Even under her self-imposed restrictions when she extended her storytelling sphere to the open space under the oak trees, she could move her audience. There she relied on hand movement, facial expression, eye contact, and an intensity that communicated itself in her voice and in subtle body movements: leaning forward or pulling away, hunching her shoulders, tilting her head.

It was at this time, while they cleared the tables or rested for a few minutes from these labors, that Grandmother Ward might finally agree to tell the story that was unsuitable for telling at her mother's graveside.

Great Grandma Lynch-Wolf's Chastity

Young women were admonished to resist temptation and not to grant their sexual favors lightly. There were biblical passages that conveyed this message, and one could assume that one's soul was in peril if petting went too far. But there were important practical reasons for remaining virtuous: men did not marry women who were not virgins. A man might wine and dine a wanton woman, but when he decided to marry, he would marry a virtuous one. "No one wants used goods" was a wise old proverb that was bandied about.

The model for the chaste female was Grandma Ward's mother. Not even marriage could convince this lady to part with her virginity. When Great-grandma was a girl of fifteen, she was pressured into marriage with an older man, a Mr. Lynch, whose wife had died. They married during a harsh winter. Several days before the wedding, the marriage bed was prepared in an upstairs room with, as chance would have it, a leak in the roof. A puddle of melted snow formed near the foot of the bed and then froze again when the temperature fell.

On their wedding night, the groom, determined not to rush his reluctant bride, stayed well on his side of the bed. The bride, upon stretching out, thrust her feet into the ice. So terrified was she of shifting positions and perhaps rousing the groom to action that for most of the night she lay with her feet in the ice, frigid in more ways than one.

Nor did her chaste story end here. The night's exposure had the effect of giving her pneumonia, which meant her virginity remained intact until early spring. As she began to reluctantly recover, she got in the habit of winding herself up like a sausage in a piece of sheet, further forestalling the impatient groom. At last the exasperated man forced his attentions through sheet and all; the result of this violent union was a sickly baby that died a few days after it was born.

Great-grandma bore three more Lynch sons before this tyrant husband died. These men, especially the infamous Fate, were boozers and womanizers, a fact laid squarely at the dead feet of the oversexed husband. Great-grandma was perhaps more receptive to her Wolf husband, by whom she had five more children, including my grandmother. She nevertheless set a sort of record for playing hard to get.

The foregoing is a somewhat cynical granddaughter's rendering of a story that even my grandmother told in a humorous, tongue-in-cheek style that I dare not attempt to imitate. As a matter of fact, I retell all of my grandmother's stories with more hesitancy than I would have felt before I did the research for this project.

It has been a shock to recognize through research that my reclusive little grandmother may have been a much more subversive storyteller than I ever suspected. Checking through old records turned up some intriguing details, which seem to contradict the story of my great-grandmother's wedding night as my grandmother told it. In the first place, the Mr. Lynch who was my great-grandmother's first husband was a young man, not much older than she, when they married, and nothing in the records suggests he had been married before. When he died (perhaps in the Civil War), she was twenty-six with two small sons (perhaps she was pregnant with or had lost a third).

My Great-grandfather Henry Wolf, on the other hand, was indeed some twenty odd years older than the young widow he married and had already fathered a substantial number of offspring. This lusty old geezer, who was still siring children well into his sixties, might understandably have been the real turn-off in bed for my young great-grandmother. He, therefore, seems the more likely villain of the wedding night story.

My grandmother obviously altered certain facts dramatically in her account of her mother's wedding night. As with the Little Mose story and others where she quite possibly took similar liberties, it is hard to know why. I am reluctant to second-guess that tiny, intense, quick-witted woman forty years after her death. Nevertheless, I *can* imagine that my grandmother would not have been comfortable with depicting her own dear papa, whom she adored, as the boorish, demanding husband of her tale, so she substituted the safely deceased Mr. Lynch.

Grandmother also made significant changes in the character and circumstances of her mother, probably for the sake of her narrative and its desired effect on her listeners. She must have known that a fearful, inexperienced, teenage virgin would be a more sympathetic heroine than a young widow who had made an unsavory marriage, probably to provide security for herself and her orphaned sons. Although the women in my grandmother's audience usually giggled at my great-grandmother's antics, there were always understanding murmurs of "Poor little thing!" and "Bless her heart!" as women related, to some degree at least, to the heroine's dilemma.

Grandmother Ward saw herself as the moral and spiritual arbiter of the family, and she was as keen on the rewards of chastity as any eighteenth-century Samuel Richardson. In fact, one of her favorite songs had a Pamela-like plot. The refrain, which is the only part of the song that I remember word for word, ran like this:

My mother was a lady
And yours, I would allow;
Perhaps you have a sister
Who needs protection now.
I came to this great city
To find my brother dear.
You would not dare insult me, Sir,
If brother Jack were here.

The story line of this song follows the adventures of a pretty, vulnerable young girl who, as the refrain suggests, goes to the city to try to find her brother and is horrified when a lecherous city fellow makes a pass at her. He is so impressed with her chaste rebuff, however, voiced in the refrain above, that he proposes marriage on the spot and assists her in locating the chivalrous brother Jack. I think my grandmother may have attempted to make her mother the heroine of a story in which a young maiden is somewhat similarly beset. Most often, the story of Great-grandma Lynch-Wolf's wedding night was told for the edification of pubescent girls, with a simple message: if Great-grandma could hold onto her virginity through several months of marriage, her great-granddaughters should be able to hold onto theirs at least until a wedding band was firmly in place.

For me, the wedding night story is troubling in all its inconsistencies. As an object lesson on the importance of female chastity, the story misfires completely. Great-grandma's celibacy created more problems for her in dealing with her husband than it seemed to solve—and the marriage that her virginity bought was decidedly unattractive. There would usually be amused agreement that Great-grandma Lynch-Wolf had carried the chastity issue a bit too far, probably because of her inexperience and the unfortunate nature of the marriage arrangements. But, as I recall, there were never corresponding warnings that girls needed to be more knowledgeable about what to expect in marital relationships or to demand more control over whether and whom they should marry.

Nor did the young wife's inexperience exonerate the inept, boorish husband. My grandmother often added the truly damning bit of information that the older man had frequently compared his young wife unfavorably to his dead one as a sexual partner. Thus, the story provided an opening for comments about men's blundering, selfishness, and lack of consideration. It also generally led to the conclusion that the "sins of the father" had assuredly been visited abundantly on Great-uncle Fate, whom the women regarded as a rogue and rascal.

Both the wedding night story and the story of Little Mose, which my grandmother always told in the same context, must have involved an unusual sort of teller-listener collusion. I therefore believe the stories may have had deeper, darker implications for my grandmother and her audiences than is evident on the surface. For instance, there must have been women in my grandmother's audiences (relatives, perhaps) who realized that the plot and characters of her wedding night story had been yanked somewhat askew, but they nevertheless listened approvingly. That story went unchallenged through numerous retellings. It seems likely that a couple of my grandfather's younger sisters must have heard my grandmother tell her Little Mose story; yet they did not, apparently, contradict her unflattering depiction of their father or correct her on other details. Quite the contrary: at some point, presumably, they must have supplied the description of the morning of their brother's birth and the lonely orphan boy's anguish. I have to wonder why these women permitted my grandmother to alter the facts and, further, if her ability to do so accounted for her popularity as a storyteller. Had my grandmother a "submerged consciousness" of the fact that "[telling stories] might constitute a subversive activity, an expression of solidarity with the rebellious [listener], a mode of social strategy—and a form of struggle"?[13]

It is my theory that the Little Mose story is a "cover-up"—both my brother's documented family narrative and my grandmother's more elaborate tale that involves violence, mystery, complex human relationships, and the supernatural. I question the account of the strange woman who appeared out of nowhere, birthed her child, and disappeared again. I believe some girl in the family got pregnant out of wedlock and carried and birthed her baby in secret. The family then decided to keep and raise the boy. When neighbors asked, "Where did this one come from?" some quick-thinking family member answered, "Well, you won't believe it, but we found this kid down by the creek!"

I think it is entirely possible that my grandmother *and* her audience knew that the story was a cover-up—a story that, no matter how accurate its details, was predicated on a lie. Their rigid social and moral system prevented any of them from acknowledging the lie and speaking the truth openly. My grandmother correctly ascertained that any story that would "cover up"—and her plot may have been quite preposterous—would be tolerated so long as she did not tell the socially disruptive truth. Her audience enjoyed their own collusion in what amounted to narrative blackmail: they were allowed the freedom to verbalize a wide range of inequities on the condition that they preserve the essential lie. If this hypothetical scenario did apply, then the narrative situation of these women was truly a mode of social strategy and a form of struggle.

For my grandmother, I believe the Little Mose story served as a way of easing into some of her riskiest material: a story about a woman who provided sexual services to men for a price and who herself paid a terrible price for defying society's strictures. The woman who presumably gives birth to Little Mose remains nameless in all versions of the story. Although the assumption is that she is a "fallen woman," since no explanation is given for her circumstances, she remains a dim, mysterious figure. The possibility that she may not be what she appears to be remains, too. In the story that follows, the woman is at least a semiprofessional whore or prostitute, so the nature of her transgressions seems irrefutable and the implacable poetic justice of her punishment the only logically moral outcome.

The Wages of Sin

Early in this century, a young woman came into the community, perhaps to visit a friend or a distant relative. At any rate, she decided to stay on permanently and make her own way, something that a lone woman would usually have been hesitant to attempt. She was a handsome thing, dark, shapely, and full-bodied—and somewhat arrogant because of her good looks. She haughtily refused to hire out for housework or fieldwork, and she did not wish to take in washing and ironing.

Instead, this strange young woman moved into a little shack down by the creek and set herself up in the world's oldest profession. Because of her beauty and the variety of her skills, she soon acquired an impressive clientele. Not only were men in the community spending money that should have gone for groceries and children's school shoes, but farmers and tradesmen who wouldn't lift a finger at home were spending their spare time mending her fences and renovating the shack where she lived and plied her trade.

Wild stories about the woman's activities and her sensual lifestyle circulated. Men arrived for their appointments bringing gifts and fine liquor, and she could outdrink any of her customers. She wore black lace underthings and expensive perfume. A big mirror on the ceiling reflected whatever might be happening on the bed with its red velvet spread. The story was that the woman plaited her pubic hair and tied it with red ribbons.

But this loose lady eventually got her comeuppance. She came down with a vicious social disease, and her clients soon lost their enthusiasm for her favors. The time came when she was alone, literally rotting away, they said, from the disease that fate had visited upon her. The very women whom she had wronged by tempting and exploiting their menfolk were her only source of help. As she lay slowly and agonizingly dying, they brought food and pushed it in to her bedside with a long pole. None of them would enter the shack because of the terrible smell and because they were certain the place must be contagious.

When the woman finally died, the men of the community, some of whom had probably been clients during happier times, put on old clothes and gloves, covered their faces, and went into the shack to dispose of the body. They simply rolled the woman's body up in her mattress, carried the whole thing out to the cow pasture, and buried it in a deep hole that had already been prepared for that purpose. After that, they removed their clothes, threw them into the shack, and burned the building to the ground.

Surely the woman paid a heavy price, even on this earth, for her arrogance, vanity, and sexual promiscuity. Often during her last days, she begged for someone to come in and remove the mirror from the ceiling so that she would not have to lie and watch herself die. No one dared do this, partly out of fear of the disease and partly from reluctance to interfere with what must have been divine judgment. Clearly, the wages of sin is death.

Both the Little Mose story and "The Wages of Sin" reveal much about the social and moral attitudes of the Long Cemetery folk group. Although the men of this group might be protective of their women and careful of offending them, there was a definite and unquestioned double standard for male and female behavior. This double standard is particularly evident in the matter of sin. The sins of the women in the stories are taken much more seriously than those of the men. Through their evil—and it should be noted that it is sexual evil—the women in "Little Mose" and "The Wages of Sin" are powerful negative influences on the community, and their punishment is severe and terrible. No one wondered why Little Mose's biological father did not show up to take responsibility for the well-publicized abandoned and orphaned boy; the blame for his unhappy life lay entirely with the mother. The fact that the handsome wench in "The Wages of Sin" was bound to have had partners, doubtless the very men who so self-righteously buried her, was glossed over. Men were not responsible in sins of the flesh. Their sins—drinking, marrying another wife too soon, laziness, having too much pride, even sometimes fighting and killing if their motives were good—could be recounted good-naturedly.

It should be noted, too, that a controlling force in nature singles out the women in "Little Mose" and "The Wages of Sin" and punishes them, in a manner that corresponds exactly to what the folk group perceived as the extent and definition of their sins.

Present-day feminists would probably note elements in the stories about Great-grandma Lynch-Wolf, Little Mose, and the tragic prostitute (and perhaps in other stories told by women in the Long Cemetery folk group) that reveal issues that my grandmother and her listeners would not have been aware of or have acknowledged. The problems involved in such interpretations are suggested by Joan N. Radner and Susan S. Lanser in their essay "Strategies of Coding in Women's Cultures": "When one identifies a 'feminist message,' one is attributing a conscious or unconscious political stance to an author, performer, or text."[14] Radner and Lanser go on to suggest some troubling questions with regard to interpretation. "What is the 'communicative context as a whole' and for whom does it have to make 'sense'? What conventions are operant in any given performance, and who identifies them?"[15]

It would be risky to attempt to resolve these questions based on my memory of stories heard when I was a child, although I am aware of certain possibilities. For instance, marriage licenses, snowstorms, and winding sheets notwithstanding, from a feminist viewpoint Great-grandma Lynch-Wolf, still a young teenage girl, is raped and has a baby she conceived against her will, who then dies. Her painful dilemma is trivialized (perhaps through a strategy that Radner and Lanser would term distraction) by the somewhat comic frustrations of the groom. The culture-at-large sympathizes with him, even while it chuckles, because his expectations are socially approved while the young bride's failure to meet them is condemned.

I do recall that the story that I have titled "The Wages of Sin" always elicited enthusiastic and often participatory audience response. It explicates a struggle between good and evil: there are no nuances, no shades of gray between the opposing poles. I do not know to what extent my grandmother and her audience realized that part of the message of the story is that there are two ways of being a woman, two alternatives, and that the price for making the wrong choice is a heavy one. I believe that at different junctures in the story, the women in my grandmother's audience identified with the fictional women at both poles. They enjoyed the idea of the whore's freedom from drudgery, and the interest they took in the list of the luxurious accouterments of her profession—"kinky" items they associated with unrestrained and forbidden sexuality—suggests that they reveled in her sensuality.

These were women whose underwear was probably stitched from bleached flour sacks and who went to the feed store to select materials for most of their dresses. It could well have been true that for many of these women the message of the story was a bitter one. Men—exactly like their husbands—provided the whore with extravagant, beautiful items that validated her sensuality and sexuality, but they denied these things to their wives, just as they denied them the kind of sensual pleasure that is represented by the large mirror over the whore's bed. Ironically, according to this interpretation, the role of the whore would be the more desirable since her sexuality is valued and paid for, her sensual needs are at least seemingly met, and she is exempt from drudgery. Except, of course, for sin and inevitable punishment.

When the punishment phase of the story was introduced, my grandmother's listeners, I feel certain, switched allegiances, now identifying with the "good women" and going from a vicarious orgy of sensation to an orgy of revenge. As the whore is systematically punished for each thing she had that the good women did not have—beauty, masculine admiration, sensual pleasure, and independence—she becomes an "untouchable" from whom the women measure their superior distance with the pole used to push her food in to her. Whether my grandmother's audience picked up on these possible implications of the story is uncertain. I have no idea whether my grandmother meant to imply or encode them. Certainly the women voiced their opinions that "it was good enough for the men" that they were the ones who must enter the stinking cabin and finally burn the clothes that had come in contact with the whore's putrefaction. The good women may be perceived as victorious, to the extent that "victory" can have meaning for lives that may have been mentally, spiritually, and emotionally circumscribed.

Were my grandmother and her audiences good women like the ones in her story? They assumed such a stance, I think, but I also believe that their storytelling allowed them to explore the space between the bars of the moral cages into which their culture had locked them. The demands of the system to which they adhered could be stern and painful, and probably most of the women had suffered enough to wonder whether such pain need inevitably be their lot.

I remember that during one of our talks, after I was old enough to "know about things," Grandmother Ward told me that on her wedding day, the girl who had been her closest friend since childhood hugged her and then burst into terrible weeping. "You'll hate me now that you're marrying Jim," she told my grandmother. "Oh, you'll never forgive me! You'll never forgive me!" Grandmother Ward had no idea what her dear friend meant until, more than a year later, my grandfather confessed that before he had been permitted to come courting her, he had gone out with her friend a few times. On one occasion, riding home in the buggy, the girl had let him fondle her breasts. My grandmother had been hurt and mortified. "And did you never forgive her?" I asked my grandmother.

"I forbade her ever to set foot in my house again!" my grandmother told me. My comment that I thought my grandfather had been equally culpable met with stony silence. Long minutes later she said stiffly, "I knew that. I could not ever love him the same again, either." The pain of those high expectations betrayed and that uncompromising judgment passed still tightened my grandmother's lips and shook in her voice. I recall that I asked my grandmother if she thought her friend was the only girl she knew who had indulged in such intimacies. She cast me a shrewd, guarded look and admitted that she had come to suspect that many women "carried such sins in their hearts."

My grandmother and her audiences were, I think, "good women," many of whom "carried such sins within their hearts." But they needed to be careful about offering compassion and forgiveness because they also had to stand in judgment of each other, and judgments were swift, stern, and permanent. In retrospect, I find it hard to believe that Grandmother Ward, shrewd and observant as she was, could have been unaware of my Aunt Dovie's socially and morally marginal behavior. Her storytelling situations gave her opportunities to take a strong moral stand while, at the same time, exploring human experiences with which my aunt and (more than likely) other women in the group were familiar.

Whether the women listening to my grandmother were experienced beyond their marriage beds or not, their collaboration in supplying details beyond my grandmother's invention revealed that they recognized, at least superficially, the clues indicating that a woman was "loose" and the trappings of that "other" lifestyle. Aunt Dovie was always a ringleader in supplying salacious tidbits: the plaited, bow-tied pubic hair was no doubt her contribution. She offered this detail knowing that an abundance of body hair on a woman was perceived by the folk group to be animalistic and a sign that the woman was "low bred" and inclined to be lewd and immoral. Out on the Ward sleeping porch, she sometimes told a story about a young lady's problem with superfluous pubic hair. Although the story would never have been told at graveyard workings, I think it serves to illuminate my grandmother's narratives.

A Spinster by Choice

There was a good-looking woman who taught school all her life in one of the small towns in the area, Campbell or Miller Grove, maybe. She was a lovely, charming lady, but she never married; people couldn't understand why she'd settle for being a spinster schoolteacher when she could have had a husband and family. But that was the way it was. When she was pushing thirty, that dreaded cut-off age in a woman's husband-hunting career, her father finally just gave up all hope and sent her off to normal college to train to be a teacher. So she went off and got her certificate and came back home and took a job teaching.

Only a few people knew the real story. It's not something anyone would talk about much.

This woman belonged to a well-off, respectable family. They had a bunch of boys, but she was the only girl. She was a very pretty, bright child, and the whole family doted on her. But when she reached her early teens and the age of puberty, she became bashful and unsure of herself. Her family was surprised that her personality had taken this turn, but they were not alarmed. They did worry a little that she was so shy with boys, for they wanted her to make a good marriage.

Eventually, though, a nice boy in the community did come courting, and the girl's family did what they could to encourage the match. It was soon clear that the young couple were much taken with each other, so everyone in town expected that any day they would announce their engagement. Months passed, however, and this did not happen. More puzzling still, the young man became increasingly vocal about his disappointment. He had proposed marriage, but the girl kept putting him off.

At last, the impatient family decided to intervene. No one had been able to get a straight answer from the girl, so they arranged a family gathering: the parents, the brothers, and a couple of the girl's aunts, the mother's sisters. The father confronted the girl: "Why haven't you accepted that young man's proposal? You've been seeing him for quite some time, and you seem to like him. You can't keep stringing a fine young man like that along indefinitely. You're going to lose him. What's wrong with you? It's not like you have men standing in line outside begging for your hand in marriage!" The girl just sat in silence, with her head bowed and her hands folded. When the father became more demanding, she fell into a fit of violent weeping. More than likely, she vomited, too. She would not have fainted—women in that part of the country didn't faint. Anyway, the family meeting came to an end.

But the women—the mother and aunts—had realized that something serious was wrong. So when the girl was calmer and could talk, they took her off in private and told her, "We can see that you must have a real problem of some kind. You need to tell us what it is." The girl was still upset, and so she broke down and confessed. She had realized from puberty that the body hair in her nether regions was exceedingly abundant, a condition that became increasingly alarming as she matured. From what she had heard and the little she could observe, she had concluded that her condition had far surpassed the bounds of decency. In short, she just wouldn't do at all. It was not a matter of dreading embarrassment. She feared that her groom would get one look at her, bolt from the bridal chamber, and spread word of her deformity throughout the whole countryside, to the dishonor of her and her family.

The mother and aunts were shocked. People were very modest about their bodies in those days, and the older women had no idea that the girl's maturation had gone out of control. This was indeed a grave problem, they agreed, doubtless a trait she had inherited from the *father's* side of the family. Certainly none of them was cursed with this vulgar defect! But they loved the girl, so they did their best to comfort her. The abnormality was not her fault, so surely they could do something to prevent it from ruining her life.

The plan they devised was to remove the excessive growth one follicle at a time with a pair of tweezers. Shaving with the father's straight blade would cause her to grow a beard, if one could judge by what happened with her father and brothers. They were under the impression that tweezing would be a permanent solution. These women proposed to schedule the tweezing over a period of several days, clearing out one section and then moving on to the next until the entire area had been brought within acceptable dimensions.

The poor girl was desperate enough to give in to well-meaning family pressure. It is not certain how many sessions she endured. But the procedure was embarrassing and dehumanizing, an awful invasion of her person—and it hurt like the dickens! A few minutes into the second or third session, she said, "Forget it! I love him, but not that much."

There was no engagement, and the girl went off to normal college in a few years. And they say she felt justified in her decision. Contrary to the opinion of her mother and aunts, the hair not only grew back but in greater profusion than before. Had she gone through with the marriage, she would have condemned herself to a lifetime of ever more vigorous tweezing.

I remember this story because it haunted me as I approached puberty. It also haunted a couple of my school chums with whom I secretly shared it, despite my mother's warnings never to repeat Aunt Dovie's stories. I do not know if the story was my aunt's own invention; perhaps she took ideas from "smutty" jokes she heard during her clandestine weekend retreats. The plot turns on a series of improbabilities; its logic is fuzzy and skewed. But I think the story did exactly what my aunt wanted it to do. From my now distanced and more experienced perspective, I am aware of the story's barely concealed rebelliousness: it systematically overturns the value system by which my aunt must have felt she was being measured.

In my aunt's story, it is a *nice* girl from a respected family who, through no action of her own, finds herself branded with one of the tangible signs that the folk group associated with lust and immorality. Important as sin (or the appearance of sin) is to the girl's family, they do not discuss sexuality openly. It is the older women's extreme modesty—a trait the folk group encouraged—that prevents them from noticing what is happening to the girl or helping her through the long years of her youthful isolation. Instead, the entire family pressures the young woman to conform to their community's stereotypical expectations.

Whatever suffering the girl must endure to achieve the appearance of respectability is considered justified and appropriate. And in attempting to make her acceptable, the older women subject the girl to the very conditions that they regard as morally offensive. Tweezing the hair is as obscene as plaiting it and tying it with ribbons. Thus, the young woman's choice of permanent virginity is as much a perversion of a natural moral order as the whore's promiscuity. Finally, the adults in the girl's family are misguided about how nature works: they have false ideas about how hair grows and, hence, about workable solutions. They assign to that growth meanings that are dangerously inapplicable.

My aunt's story is, I think, an extended metaphor for (or a nearly allegorical representation of) her own resistance to the prevailing patriarchal social and moral order. Although my aunt delighted in describing her "nice" girl's discomfort during the male-dominated family confrontation and the female-implemented tweezings, she nevertheless empowered her heroine by having her choose finally an autonomy that freed her from the social and moral cages that imprisoned her. My aunt may well have felt similarly freed. Most assuredly, her final point is emphatic: marriage would have condemned the girl to a lifetime of submitting to ever more demanding modifications of her most private self in order to measure up to an ideal that was false in the first place.

So open a statement of rebellion (not, I suspect, the story's naughtiness) made it too daring for graveyard working day audiences. However, examined in light of my aunt's story and considering the opportunities for embellishment given my aunt as an audience participant, my grandmother's stories are all the more obviously not just simple moral treatises, even though the morals were drawn. My grandmother did not use what feminists such as Sabine Broeck-Sallah and Rachel Brownstein would call "love and marriage plots."[16] Her memorable female characters possess a terrible autonomy, although they may be "devil women" operating outside the ideal "women's sphere." Little Mose's mother displays strength, independence, and mobility, entering the folk group alone, serving food while she must be in the early stages of labor, bearing the child unattended, and walking away from the duties and emotional ties of motherhood; the whore refuses traditional menial work, enjoys material luxuries and sensual pleasure, manipulates the men, and imposes her illness and burial on the unwilling community; Little Pearl, in both her living and her death, controls the people around her and manages to see and report what may lie beyond the grave; even my great-grandmother—because Grandmother Ward rearranged the facts—thwarts a husband demanding his "rights": a husband who, though he eventually forces his demands, will not long survive either in person or good reputation.

Having raised these magnificent specters, it is small wonder that my grandmother felt an uneasy need to find safe closure, to "bury" them in tangible graves. Her audiences colluded with her in this need, nodding wisely as she pointed to a lonely mound far out in a pasture (the whore's final resting place) or to two uninscribed graves in an obscure corner of Long Cemetery.

The fact that such collusion between teller and listeners must have shaped the storytelling sessions that so impressed me during my childhood has been, for me, a gradual realization, dawning and developing as I have relived and reexamined those times past and have researched and rethought them. In this area—and in interpreting the stories through new insights and discoveries—truth seems to me most fragile. Again I wish for "sharers," tellers and listeners from that time and place, who might affirm or deny what I have come to believe happened when those women nearly a half-century ago got together and talked and listened. If only Aunt Minnie had been willing or able to share her thoughts and feelings about those events!

Instead, I must rely on the memories of a young girl whose observations cannot entirely be trusted. I can be reasonably certain that when my grandmother told the story of the prostitute in "The Wages of Sin," her audience relished both the whore's socially unacceptable lifestyle and her punishment for that lifestyle. I recall once asking my mother, "Are you women for or against the lady of ill repute?" So I can assume that the duality, the contradictory reactions, *were* part of that reality. I can also feel fairly safe in saying that the story reflects community values but at the same time offered opportunities for women to express their desire to be free of the restrictions those values placed on them. In offering such an interpretation I am supported by the likes of John G. Cawelti, who states that various types of formulaic stories "enable the audience to explore in fantasy the boundary between the permitted and the forbidden and to experience in a carefully controlled way the possibility of stepping across this boundary."[17]

To readers who are not in my predicament—a prodigal daughter (and granddaughter) trying not to twist, manipulate, and distort truth—my interpretation may seem too neat a little package: surely it does not fully explore the complexities of the cultural processes of storytelling. I readily admit this shortcoming. I have simply taken this interpretation (and those of other stories) as far as I feel I honestly can based on childhood recollection. The same problem confronts me when I attempt to analyze teller-audience collusion, although I was somewhat aware that it existed years ago when I sat among the women, watching and listening. I am now more thoroughly convinced, having considered my grandmother's storytelling as an experienced, educated adult. Still, I am conscious of the fragility of truth—my grandmother's truth, her listeners' truth—and I cringe at the possibility of misrepresentation.

I can speculate, for instance, that my Aunt Dovie's haughty, distanced snobbishness at public events such as graveyard workings may have been a defensive stance that she assumed because she felt the other women's rejection and disapproval. Perhaps, in attempting to share a story in this public sphere, she would not only have gone against my grandmother's advice and wishes, but she might well have experienced group censure of herself as teller and of the story she told. Truly, I think, women of that time and place could not relate to each other with ease and confidence in those rare and highly treasured opportunities to get together with other women.

Pointing out that cross-culturally, segregation by gender is the rule, Nancy Chodorow notes that an important way in which women fulfill their needs for love, emotional gratification, and female identity is "through the creation and maintenance of important personal relations with other women." However, Chodorow acknowledges that "deep affective relationships to women are hard to come by on a routine, daily, ongoing basis for many women."[18] This must have been especially true of women in this section of Hopkins County in the first half of the twentieth century, given that most of them lived on isolated farms where, for weeks at a time, their only human contacts were with husbands and children.

A troubling, underlying theme in both my grandmother's and my aunt's stories involves the role played by the "community" of good, decent women in each story's outcome. Both stories revolve around peripheral women: the one who is promiscuous, the other who is a spinster. In both stories, the protagonists are maneuvered into this peripheral position through their desire to avoid some aspect of the patriarchal society in which they live: drudgery, dependency, shame, loss of autonomy. In both stories, the "good women" enter at the point of the inevitable clash between female rebel and the prevailing value system, and in both stories their intentions are well meaning: they are there to alleviate suffering, to provide solutions.

In both stories, these women become extensions of the judging, punishing social system. The introduction of intrusive, phallic instruments, such as the pole for pushing food to the whore and the tweezers, manned (pun intended) by women, emphasizes the disturbing nature of their presence in the plot. Their actions serve ultimately to seal the unhappy fate of each story's protagonist. Both stories are, thus, partly concerned with women's failure (or ineffectuality) in nurturing, or saving, members of their gender. Chodorow also argues that relational abilities and preoccupations are extended in women's development and curtailed in men's; thus, women serve as cultural mediators.

Whether it was the tellers' intentions or not, it seems to me that both of the stories I have discussed demonstrate that filling the role of cultural mediator can be hazardous. It can, ironically, have an effect opposite to the female group's humane intentions. Probably, in gathering together and sharing stories, my grandmother, aunt, and graveyard working day audiences faced a dilemma that mirrored the dilemma faced by the good women in both of the stories. As noted earlier, women needed to be careful about offering compassion and forgiveness because as cultural mediators, they had to stand in judgment of each other, too. It was, I believe, within this rather perilous framework that teller-audience collusion took place. Women had to be prudent in their choice of storyteller, and that narrator had to exert the utmost insight and responsibility in selecting her tales. The questioning and undermining of prevailing values had to be subtle—so subtle that I as a childish listener did not recognize what was going on. Or perhaps I did unconsciously, and that was why the stories stuck in my mind. I left, and I have never exactly aligned myself with the community of good women in any place where my wanderings have taken me.

Teller-audience collusion was especially important in the evolution of the stories that women told about Great-uncle Fate. The Uncle Fate stories allowed women storytellers to openly express their dissatisfaction with their lot and their disapproval of masculine attitudes toward and treatment of them. My grandmother never told stories about her older half-brother, quietly refusing to participate in maligning him out of family loyalty. Other women told these stories. But they told them during my grandmother's storytelling sessions, and her silent submission to their narratives—with their accumulation of wives buried and quickly forgotten, loose women wooed and flaunted, and neglected children dead in infancy—lent authority to their probably fanciful content. This may have been my grandmother's most subversive tactic, for she retained Uncle Fate's lifelong devotion even while (through her martyred acquiescence) she helped to undermine his reputation within the family and throughout the community.

Women told a number of stories about Uncle Fate's less-than-honorable antics: refusing to kick the mud off his boots before walking across his wife's freshly mopped floors, hitching a freight to Dallas for a weekend of boozing when his wife was going into labor, abducting a lady friend's other suitor and leaving him naked and horseless down on the creek. A story that was often told, and one that my grandmother especially liked—probably because of its supernatural elements—concerned two of Uncle Fate's wives who were presumably buried in his plot in Long Cemetery. I am including the story in this chapter because it is part of the women's repertoire and would not likely have been told with men present.

Uncle Fate's Jealous Wives

Uncle Fate lived a long, busy, and procreative life. Three wives and several of his small children had been buried in his family plot before he finally joined them there. (According to legend, at least two other wives had chosen other burial arrangements.)

When Uncle Fate's first wife was lying terminally ill, a young niece was brought in to tend her. Love blossomed between Uncle Fate and his wife's attractive nurse, and the dying woman was bitterly aware of the affair.

Uncle Fate waited only a fraction of the "decent" mourning time to marry his new love. But that marriage, too, soon came to a tragic end: that woman got milk leg after the birth of a child and died, and the baby died soon after. Although family and neighbors protested, Uncle Fate buried the second wife beside the first. He provided both wives with store-bought tombstones.

Strange things, however, kept happening to the succession of tombstones that he placed on the second wife's grave. The first sank into the grave after a heavy spring rain; a second fell from its pedestal and crumbled; a third disappeared completely. As other wives and additional offspring occupied more and more of Fate's time and energy, he eventually admitted defeat and marked the favored second wife's grave with a bois d'arc post.

What had happened to the second wife's gravestones remained a mystery, but many people believed they knew the answer. Surely it must have been the angry spirit of Fate's first wife, indignant that she must rest beside her hated rival for all eternity.

This story, like a number of other stories told about Uncle Fate by women, emphasizes and very probably exaggerates Fate's misdeeds and characteristics. Men listeners would have scoffed at the supernatural element in the story, although the possibility of a "spirit" is merely suggested and not insisted upon. It is this possibility, however, that makes the story satisfying to female narrators and listeners. Women probably felt helpless and without recourse confronted with the kind of selfishness and insensitivity assigned to Uncle Fate by these tellers. In this case, however, the woman manages to assert herself and strike back, albeit in death.

Chapter Eight

Coming Home Feet First

LONG CEMETERY LEGENDS II

Great-uncle Fate died up in Oklahoma, so they hauled his body back to Cumby for burial in Long Cemetery. Just what the old outlaw's wishes would actually have been in this regard is hard to say. Were his family loyalties such that he was determined to join in death the congregation of siblings, wives, and children already buried in the bleak little rural cemetery? He had, after all, chosen to spend most of the last two decades of his life in Oklahoma, ending his own migrations between Texas and that place of origin (real or presumed) that strangely maintained its hold on Wards, Wolfs, and Lynches. He had in his dotage acquired another wife—his seventh or eighth according to the "living legend" that had attached itself to him during his lifetime—and she was a native Oklahoman. Perhaps she refused to accompany him back to Texas, and his exile was involuntary.

Whatever the case, Fate's place in Long Cemetery had been reserved for him for a number of years. A decent monument, suitable for the family patriarch and certainly more imposing than the dinky gravestones and bois d'arc posts that marked the graves of his wives and children, had been erected for him in his portion of the family plot. No one seemed certain whether Fate had participated in the selection and purchase of the monument or whether certain manipulative kinfolk had devised this means of ensuring that the incorrigible Fate would, if only posthumously, assume his proper role and acknowledge familial responsibilities. At any rate, the monument was there, and a space large enough for an adult male's grave was staked out.

Possibly, Fate's body was shipped into Greenville by freight, and there a mortuary and funeral home took charge. On the other hand, the hearse and its little cortege may have driven into Cumby that day all the way from Oklahoma. I was quite young at the time and do not recall these details. Whatever the exact arrangements, various Texas family members and friends gathered in Cumby to await the arrival of the hearse. When my family parked in a space in front of the post office, a number of other carloads of people were waiting with considerable impatience for the proceedings to begin.

It was a Saturday afternoon in late August, quite fall-like because of a rare cool spell. Saturdays were usually not considered appropriate for funerals. On Saturdays, rural folk traditionally "went into town," a practice that involved bringing produce to sell, stocking up on groceries, getting haircuts, hanging out at the feed store, and perhaps viewing a serialized western at the local "bloody bucket." The theater was so called because the B movies shown there and at others like it contained what people at that time considered a lot of gunplay and bloodshed. The brisk pace of Saturdays, with their built-in irreverence, did not coincide well with the solemnity of most funerals. But a corpse being transported from out of state had to be dealt with at whatever time it managed to arrive—and so Great-uncle Fate's funeral was scheduled for a Saturday. As one of his Cumby cronies commented, "It's fittin', it's fittin'! Fate always came into town on Saturdays—and when they saw him comin', there was always a few that ran in the opposite direction as fast as they could!"

But because it was a Saturday afternoon, the small town was relatively crowded with people, many of whom milled about the narrow sidewalks awaiting, out of curiosity, the arrival of the hearse. They knew Fate by reputation, despite his long absence. Groups of men stood around talking and sometimes laughing, more than likely recalling some of Fate's escapades. Children whined for ice cream or soft drinks, and anxious mothers—even several from the carloads of mourners—relented and took their restless offspring either to the drugstore fountain or to get an orange soda at one of the two grocery stores. One enterprising man went around from car to car tying black crepe paper streamers to the hood ornaments of those that were going to follow in the funeral procession.

The somewhat carnival-like atmosphere disturbed my grandmother. "You'd never guess that we are here to bury the dead!" she exclaimed indignantly. Many of the other relatives, however, especially the children, rather enjoyed sharing the spotlight with Great-uncle Fate. He seemed, for the moment, a very important personage, with a whole little town awaiting his homecoming. Most of Fate's kin hardly noticed the remark of one old fellow that so shocked my grandmother with its insensitivity: "I always said Fate would come back to Cumby one day, even if it had to be feet first!" Great-uncle Fate was a very old man, nearly ninety, who had lived a life that had been "a bit too full," in the opinions of some good people. He had been gone long enough from the area that his death did not leave a vacancy in community affairs that would make his presence missed. Even relatives and former friends could not feel (and did not see the need to express) the kind of sentimental grief and regret that my grandmother considered appropriate.

Someone spotted the hearse when it was still some distance down the highway, and then an eager hush finally settled over the crowd as they waited for the little cortege to come into town. The hearse rolled in smoothly, long and shiny black, followed by three funeral home limos in smoky gray and two or three other vehicles. It was a grand moment. The black drapes at the windows of the hearse were pulled back, so that one caught a glimpse of the casket in its grim dignity surrounded by barely visible mounds of floral offerings. People moved forward, craning their necks to get a view of the casket and to see if they could recognize anyone among the Oklahoma mourners. The hearse was directed to move in its slow majesty on down through town to the little farm road that led south to Long Cemetery. There it and the rest of the brief cortege was stopped in the middle of the highway while the constable prepared to route traffic around it.

Funeral processions offered rare opportunities to people around Cumby for a touch of pageantry—rivaled perhaps by those other significant rites of passage, high school graduation and baccalaureate exercises in the spring. The funeral procession has its basis, of course, in an indispensable physical act: the transportation and burying of the corpse. But as Robert W. Habenstein and William M. Lamers note in their definitive history of American funeral directing, the procession to the grave is a solemn social act that imparts "importance, dignity and profundity to the ceremonial disposal of the dead." As funerals in America became more involved and the journey to the grave became longer, the task of directing this extended service—arranging the procession and successfully moving it, leading it to the burial ground, and assisting in the committal of the body—naturally fell to professional funeral directors.[1]

Great-uncle Fate's burial posed special problems, however. An out-of-state funeral director (or at least one hired by out-of-state mourners) who had traveled a considerable distance to an unfamiliar community was forced to rely on assistance from members of that community in making some of the arrangements. The ingenious individual who had designated with black paper streamers the vehicles that would form the funeral procession had also determined the exact relationships among Fate's kinfolk. He had prepared a list in descending order from the closest in kin to the least, ranging from intimate friends and professional contacts to mere casual acquaintances. Pallbearers, though no blood kin at all, rode in a vehicle near the front of the procession. Being improperly placed in the procession could be taken as an insult by someone who felt he or she had not been duly recognized.

Thus, carloads of family mourners were directed, one by one, to pull in behind the hearse in the predetermined order. The hearse began to creep forward along the sandy farm road in order to accommodate an ever-lengthening procession. Several of the men were heard to comment with considerable pride, "It's going to be one of the longest funeral processions we've ever had in this part of the country!" The length of the funeral procession—even more than the number of people at the wake or funeral—was taken as an indication of the deceased's position in the community and the importance of his or her accomplishments. As a matter of fact, most families in this region did not hold wakes as such; friends "sat up" with the dead, serving in shifts, while others lingered outside the home or funeral parlor.

When I was a child, the embalmed corpse in its casket was still often taken back to the family home and "laid out" in the best room there. This practice became less common as funeral directors, daunted by nearly impassable country roads and eager to avoid the inconvenience of extra trips and moving of the body, managed to convince people that the funeral parlor was more gracious and convenient than returning the body to the home to await burial (and that leaving the body in the mortuary could be more economical, as well). On the day of his funeral, Great-uncle Fate's kinsmen tended to forget that his notoriety was not exactly of a flattering nature.

Incidentally, my grandmother was invited to leave our vehicle and join the widow in the limo directly behind the hearse. This was an honor that she probably owed less to being Fate's half-sister than to the enmity between some of Fate's offspring and other kinfolk and the woman he was married to when he died. My grandmother did not approve of Fate's last wife, either, so she was hesitant. But she finally decided firmly, "It is my duty, out of respect to Fate!" She took the funeral director's arm and walked to the head of the procession with the air of a queen.

Once the procession was in line, the hearse picked up speed, but progress was, nevertheless, slow. The big hearse rocked as it maneuvered the narrow, rutted sandy road, and the cars behind it kept a respectful, cautious distance. Following several cars back in the procession, my family caught sight of the hearse from time to time as it rounded a curve. Otherwise, we were held hostage between the cars in front and in back of us and enveloped in thick, smothering clouds of sand stirred up by the moving vehicles. We drove in absolute silence, which was regarded as correct behavior considering the seriousness of our mission, so it seemed a lengthy journey.

Long Cemetery lies to the left of the farm road going south, down a private dirt lane. At the time of Great-uncle Fate's funeral, a grove of stately oak trees distinguished its entrance; now only three of these trees remain. There was a problem finding parking space for all the cars in the lengthy procession; some of them were forced to remain on the farm road, pulling almost over into the ditch in order to clear the road. Certain kinfolk and community members were already there, waiting for the procession to reach the cemetery. Some of them had, of course, dug the grave. They had set up benches and an old pulpit under the shade of the oak trees, and local floral offerings had already been delivered and arranged about the area where Fate's last services would be held. The hearse drove in relatively close; the director and his assistant took out the flowers first and arranged them among those already there. The casket was brought out last and placed on a portable stand in front of the pulpit.

The funeral directors had probably expected to provide a brief open-air viewing of the corpse, but they were upset with the ambitious plans that Fate's kinfolk had made. Because Fate had died out of state, there had been no chance for family and friends to gather in his home or in a funeral parlor or church. To the funeral directors' dismay, the family proposed allotting time for such a gathering before the actual funeral service began. The directors objected as strenuously as they dared: they had, after all, traveled a long way and must go back where they came from. They wanted to move along with the services as originally planned.

But the Texas kinfolk remained adamant. They possibly felt under more pressure than the funeral directors could imagine. Many of those who had joined the long procession had come mainly to get a first or final look at the man they had heard so much about—and the disappointment would have been keen had they been denied the opportunity. Great-uncle Fate's casket was opened, and a period of viewing the corpse and of shared mourning began. At last there were tears on the part of many of the older women and of the old men who had been Fate's youthful partners in crime and who had been selected to serve as pallbearers. Families intermingled, paying their respects with solemn formality and offering each other consolation.

At the casket's first opening, the crowd moved back and allowed my Grandmother Ward a few minutes of relative privacy with her half-brother's body. She was joined at the casket shortly by Fate's last wife, a wiry little woman with frizzy hair who was probably some twenty years younger than the deceased. My grandmother had not seen her half-brother for a considerable time, so she found him much changed. "Oh, poor old Fate!" she wailed. "He looks so frail. How he must have suffered!"

"What are you talking about?" Fate's wife exclaimed. "He looks better than he's looked in years!"

Thus began the story that would be repeated by the women in

the family for years to come, the tale of the scandalous performance of Fate's last wife at his funeral. Fate's widow was dry-eyed and in good spirits. But she had a habit of conversing loudly with her husband's corpse—and of appearing disconcertingly oblivious to the fact that these conversations were one-sided and very disturbing to all the other mourners. At one point she went to the graveyard fence and looked in, pointing to the gaping, newly dug grave among the bois d'arc posts and meager markers. "Well, Fate," she called back to the casket, "They're out there waiting for you!" As she followed the pallbearers to Fate's open grave, she again took note of the shabbily marked graves of his wives and offspring. "Just look at that!" she scolded. "Now that's a shame, Fate! Sticks of kindlin' wood for tombstones! I bet you don't know one of them kids from the other—or maybe any of them wives, either. You're going to get up *there,* and none of you will even be acquainted. You sure ought to have kept up with their names, Fate!"

Although he was just a small boy at the time, my brother, James, remembers the August afternoon when Great Uncle Fate was buried.

> You know, I was *there.* I went to Fate's funeral. He was an old man, and he was living up in Oklahoma somewhere. And they brought his body in from Oklahoma to be buried there in Long Cemetery. They just had the service under the big oak trees there at the old graveyard.
>
> They had a preacher that said a very few words. And at that service there were a few of Fate's old cronies that were still left. They gathered around his casket and sang his funeral songs. And it was sort of ironic listening to them, *knowing* the type of people that they were, knowing how tough they had been and how they had fought when they were young and just wrecked the town on occasion. These old fellows gathered around the casket, and they sang the most *beautiful* songs that you ever heard in your life. Their voices blended so well. They just sang such *sweet* music at this man's funeral.
>
> Looking back, I can't help laughing at how really preposterous the whole thing was. Here were these old pals who had wrecked the town when they were young—you know, they'd come riding in and scare everybody half to death. You sure didn't want to be their enemy! Or that's the way I've heard those Lynch cousins of my mother tell it—and I've heard some of the Warren men talk about it, too. And now they

were gathered about, watching one another pass away. And here was Fate being properly issued out of the world by these old friends of his.[2]

As my brother recalls, the preacher at Great-uncle Fate's funeral said only "a very few words"—an incidence uncharacteristic of that time and that place. In rural northeast Texas then, preachers still delivered long funeral sermons, working on the emotions of their captive audiences either with tear-jerking reminders of the deceased's good deeds and hopes for the hereafter or by using his or her death as a means of exhorting members of the audience to prepare for their own. I have heard preachers describe in minute, painful detail the last moments of the deceased (provided by some family member or friend presumably at the scene) in order to achieve dramatic effect.

Great-uncle Fate's funeral, however, was only in the very remotest sense a religious event: it was a public ceremony that had fallen, somewhat spontaneously, into place according to certain broadly understood rules of conduct. To the extent that the funeral was religious in nature, it was Protestant. In *The Living and the Dead: A Study of the Symbolic Life of Americans,* W. Lloyd Warner makes the point that for many Protestants, funeral orations and sermons by the minister are believed necessary and important. The primary function of the eulogy is to "translate the profane person in the feelings of those who mourn from secular living into the sacred world of the dead and the Deity."[3]

If the eulogy was expected to serve this primary function, Great-uncle Fate presented the unfortunate officiating minister with insurmountable difficulties. As Warner points out, "The whole group of mourners is composed of individuals who have considerable knowledge of the habits and activities of the deceased," some of which might cause an entirely just judge "to refuse the candidate admittance to a happier life."[4] Great-uncle Fate's well-known habits and activities had been all of this sort. His half-brother Wood, for instance, refused to attend the funeral—and had issued a warning that none of his offspring should attend—because the brothers' lifelong violent and often bloody brawling had led to permanent enmity. Further, Fate's reputation for drinking, fighting, and womanizing precluded "touching lightly on his earthly traits" and "moving gracefully over to his positive virtues and spiritual qualities," a technique Warner indicates preachers may use. The task of his minister was indeed a delicate one. The least said the better.

Certainly, the preacher at Fate's funeral was given few options by Fate's Texas kin. During the open-air viewing of the corpse, there was an intense flurry of last-minute debate and instructions as my grandmother and Fate's last wife were drawn into making arrangements with the preacher regarding a suitable sermon. The widow assured Fate's kin, and the preacher, that Fate had, in fact, been belatedly "saved," but she could give only vague and indefinite details of this momentous event. My grandmother yearned to believe in Fate's salvation, but she relinquished that hope as it became clear that even if Fate had repented in his old age, he had affiliated himself with a group not in good standing with either my grandmother or the preacher. She, in turn, was certain that Fate must have been baptized at some camp meeting or other when he was a lad. However, in view of the way Fate had lived his long life, they were all forced to admit that any such early cleansing of his soul had obviously not "stuck."

Absolutely nothing reassuring could be said about Great-uncle Fate's spiritual status. Family members cautioned the preacher against a hellfire-and-brimstone approach because any mention of sin would be taken as direct criticism of Great-uncle Fate and was totally unacceptable to them. Nor did they want much mention made of any of them—here displaying their usual reticence in matters of kinship. Considering Fate's complicated family life, they felt that the barest mention of his living offspring would suffice.

The poor preacher was left with nothing much to say. Fate's old cronies, however, came to the minister's rescue by urging him to talk about what a good friend Fate had been to them all. The grateful clergyman did just that, delivering a brief declamation on the value of earthly friendships that, in content and language, reflected the influence of Tennyson's *Idylls of the King* much more than that of the Bible. The old fellows sat with tears flowing down their creased cheeks throughout the preacher's impromptu performance. The preacher was subsequently rewarded with pats on the back by members of the family and assurances that his words had been in "very good taste."

After the sermon and song service, the pallbearers—the same old men who had done the sweet harmonizing in honor of their departed friend—bore the carefully closed casket to the grave. There the funeral directors, doubtless relieved to have the ordeal nearing its finish (or so they thought), succeeded in lowering the casket without incident. In Long Cemetery at that time, it was customary for family members to stand at the grave until it was filled and the last clod of dirt patted into place on the mound with the back of a shovel. After the grave was filled, relatives generally heaped flowers on the grave, sometimes reserving a blossom or two for keepsakes—or even entire branches to place on graves of other kinfolk.

Violent outpourings of grief might occur during this process, for it constituted tangible closure, quite undeniable finality. When the first hard clods of earth hit the wooden frame over Great-uncle Fate's casket, however, the voice of his last wife rang out: "Well, this is it, Fate. This is the end of the line. Sweet God in heaven be praised, you didn't get to put me out here in the back-end of nowhere! I'm leaving you here, Fate, with all of *them*. And I won't be coming back. Dead or alive, I won't be coming back!" People gasped, and my grandmother swayed as if she might faint in her horror. The funeral directors and two of the women forcibly carried the last wife away from the grave and out of the cemetery, treating her as they might have had she become suddenly crazed with grief. Quite the contrary seemed to be the case. The widow handled this indignity, as she did all of the hitches in the funeral proceedings, with equanimity and appeared very much in control of her faculties. As she at one point told those around her, "We just don't think alike, is all."

As soon as Fate's grave was filled and the raw earth smothered under its bank of steaming chrysanthemums, gladioli, and roses, the members of the immediate family formed a sort of "receiving line," and the other guests or mourners filed by offering condolences. Normally, such condolences depended heavily on references to an assured hereafter, to release from troubles and pain, and to biblical promises of strength in the face of loss and suffering. Such reassurances did not ring true, however, in connection with Great-uncle Fate. Those offering consolation were reduced to murmuring things like "He lived a long life, and he was active up to the very last" or "He is in the hands of a merciful God who knows better how to judge than we on earth do." The uncertainty of Great-uncle Fate's eternal destination made for some awkward moments among those who had gathered to dispose of his remains with due ceremony.

With their condolences offered, the crowd fanned out over the graveyard so that each individual could "pay respects" at the graves of his or her closest kin. This was a nearly ritualized part of any visit to the cemetery. In this process people usually drifted together in small groups, often separating along gender lines: the women to catch up on family gossip, perhaps, and the men to indulge in harangues about war or politics or the latest fiasco with the county agricultural agent.

Historically, the funeral in America has had important social implications. Leroy Bowman notes that one of the functions of the funeral, especially in small communities, is its fulfilling of people's desire "to re-experience total group association" and to "strengthen the sense of community solidarity" as people "of various faiths, of various vocations and economic levels come together in the wake or religious service."[5] Only in the most superficial way did the funeral of Great-uncle Fate serve to "strengthen the sense of community solidarity." True, people from the vicinity who were not normally close associates were drawn together at this event, and far-flung relatives "touched base" with their families of origin and their place of birth. The agendas, however, varied: family loyalty, self-justification, simple curiosity—even, perhaps, revenge. Not surprisingly, once the ritualized portions of the service were finished, the momentary unity of the crowd vanished and the more usual stratification manifested itself.

Even so, the relatives who went to considerable trouble to transport Great-uncle Fate's body back to Texas to be buried in the family plot and the Texas kinfolk who met the body and its Oklahoma mourners in Cumby were maintaining a longstanding American tradition. People in America have historically felt a need to gather beside the bier of a departed relative and to share in the social gatherings that automatically followed the get-together of scattered relatives and friends who seldom met except on such an occasion.

This need to allow time for far-flung relatives and friends to travel to the funeral gave rise, Habenstein and Lamers suggest, to the development of a variety of methods to preserve the corpse. It culminated, finally, with the introduction of embalming in the early to mid-nineteenth century. Several of the stories that were often told at Long Cemetery suggest that the practice of embalming did not catch on as rapidly among the rural folks around Cumby as it did in other parts of the country. But by the time of Great-uncle Fate's funeral in the 1940s, it was common procedure to turn the deceased over to professionals who embalmed the body, laid it out, and orchestrated the funeral. Interestingly, Great-uncle Fate—ever the rebel, even in death—turned out to be the one to make the long journey so that relatives could gather beside his bier. His death and burial, nevertheless, pulled together a group of people who rarely had an opportunity to be together, and a social gathering ensued.

For the people who buried their dead in Long Cemetery, a funeral offered the chance to maintain contact with family members whom they did not often get to see. The quality of their socializing varied from funeral to funeral, depending mostly on the age of the deceased and the manner of his or her death. If the deceased were a young mother, perhaps, or a child, or if death had been long and agonizing or sudden and violent, the socializing extraneous to offering comfort to the bereaved was muted and kept at a minimum. In the case of someone like Great-uncle Fate, however, death was regarded as natural and to be expected. The socializing connected with the event of his burial, therefore, could be quite open and extensive. (The Long Cemetery group's tendencies to gear the nature of the funeral gathering to the age and manner of death of the deceased have close parallels in Hungary, as noted by Linda Degh in *Folktales and Society: Story-Telling in a Hungarian Peasant Community,* and in Ireland, as noted by Sean O'Sullivan in *Irish Wake Amusements.*) These gatherings constituted important storytelling situations, as well, because people found comfort in recounting familiar stories or in telling them for the first time to offspring paying an unaccustomed visit to the family plot.

Most of the stories connected with Great-uncle Fate seem to me to have been told by males. It seems significant that I had not heard several of the stories during my own childhood (being a girl child attended primarily by women) but that my brother had heard them told among the men on several occasions. Typically, after the grave had been filled in, several of the men would gather in the shade of one of the bois d'arc trees that were still, at that time, scattered throughout the graveyard. While they smoked or chewed tobacco they would tell stories, often heatedly debating the truth or accuracy of each teller's version of a given event or string of events.

It was usual, when a person had just been buried, to recount some of the most memorable things that person had done when he or she was alive. Apparently, although men storytellers tended to steer clear of details that might reflect in some damaging way on the deceased person's survivors, they nevertheless enjoyed telling about preposterous and often humorous things that the dead person had supposedly done. My brother is fairly certain that it must have been at Great-uncle Fate's funeral that he first heard several of his favorite stories about this colorful kinsman—like the following story. James retells it as he recalls hearing it told by men in my mother's family and other men in the community who joined in their storytelling session.

Uncle Fate's Saturday Night Fights

It's kind of funny how people back in those days were sometimes *later* made into heroes because of some crazy things that they did. One of these characters was Great-uncle Fate.

Because of deaths and remarriage, my grandmother's family included both the Lynches and the Wolfs, and Uncle Fate was her half-brother. This family was a mixture of Indian and Caucasian—and all kinds of bloodlines intermixed—and it seemed as though the stew of that mixture of bloodlines sometimes became pretty hot.

At this point in time, I do not know whether "Fate" was my great-uncle's actual name or whether it was a nickname. I *do* know that old Uncle Fate, as they referred to him, *was* like "Fate coming upon you." They said that he was one mean sucker! When it was reported that Fate was coming into town on Saturday night, there were certain individuals who would literally get up and leave town. They knew he was not someone they could mess with, and they didn't want to take any chances.

When Fate went into town on Saturday nights, he had some cronies that he hung around with, and did they ever love to have fights. There was a story that my mother told about picking cotton with a Mr. Jim Warren who had known Uncle Fate in the early days. At the time my mother knew him, old Mr. Jim was so old he could barely get around.

> But he told what a *fine* man Fate was. "Fate and I had some of the *finest fights* that you ever saw!" is what he said to my mother. He really and truly looked on the fights they'd had as some sort of great fellowship that they had shared. They would go into town on Saturday nights, and they'd go out in the wagon yards and they'd just flat bust heads and fight! It seemed as though old Mr. Jim had really enjoyed their fighting—it was their sport. Of course, they probably did a little drinking while they were at it, too.[6]

Such an account as the foregoing, relatively plotless and documented with at least one quote from someone everybody knew and recognized (and everyone in Cumby knew or at least knew *about* old Jim Warren), served to establish Uncle Fate's reputation as a fighting man who was rough, tough, and admired by those who dared claim to be his peers. As an introduction to storytelling, such background information was certain to be followed by accounts of particular or specific events, loosely plotted. This had the effect of demonstrating that although he was "mean as the dickens," Great-uncle Fate was human, fallible, and in his own way lovable—in the same way that a grizzly bear may be thought lovable. Stories about Great-uncle Fate's tangles with women often combined all these elements. My brother recounts another of the stories that he believes he first heard at Great-uncle Fate's funeral, one in which Fate emerges as a rather dangerous Don Quixote on a misguided mission.

Gallant Uncle Fate Rescues a Mop-Wielding Lady

> There are certain stories that are told about Uncle Fate's escapades, mostly involving his fighting and getting tangled up with women. Being a man's man, so to speak, Fate felt obligated to be very gallant and rescue the ladies, and there were times when he did that very thing. He rode about over the country, and if he found someone in distress, well, he was the person who would help them out. He just really had a lot of high self-esteem!
>
> Well, he happened into a situation one day. He was riding down an old country lane on his horse, and he heard this woman just a-screamin' bloody murder. I mean she was screaming for the help of the Lord. Well, Fate just couldn't imagine what in the world, so as he comes closer, he begins to realize that this woman is being beaten by her husband—

and I mean the old boy was really givin' her a good whippin'. So Fate just rides up on his horse, dismounts, goes over, gets the man by the collar, and raises him up and knocks him cold as a wedge.

Well, when you enter into these domestic squabbles, you're likely to get into trouble! Yes, he'd knocked the man completely cold, see; he didn't have any trouble out of the man. But the *woman* took up a big old wet mop, and she went after Fate. She hit him over the head with that wet mop—just wrapped up his head in the smelly thing. She beat the livin' daylights out of Fate till he managed to get on his horse and ride away.[7]

Although such a story casts the infamous Fate in a somewhat unflattering, comic role, one can deduce that the narrator's purpose was, in part, to mitigate the view of Great-uncle Fate as a pugnacious, insensitive rounder, hard on his women and indifferent to his unhealthy offspring. It thus, perhaps, cast a more favorable light on his reputation.

It is difficult for me to visualize the Great-uncle Fate that we buried that August afternoon many years ago as the hero of an episode like the one just recounted. During the open-air viewing, I spent several minutes peering curiously into Great-uncle Fate's casket. So far as I know, this was the first and only time that I ever saw the man. He had made his permanent move to Oklahoma before I was born, and although he may have visited Texas at some time, I have no recollection of him. But like everyone around Cumby, I knew him by reputation—and I had imagined how he must look.

The man in the casket was a shock and a disappointment. I have always thought that my uncles, Bernice and Elmer, and my Great-uncle Wood looked like old Indian warriors. Great-uncle Fate bore little resemblance to any of them. The funeral parlor had laid him out in a nice gray dress suit over a pale gray dress shirt with a dark tie. The casket, too, was gray and lined with white satin, so everyone commented on the color. Whatever might be her other shortcomings, most of the guests agreed, his last wife had good taste—although she might have fixed Fate up so that he seemed more human, more like himself. Fate, they were certain, would never have worn a dress shirt and tie.

Great-uncle Fate had a thin, firm jaw, a full, white mustache (with no nicotine stains), a prominent nose, a high forehead, and a shock of long, white hair. He had the rigid, pontifical air that death and embalming often give a corpse. More than anything else, he looked to me like one of the deacons in the church my family attended when we went into town. If there was any clue to the kind of man that he had been, it was the right hand that had been placed at an angle across his breast. It was an extraordinarily large hand on which the veins stood stark against big bones, with long, big-knuckled fingers. Although the nails were trimmed, they were cracked far back into the quick. It was a hand that could clench itself into a fist and knock a man across a room, or curl itself around a knife, or pull a trigger. But this calm, austere old gentleman fending off an angry woman's wet mop—unlikely! And yet my brother tells a similar story of still another of Fate's misadventures.

A Dallas Rescue

Fate left the Cumby area, eventually, and lived in Dallas for awhile. I don't know how old he was at this time, but he hadn't given up on the business of being the gallant man who helped in time of need.

The story is told that in downtown Dallas one day, Fate saw a fight going on. There were two men who had ganged up on this little fella—and he didn't look like he was a very healthy guy, anyway—and so they were really giving him a bad whippin'. Fate stopped his buggy, and he goes over and starts workin' over the two men that were whippin' the little fella.

About that time, here comes a lady out of a shop there somewhere, and she had an old hatbox. She crowned that hatbox down over Fate's head. He went ahead and finished the fight with his head sticking up through the bottom of this hatbox. And he whipped the guys. Now that's the story that's told. From the way they told the story, it seemed that Fate never lost a fight in his life.[8]

My brother, through youthful years of patient listening while the men in both branches of our family railed each other and told stories about their kinfolk, and now through extensive practice as a storyteller in his own right, has mastered the oral style and techniques peculiar to the men in both families. I think he leans more toward the Winniford-Alexander storytelling mode, probably because he listened most often to our father. In that mode, the audience deferred to a single storyteller who "held forth" without interruption except for appreciative reactions from the other men (and women when they were present).

As I recall from my own years of listening, male storytellers on both the paternal and maternal sides of the family valued an ironic and often humorous distancing from their materials. It seemed important to them not to pass judgment on the heroes of their tales and not to moralize. In fact, when they recounted the adventures of the various "black sheep" on both sides of the family, by tone and inflection—somewhere between mock horror and amused indulgence—they managed to convey the impression that their outlaw-hero was really not all that bad. In fact, under some other value system stemming from a less misguided society, the person might even appear admirable.

In their storytelling, these narrators succeeded in changing Fate and other characters like him from a "bad" person to a "bad boy," which, as Warner points out, is a very different thing. Warner states that the "bad boy" symbol or label is highly valued in our society. The bad boy is someone who is indulged and often liked for behavior that is ordinarily disapproved. People identify with the bad boy, whose ingenuity is usually directed against persons and restrictive rules that the public finds irksome and from which it needs emotional release. The bad boy dares do things that those around him might easily wish to do, and the consequences of his deeds are events they might wish to see happen.[9]

In the content of the stories he told and in the manner in which he told them, my brother reflected the "bad boy" interpretation of Great-uncle Fate's character and actions that he had picked up from other male storytellers in the family. In fact, in what he knew to be a collecting situation, he may have been more self-consciously anxious to present Fate in a sympathetic light. Once when my brother was telling the Great-uncle Fate stories, our Aunt Minnie Martin Foster called attention to this fallacy in male storytelling. She countered with a story of her own that certainly offers a different view of Great-uncle Fate's relationship with the opposite sex.

Fate and the Liberated Female

Old Fate wasn't any knight in shining armor—I don't care if there *are* stories about him rushing in to help someone. And he sure never did treat women right—except your grandmother; he was nice to her. But he was mean and no good.

Now he must have been a young man when this happened. I think he was between wives. I'm not going to accuse him of *that.* I'm not going to accuse him of running around on one of them. I won't do *that.* But there was this gal in town, and she was good-looking, but she was wild and headstrong and forward. Brazen, you know. There is another word they have for women like that, but I won't say it.

And she set her cap for Fate. I don't know why. Women liked Fate, and I've never understood that. But she did, and old Fate thought he'd oblige her, I guess, and they got this courtship going, hot and heavy, and it looked like she would probably be his next wife. She came from a good, well-to-do family, but she was just wild.

This gal was used to having things her own way and doing whatever she wanted to do. So one day Fate was out somewhere, and this gal rode up on a big, fine horse—and she was wearing a pair of men's pants. Well, she was a buxom gal. Fate got one look at those hips of hers in those men's pants, sitting in that saddle—and he pitched a fit. He told her that no woman of his was going to go around flaunting herself like that, and he ordered her to go get into some decent clothes.

The gal just laughed and told him to get used to it—she'd wear whatever she liked. Of course, old Fate was accustomed to having his women meek and mild, so he really started ranting and cussing then. Well, she just turned and rode off—and being the sassy sort, she reared up in the saddle and patted her butt at him, real defiant, you know.

Fate couldn't stand it! He had his shotgun with him, loaded with buckshot, and he just raised his gun and shot both the gal and the horse in the butt with buckshot. It didn't kill her, of course, but the horse got scared, and she had the ride of her life. And naturally old Fate got in trouble with her daddy and brothers.

But any man who'd haul off and shoot a woman in the butt with buckshot is no gentleman.[10]

As Aunt Minnie tells this story, it fits, of course, into a pattern characteristic of female storytellers, stressing either overtly or implicitly a particular moral stance regarding human sexuality and condemning Great-uncle Fate for all of the character defects for which he was famous: frequent marriages and general faithlessness, arrogance, crude manners, and violence. Female stories about Fate measure him by how women, specifically women family members, reacted to him. As some of Aunt Minnie's remarks suggest, women outside the family often liked Fate and were attracted to him. Certain elements of the story, however, suggest that it may, in fact, have originally been one of the tales told mostly by men. Women storytellers seldom employed the broad humor that underlies the action of this story. With other trappings than Aunt Minnie's indignant moralizing, this could be a rousing, somewhat bawdy tale of the hero's getting the best of a woman who "deserved her comeuppance."

That Aunt Minnie's story was part of the masculine repertoire is borne out by my brother. He was familiar with the story, and he offered some good-humored corrections and commentary. If Great-uncle Fate had fired a shotgun load of *buckshot* at his sassy-mouthed sweetheart, both woman and horse would have been minus rear ends; the shot would have been fatal. Uncle Fate had, of course, used *birdshot,* which meant that he was hot-tempered and rash and perhaps a bit rude but not brutal. According to my brother, the men telling and listening to the story would have understood Fate's dilemma. In the other stories about Fate and angry women, the women were peripheral to the main action and Fate's mission or purpose. He therefore endured their attacks as one might a pesky gnat, brushing them aside and going on about his business even though they detracted momentarily from his manly dignity. But when a woman with whom he was romantically or sexually involved defied him with her very sexuality, that was a confrontation that engaged his ego, his pride. He could not permit her to triumph.

From a male standpoint, the woman's already unsavory reputation, and especially her obscene gesture, invited Fate's quick, nearly righteous retaliation. Further, the woman herself was rash: first, in setting her cap for Fate, and then in tempting his temper. Everyone knew that Fate was mean and that he overreacted. Men respected this and stayed out of his way. The woman should have had better sense. Thus, Aunt Minnie's story is one that men would probably have enjoyed telling—perhaps not at Fate's funeral, but under less decorous circumstances.

Great-uncle Fate's funeral was destined, probably from the very beginning, to end on a discordant note. Certain incidents shattered the good-natured conviviality among the mourners and guests who lingered in the graveyard after Fate had been laid to rest. One such incident was his widow's confrontation with the undertakers.

For the probably weary and stressed-out funeral directors, who had likely driven in all the way from Oklahoma, nothing about Great-uncle Fate's funeral had gone according to schedule from the time the procession left Cumby. Time had been lost arranging for parking space, the open-air viewing had developed into an hour-long wake, and the song service had been unexpectedly lengthy. Now the Oklahoma mourners, delighted to be among friends and kinfolk, showed no signs of leaving the graveyard until sundown finally forced them to disband. So at last the exasperated funeral directors determined to take a firm hand: they were ready to pull out, they announced. Believing that some ultimatum was in order, they declared that they would pull out whether the vehicles were full or empty.

The attitude of the directors had rankled the crowd from their first arrival at the cemetery. This final development made these professionals most unpopular with all concerned. The Oklahoma mourners were embarrassed and indignant at being so ordered about. Their Texas kin and friends supported them enthusiastically in their rebellion against these "fancified city folk" who were attempting to dictate in so important and personal a matter as a family funeral. The general feeling was that the funeral directors needed to understand that they were "hired to do as they were told." Because she was the one with leverage, Fate's last wife became the group's champion.

"You drive off empty if you're a-mind to," she dared the funeral directors. "You go right ahead. But your pockets will be as empty as them old limos—I promise you that! *I'm* the one paying for this shee-bang. It's my name has to go on the check. You drive off empty—and we'll thank you kindly for giving Fate a *free* ride back where he belongs, and that'll be that!"

So the funeral directors hunched their shoulders in defeat and went to sit dejectedly on the hood of the big hearse, waiting in the long shadows of the big oak trees for the slow summer Texas sun to descend.

In a chapter titled "The Modernization of Funeral Service," James J. Farrell, in *Inventing the American Way of Death,* 1830–1920, comments that in their quest for financial rewards and social status, undertakers "created the culture of professionalism, in which the able citizens of a democratic society deferred to the decisions of an educated and (eventually) economic elite." "Able citizens" of rural northeast Texas—at least those living forty to fifty years ago—were by nature suspicious of any profession that expected them to believe that, as Farrell suggests, "there are better methods than have been prescribed by custom" and to defer in matters of propriety, unquestioningly leaving the arrangements for the burial of the dead to the undertaker who "best knows how to proceed."[11]

As stated above, the people who buried their dead in Long Cemetery were slow to adopt the practice of turning their dead over to undertakers even after the funeral parlor became popular in most of the country. As the fad caught on everywhere else, however, they grudgingly relented. Embalming had its advantages, not the least of which was the assurance that, once embalmed, one no longer faced the danger of being buried alive. Too, embalming eliminated other messy, time-consuming methods such as the cooling board, ice, and the removal of organs. Funeral parlors exerted considerable pressure on clients to accept a "package deal," which involved not just embalming and a casket but the remainder of the funeral service. Also, as working conditions and lifestyles gradually changed in the country around Cumby, people found that they could depend less and less on friends and neighbors to assist in all the tasks demanded by a home-oriented burial. But even when, for the sake of convenience, these people finally relented and began turning their dead over to professionals in the field, they did so with reluctance and skepticism.

It was, therefore, nearly impossible for an undertaker or funeral director to satisfy the Long Cemetery group. Much of the talk one overheard throughout the proceedings connected with death and burial involved dissatisfaction with the professional handling of the corpse and its final interment. Among these people, criticism of the undertaker's procedure for preparing and burying the dead usually began even before the corpse had been removed from the deathbed and often continued well past the interment of the body and the departure of the hearse. The corpse was either "gussied up" too much so that the deceased did not look natural or the undertaker had failed miserably at concealing the ravages of fatal disease. The casket was either too ornate and ostentatious (for which the bereaved had been pressured into investing more than they could afford: a real concern with the Long Cemetery group, who distrusted funeral directors as "slick talkers") or it was too cheap and plain (and the bereaved had been ill-advised or were selfish and parsimonious).

The funeral director himself was either overdressed, sissified, pushy, and overly solicitous—or he was drab, stuck up, and unconcerned. If the Long Cemetery group employed the services of the funeral parlor grudgingly, they felt outright hostility toward the men who administered those services. The very characteristics that were considered essential to a funeral director's professionalism (Farrell includes delicacy and tact, urbane manners, being well-dressed and well-groomed and alert to appearances, in short, being a "gentleman") made him just the sort of man that rural people, especially the men, distrusted and wanted to "whittle down to size." Funeral directors might have attained financial clout and social status in other parts of the country, but among the Long Cemetery people they were "hired help" who had a habit of forgetting their place and getting out of line.

Therefore, a number of stories involving undertakers and disastrous professionally conducted funerals circulated among the Long Cemetery group. And late that August afternoon, while Uncle Fate's unhappy funeral directors brooded by their empty hearse and the crowd reluctantly began to break up and head for their respective vehicles, several of these familiar stories were told again with special relish. A favorite story concerned what was reputed to have been the first professionally directed funeral in Long Cemetery. My brother recalls that only snatches of the story were mentioned that afternoon, doubtless because all of the men were familiar with the tale and did not need to go through it in its entirety. Both my brother and I have heard the tale told a number of times and by several different tellers, and details have varied from one narrator to the next. The following is a reconstruction based on multiple tellings.

A New-Fangled Funeral

One old farmer had managed to be more prosperous than his neighbors. As the years passed and he entertained the idea of dying, he planned an elaborate funeral that he felt would be in keeping with his means and status. He arranged with one of the new-fangled funeral parlors—with its motorized hearse—to do the honors. Unfortunately, the man died in the spring after a long, wet spell.

He had requested funeral services in the church instead of at graveside—and even there matters got out of hand. Everyone wished to ride in the funeral parlor's two limos, so although the widow and sons were helped into the first vehicle following the hearse, there was a general free-for-all among other relatives over who qualified to ride in the second.

None of them was destined for a high-speed joy ride, however. The hearse and the two other motorized vehicles were forced to creep along to accommodate the rest of the mourners, who were in wagons and buggies. About halfway to the cemetery, the hearse got stuck in the mud. Although men got out and pushed (and were thoroughly mud-splashed in the process), the hearse would not budge. The hysterical widow refused to let the casket be transferred to a wagon, certain that her husband's spirit could never rest thereafter. Finally, horses were unhitched from two of the wagons, and they began the slow business of pulling the hearse to the cemetery.

The rest of the mourners went on ahead in their wagons and buggies. Several of the dead man's buddies had stocked up on bootleg booze so they could drown their sorrows once the funeral was over. With nothing to do while they waited, the men broke out the booze and shared it with the other mourners. The whole crowd was in a state of loud hilarity by the time the hearse arrived with the body. The man's funeral was remembered as the joke of the county.

❧ This story is typical of much of the Ward-Wolf material in that it apparently became increasingly generic with each retelling. The identity of the central character is omitted as are many other details that might assist a listener in checking out the truth of the incident. Quite possibly the story is also geographically displaced and describes an occurrence that, if it happened at all, did *not* happen a few miles south of Cumby; yet the events were generally attributed specifically to Cumby and Long Cemetery. Interestingly, I have never talked to anyone who has been able to say for certain who the deceased man was or to point out the grave. Nevertheless, the tale exemplifies certain themes that would have been important to male storytellers in that area at that time: the old farmer who becomes self-important and ostentatious with success makes a fool of himself; the high-tech professional approach to burial proves inferior to the old, traditional, and basically rural methods.

Another story often recounted by men also emphasizes the importance of rural customs that were vanishing but were relinquished with regret. In a subtle way, it criticizes the modern tendency to turn the tasks involved in the preparation and burial of the dead over to outsiders motivated by financial gain.

The Corpse That Refused to Be Buried

The custom was for close friends of the deceased (menfolk, of course) to dig the grave. It was an insult to the memory of the departed if paid grave-diggers were required.

One unlucky man had, as everyone put it, a "sorry, good-for-nothing" friend. Knowing that the people of the community expected him to prepare the ground for the man's burial, this lazy friend and his equally lazy son hired a couple of tramps to slip in and do the honors.

When the graveside services were over and the time came to lower the casket into the grave, the rigging jammed. Repeated efforts to get the equipment to work failed: either the casket would not budge at all, or the rigging on one end would give and threaten to upend the casket and dump its contents.

The guilty parties realized that the indignant corpse was not going to submit to burial in a grave dug by strangers, so the two finally admitted their duplicity. The quick-thinking preacher led them and the gathered mourners in a prayer asking forgiveness, and the casket was lowered without further complications.

❧ It is interesting that in the process of retelling and of rendering tales increasingly generic, narrators have sometimes confused the identities of Great-uncle Fate and Great-uncle Wood. This circumstance would have distressed poor Wood, who, although his youthful adventures rivaled Fate's, in his maturity became a gentle, if eccentric, truck farmer mainly interested in the size of his tomatoes and the beauty of his nasturtiums. One story purports to describe the antics of pallbearers at Great-uncle Wood's burial. These rickety old men, determined to carry out their sacred duty as lifelong friends and dig Wood's grave for him, went out to the cemetery on the day before the funeral to apply themselves to this task.

Fearing that their strength and determination might wane, the elderly friends had come fortified with several jugs of bootleg booze. By late afternoon the grave was finished, and after they had rested a bit, the old fellows loaded up picks and shovels and left. All but one—an exhausted old codger who had acquired a jug, crawled back into the grave for some solitary sipping, and fallen asleep. Visitors to the cemetery the next morning were startled to hear sounds coming from the open grave. There they found the old man, monumentally hung over and struggling to get out of his friend's grave.

In view of Great-uncle Wood's changed lifestyle, it seems unlikely that such an incident occurred in connection with his funeral. Jokes turning on the theme of the drunk in the grave are extremely popular in southern rural culture. For instance, W. K. McNeil in *Ozark Mountain Humor* recounts an incident similar to the above story. Probably the appropriation of this familiar plot was inspired by the active part Great-uncle Fate's loyal drinking and carousing buddies played in the proceedings of that memorable August afternoon when they "brought him home feet first."

One final incident brought Great-uncle Fate's funeral to an ironic but strangely appropriate close. The sun was low, hovering just above a bank of purple clouds that had formed in the west. There were occasional nervous little twitches of lightning within the purple, and people argued over whether it was just heat lightning or an honest sign of rain. The cool spell had not broken the drought, but maybe "more weather" was on its way. Great-uncle Fate was buried. There were people with cows to milk, hogs to slop, and chickens to feed. So the crowd started thinning out. The Oklahoma mourners loaded into the limos, and the empty hearse crawled awkwardly across the rough terrain and down to the road to lead the little cortege away.

It was in those final moments that an old pickup truck pulled to a stop under the oak trees. A thin, dark-haired fellow got out, ambled through the cemetery gate and over to the new grave, and stood there a few minutes by himself.

"That's one of Uncle Fate's sons," my mother said, and my grandmother agreed. We were all in the car ready to leave, but we waited until Fate's son headed for his truck again, and then my mother called out to him. He came over to the car, and I remember searching for some resemblance to the gray-clad dignitary in the casket we had buried. I saw none. This man looked tired, needed a shave, and had two black eyes, the bruises extending down along his nose and ending in bloody smudges on his high cheekbones. He explained the black eyes with less embarrassed fidgeting than he accepted my mother's and grandmother's sympathies in the loss of his father. It seemed he had got into a little altercation in Oklahoma City the night before, but not to worry—and he managed a tight-lipped grin—they ought to get a look at the other guy!

Discussing the function of the funeral in the strengthening of devotion to group ideals, Bowman postulates that "in the car, on the way to or from the cemetery, or later in informal groups, conflicting opinions on an individual basis are expressed about the advantage of living a righteous life."[12] I can hear my grandmother sighing as we pulled out on the road to begin the drive back to Cumby, "Like father, like son!" It was the sort of thing one would expect her to say. Many years later, my brother recalls the meeting with Fate's son and comments, "We figured that, quite likely, he was still carrying on the old family tradition." As we drove along, the adults pondered the effect that Great-uncle Fate's irresponsible, often violent life might have had on his children and on other people who knew him. It was probably my mother's brother who reminded all of us of the details that my brother still recalls:

A Family Tradition

The story was told of how Fate and his brothers would fight with one another. Now they would literally fight like a bunch of wild Indians. It seemed as though that was one of the main things that they were remembered for: their ability to "get down with it."

By old Indian tradition—they were part Cherokee—most of them carried knives. And they told about how Fate and Wood, who was a half-brother, got in a fight with one another down at the horse barns. Fate was a little bit older, but Wood, he was a younger one. So Wood brought out the knife and drove it all the way through and *out* on the other side of the calf of Fate's leg—and, of course, they told about how bad that was.[13]

This part of Fate's legendary life I had heard. The images of two young brothers going after each other with drawn knives made me shudder to think of a "family tradition" of violence that had produced Fate and that might continue through sons such as the likable but troubled one we had met. But there were alternatives to following such a course in one's life, no matter how conditioned or "fated" one seemed to be by the circumstances of one's birth, whether hereditary or environmental. I think that male storytellers, both in the family and in the community at large, sought those alternatives through the very process of recounting their generously embellished versions of the adventures of men like Great-uncle Fate.

Most of the men who relished telling and listening to the Fate family saga (and who vicariously enjoyed his impudence and strength, his uncontrolled vitality and assertiveness, and his command of the grudging respect of those who feared him) had, after all, already turned their own lives in a different direction. They were hard-working, law-abiding citizens whose violence probably extended not much further than cursing their mules or kicking the rattle-trap old Ford when it got a flat tire. Tales about Fate and other men like him, especially when told in the context of his humorous but nevertheless bleak and subdued leave-taking, validated them in choosing order and conciliation. Women storytellers had no vested interest in such tales: drinking hard, fighting hard, and loving hard had never been perceived as within their spheres.

Chapter Nine

Conclusion

WANDERINGS IN TIME AND SPIRIT

> Life ends in the cemetery. It begins here. Some night during your senior year, you climb the Cumby water tower and paint your initials on the tank, along with your date of graduation. If you are not brave enough to climb the tower, then you are not brave enough to catch a bus to Dallas and get a job. It is a rite of passage—a usually accurate test of your potential. That night the world spreads out beneath you, and more things are possible than ever will be again.

Negotiation of Truth

The night that I climbed the Cumby water tower began my wanderings. I leaned against the rail and studied the world spread out beneath me—but I concentrated on the far horizon. It has been an eerie revelation that I am a Great-uncle Fate, not a Great-aunt Becky. When I left the farm, I did not expect to go back. Even had my ambitions been tied to the land, for a woman at that time to think of buying her own farm and running it would not have been very realistic. In spite of the hardships our family had endured on the farm, my memories of those times were and are pleasant; I continue to live by most of the values I was taught. Still, I never cherished the idea that I would "get me a farm" and "show them" by being a more prosperous farmer than anyone in that old childhood community ever dreamed of being.

My break with the farming lifestyle was fairly complete. In many

The Cumby water tower

ways, my break with the family was complete. This fact distances me from the customs and traditions of my childhood community and from the beliefs and history of my family of origin. I think it is interesting that Great-grandma Sarah may have shot a renegade who was stealing her horses, and I admire her spunk and hope I could be equally courageous in some similar situation. I do not, however, see her actions as a reflection on me. I enjoy the old stories—probably as a form of literature—and welcome their superstitious, off-color details.

My brother, without whose help my project would have been nearly impossible, has, on the other hand, made a concerted effort to remain within the tradition in which he was brought up. It is part of his idea of successful manhood that he has managed to own land, build a nice home, and achieve a status that, I suspect, he feels our parents did not achieve. In effect, he is master over the life situation that ultimately defeated them. Furthermore, he is a male, and he sees himself as carrying on a tradition that, so far as he is concerned, is unbroken. The folk materials still retain a great deal of immediacy for him. His emotional involvement is still intense.

Until the Winniford land was parceled out and sold, James retained a sentimental attachment for it, although he was too practical to wish to own it. What he decided was that no farmer could be successful on that particular land. His dream could not come true there. But he has preserved pictures, family records, and pieces of furniture, prominently displaying in his home items that he has cleaned up, shined up, and repainted. Perhaps the notion that the oral materials had real value did not occur to him until I started collecting the cemetery stories. Now, however, he is applying himself to what he definitely perceives as a duty to preserve the body of lore that was passed down to us by our parents and other members of the family.

Consequently, my brother wants this thing done right. Just as he cleaned up and revarnished the old washstand that used to sit on Grandma's back porch, so he wants to lend a strong air of respectability to the old family stories. They are family history to him, and they reflect on who he is. He wants these stories to measure up favorably—not just in their original context, but in the framework of present-day social attitudes. Listeners questioned how Great-grandpa Ward could be so lacking in compassion that he would turn Little Mose out of the house when he was given a son of his own. Thus, a more recent version of the story in which the orphan child was raised to manhood by another branch of the family appeals to James, and that is the version he tells. It is permissible for the spunky old maid Aunt Becky to kill renegade soldiers: she did not become anyone's mother. But James conveniently omits Great-grandma Sarah's participation in this questionable act. During a telephone conversation, he admitted hearing that Great-grandma had gunned down one of the renegades—but he will not likely put such a thing on tape.

For both my brother and me, the shared past experiences, together with the customs, traditions, and family history that we learned while we were growing up, have always served as a means of establishing contact, of reconnecting after periods of being apart. They are the "base of operations" from which we move into some new phase of our relationship with each other. My interest in the Long Cemetery stories came at a critical time in our relationship. During the troubled last years of my marriage and, as I worked through the problems that I faced during and after the divorce, we drew apart. He could not relate to much of what was going on with me. The gap between us seemed very wide. Then I started contacting him about the Long Cemetery stories, and the gap was spanned. Despite the disparity in our adult experiences, we have the same roots, and the significance of that is deeply ingrained in us. My decision to expand my study to include materials from both the maternal and the paternal sides of our family certainly reflects my brother's enthusiasm for those family stories.

The negotiation of truth has been a problem for my brother and me as we have worked together on this project, as I think it must have been for the original storytellers in both branches of the family. The need to communicate his or her truth and to have that truth validated by listeners has been, I suspect, a strong factor in the evolution of my family's folk materials. The stories about Great-uncle Fate—and the perceptions of Fate as a legendary family member—represent unresolved tensions in two areas: first, between ways of approaching "truth"; and second, between modes of storytelling that can be differentiated along familial as well as gender lines.

These are the same tensions that remain unresolved in the two vastly different versions of the Little Moses story. There is the more recently developed rendition preferred by my brother, with its emphasis on family solidarity, sacrifice, and success, and the older account told by my grandmother (which I prefer because I consider it a more exciting story) with its emphasis on the supernatural and on moral precept.

These stories are part of the Ward-Wolf repertoire. As such, they differ in their negotiation of truth and in their intent from the Winniford-Alexander family saga, whose items usually adhere as closely as possible to what is regarded as documented historical fact. My brother, being male and leaning toward the Winniford-Alexander storytelling mode, tends to pattern his retellings of the tales from both repertoires according to the broad prescriptions implied by the combination of his maleness and his familial preference. I, being female and leaning toward the Ward-Wolf storytelling mode, tend to follow the prescriptions implied by my femaleness and my closer alignment with the Ward-Wolf approach to storytelling. Finally, my interest in all the stories is primarily literary, and I do not regard the materials as family history that affects me directly. James takes a pragmatic, scientific view of the family folk tales, examining them as part of a documented tradition in which he is still intricately involved.

In the ongoing debate about authenticity and accuracy in relation to family stories—about truth—my brother and I recalled a childhood incident and wondered if, perhaps, repeated retellings had moved the account of our experience over into the realm of legend. If so, the little "legend" that James and I helped create—at least in its germinal stage—demonstrates the sometimes disconcerting evolution of a story as various tellers negotiate their particular truth.

Something from Heaven

One balmy night in early autumn, my brother and I were sitting out on the back porch of one of the Winniford farmhouses where we lived for a number of years. I was in sixth grade, but I had been double-promoted at least once, so I was probably about eleven years old, and my brother was nearly three years younger. Our parents and our blind Great-uncle Sam were in the front room of the house reading and talking. My brother and I were entertaining ourselves by singing together, a little competitive game where one of us would sing a snatch of some song and the other would join in if he or she knew the words and tune. The object of the game was to find a song with which the other was unfamiliar.

It was one of those empty spaces in time that often characterized isolated farm life, when the vast silence and stillness demanded that something surely must happen.

Suddenly, something extraordinary did happen. A flash of white light brightened the dark sky momentarily, and a large, very bright ball of fire, a meteorite (people called them "shooting stars"), streaked past overhead, arching, or so it appeared, down toward the earth. At the time, my brother and I were convinced that the heavenly object had made a strange hissing or swishing noise as it went by over us. We sat awestruck for a couple of minutes, and then, of course, we jumped up and ran into the house to tell our family about this unusual experience.

Shooting stars were a common occurrence, easily observable on any clear night because no big-city lights interfered with their sighting. Unless there was a whole shower of them, then, farm folk paid no special attention. The three adults to whom my brother and I reported our glorious "truth" hardly looked up from what they were doing, dismissing our intense excitement with a grunt and an indulgent nod. I recall that my brother and I looked at each other and made an instant, spontaneous decision. We *would* have our truth validated. We would have the importance of our experience recognized. I do not recall which of us rushed on, "And it landed somewhere in the field out back of the house!" The other quickly supplied supporting details: "It kind of flared up for a second or so, and then it just sat there and sputtered and shot out little sparks."

At last our story had its desired effect. The adults leaped to their feet and headed for the back of the house—even Great-uncle Sam, who kept demanding, "Can you see anything, can you see anything?" There was nothing, of course. The night was still and dark. We all walked around through the edge of the field looking for whatever we imagined might be the signs of a meteorite's landing spot, but very little could be determined in the dark. "How far out in the field do you think it fell?" my father asked several times, but my brother and I were judiciously perplexed and silent.

Early the next morning, the search continued. By morning my brother and I were convinced that the meteorite *had* landed in the field—where else *could* it have gone?—and that we had only stretched the truth a bit with the "sputtering" and the "sparks." Thus, our searching was in dead earnest, and it became more desperate as we responded to what we perceived as pressure to produce something concrete that would support our story. My parents finally lost interest in the search and went on with their morning chores, but my brother and I kept walking back and forth over the field in our determination to find some kind of fallen star. It seemed very important to be believed and not be accused of "just imagining things."

About mid-morning the search paid off. We found a rock unlike any others we had come across. As we examined it, we became increasingly convinced that it must have come from some place other than earth, and we eagerly noted features that we believed distinguished it from other, earthly rocks. However, previous experience had already shown us that mere conviction was not enough. The rock needed a little help—there was no need to take the chance of having our find dismissed as inconclusive.

So we set up shop, so to speak, in a concealed area in back of the barn and worked on the rock. We built a small fire and alternated between roasting the rock and letting it soak in a small bowl of lye water. When I called my brother to ask permission to tell about this escapade, he insisted that I was the one who decided that the rock needed a few finishing touches and thought up the fire and lye water process. He is probably correct. Such a project would have been in keeping with my "artistic and creative" nature and my strong tendency to want to "fix things." But James liked to build and tend fires, so I am certain that he was at the very least an interested onlooker during the hours that it took to "fix" the rock.

James had driven a stick into the ground at the spot out in the field where we had located our meteorite, and I had tied one of my hair ribbons to it. I then saved a few of the ashes from our campfire to sprinkle on the little excavation in the furrow from which the rock had been taken (which we had inadvertently enlarged somewhat looking for other heavenly evidence). All other signs of our fire and lye water operation we carefully covered up.

We wrapped our now pretty impressive "meteorite" in an old dishtowel. When our parents came in from their labors, we proudly showed it to them. Whatever reservations they might have had about the thoroughly traumatized pebble vanished when we took them out to the place where it had "fallen." Anyway, ordinary rocks do not leave smudges on the fingers if one rubs hard on them, and, as Great-uncle Sam observed, it "stunk to high heaven."

My brother and I considered that the episode had been maneuvered to a successful, happy resolution. We were mistaken, however. Our adventure was just beginning. Great-uncle Sam asked to be allowed to take the meteorite into town to show to some of his old cronies. James and I understood at once that the situation was getting out of hand, and we resisted this turn of events as best we could. We wanted to keep our "fallen star" and were afraid it would get lost. But we could not afford to protest too much lest we raise suspicions, so my dad decided that we must "humor the old man" and let him show off the rock. So we watched in secret dismay as Great-uncle Sam put the rock, still wrapped in the dishtowel, into a paper sack and headed eagerly for Cumby, walking briskly and swishing his white cane before him.

If we had wanted to advertise our discovery (which we did not), we could not have selected a more effective means than Great-uncle Sam. Because he was widely traveled and considered worldly and sophisticated and because he had a reputation as a fine musician and a scholar, of sorts, he always had an attentive, respectful audience. After Sam's trip to town, our situation became complicated and fraught with danger. The local newspapers decided to print the story, and my brother and I found ourselves recounting it over and over again for local and semiprofessional journalists. Being some three years older than my brother, I bore the brunt of this unwelcome publicity, which perhaps was fitting if the fire and lye water process was entirely my idea. I was asked to give a presentation for the high school science classes, which I repeated for the PTA. It looked for a time as if the whole thing would never end.

What I wanted to do was get hold of the rock. I understood that I would be wise to dispose of it before other developments occurred. But although I was permitted to use it for my various public presentations, some authority figure always retrieved it, and my hopes of ending the hoax were thwarted. The rock was finally put on permanent display in the window of one of the grocery stores, along with a placard—which over the years grew yellow as the rock became dull and dusty—explaining where the "meteorite" had landed and who had found it. The mere existence of that rock, so pitifully vulnerable to public scrutiny, haunted me for years. I had nightmares that a scientist somewhere would get hold of an old copy of one of the local papers and come to Cumby and expose the hoax. I was not certain what the punishment would be for a criminal act of this nature, but I imagined it would be severe.

About the time I thought that all the hoopla about the meteorite had died down, it would surface again. When I was a sophomore in college, a journalism major in one of my classes informed me happily—in front of the entire group—that she had come across the article about James and my "contribution to science" in an old copy of the *Commerce Journal.* The episode shattered my serenity and may have accounted, more than I cared to admit, for my general restlessness and my conviction that I probably needed to get out of Cumby and not come back.

In discussing this episode as a possible "Cumby legend," my brother and I puzzled over the factors that had contributed to its evolution and the function it must have served for the various tellers involved—starting, of course, with our childish desire to be taken seriously. Great-uncle Sam enjoyed being the center of attention, and with age and blindness, his opportunities for showing off had greatly diminished. Also, he had an active, curious mind, and the idea of touching and smelling a meteorite would have appealed to him. My brother and I had made available to him a concrete object that could be examined through his remaining senses, and this was important to him.

Wasn't there, my brother and I wondered, someone in town with enough scientific background to look at the rock, listen to the story, and realize how implausible were the claims regarding them? Probably no one cared to inspect either the rock or the story that carefully. Cumby did not get in the news very often. Cumby needed to be taken seriously just as my brother and I did. The feeling of being involved in something of even minor importance was satisfying, and the story gave people something immediate, something local, to talk about.

It was the issue of truth, however, that intrigued us, because this had been a problem for us during the course of our work on my project. As Elliott Oring suggests, the narration of a legend is "in a sense, the negotiation of the truth" of the episodes recounted.[1] My brother and I had debated the accuracy of different versions of certain tales and whether others recounted events that had happened at all. In the case of the foregoing story, James acknowledged that the documentary evidence, such as it was—the rock, the newspaper articles—supported a misconception and not the "truth" as he and I knew it to be. Documented "truth" is not infallible.

At the core of the story, however, is a truth: my brother and I did, in fact, see an impressive, unusual thing that affected us mentally and emotionally, and we wanted to share that experience. If we had not been convinced of the necessity of negotiating that truth in order to be heard, there would have been no story. That is, if our parents had exclaimed, "Oh, wow! How wonderful! Not many people get to see a meteorite that comes so close to the earth. We wish we could have seen it, too," the event would have ended there, and no story would have developed. Given the impetus of our truth negotiations, and evolving through a series of other tellers, a story developed.

Probably this same phenomenon accounts for many of the Long Cemetery stories especially, which are more suspect in their truth status than are the items in the Winniford-Alexander family saga. The core of truth is there, but that truth had to be altered in order for it to be received and elicit the response that the teller intended. Possibly my grandmother pointed toward handy bois d'arc posts, devised the circle of ground where no grass would grow, and invented the spirit of Fate's first wife for the same reason that my brother and I searched for a suitable rock and, lest that still not be sufficient, subjected it to fire and lye water.

When James and I began working together on my folklore project, we were surprised to discover that, although we had both grown up in the same family, we had not experienced that family's lore in the same way. This was at first a disconcerting stumbling block that interfered with our handling the materials successfully. We assumed that each story had to be told either accurately or inaccurately, that there was either a right or a wrong way for each tale to function for teller and listeners. Through a gradual understanding that truth had been—and continues to be—negotiated in the recounting of even the Winniford-Alexander family legends (most of which have some grounding in documented fact), we came to accept the entire body of material, with all its conflicts and contradictions, as the legacy of our family and the little town where both of us were born and grew up.

This acceptance, which permitted us finally to work comfortably together on the project, does not mean that we do not still prioritize our own versions of the stories, our own perceptions of what those stories were intended to mean, and how a listener or listeners generally responded. Because the project is mine, and because I regard the stories as folklore and as literature, both consciously and subconsciously, I valorize my telling of the tales over my brother's. I do, however, respect his desire to ensure that the stories have validity as family history. Such valorization seems unavoidable.

I acknowledge readily, however, that as family history, what I choose to call family folklore has—along with other aspects of his training and upbringing—worked well for my brother. Like our ancestors, he struggled to establish "place permanent"—not on the original Winniford-Alexander land but on land of his own choosing. Once established, he became the kind of patriarch that the men in our family, particularly on the paternal side, aspired to be: a gentleman farmer who combined a certain rugged individualism with refinement and social commitment. He avoided the mistakes he felt his forebears had made, and he took advantage of the opportunities that they failed to recognize.

The home he built for himself is the kind of home they probably dreamed of building, his cattle are fat, his grass is green—and when speculators drilled for gas and oil on his land, they found it. He has been a considerate, faithful husband, a loving, protective father, and an upstanding member of his community. I expect that he will comment jokingly that what I have written about him sounds like a rather corny obituary, and no doubt any such final assessment of him will conclude that his was a life well lived. Although people sense that it would not be a good idea to cross him, and he has a reputation for being tough, stubborn, and independent, I do not know of so much as a breath of scandal connected to any of his enterprises, public or private.

Like the Wards and Wolfs, who probably because of their mixed blood could lay no claim to "place permanent," I have felt betrayed and disenfranchised—not by race but by gender. When I climbed the Cumby water tower that night and looked out on the world, knowing that I would leave, I could not have anticipated the intricacies of my future migrations, my wanderings—like Zora Hurston, not so much in geography as in time and spirit. At that young age, I did not comprehend the limitations imposed by my being female. During the time of my girlhood and young womanhood, society at large expected that even an educated woman would work at a suitable profession for a time, perhaps, and then marry, have children, and lend her efforts to the more socially viable goals of her husband. When one casts one's lot with another human being and accepts that person's idea of direction, place becomes very "portable." Husbands and lovers travel tangled roads.

I do not think that for me "self" was less intact than for my brother, but like the Wards and Wolfs, that "self" had trouble knowing where to be. The Ward-Wolf stories sought, in part, to preserve an integrity of self that transcended place. My grandmother could thereby transport an incident from any point in the geography of her migrations, superimpose it on Long Cemetery, and make it real and relevant. "What" and "how" mattered in ways that "where" could not; truth was private, personal, and internalized instead of public, general, and externalized through society's judgment of who one was in relation to where one was. My private, personal, internalized truths, my "place portable," made my survival possible, but the record of my wanderings will not lend itself to an impressive obituary.

Both my brother and I have responded throughout our lives to the overriding implication of all the family lore that some greater design and purpose controls the individual human activities that the tales record: primarily historical in the Winniford-Alexander family saga and moral and supernatural in the Ward-Wolf cemetery legends. We also believe that this greater design or purpose obligates the members of each generation to duties that extend beyond self and family. The fact that we both became teachers may have had as much to do with the accessibility of that profession, in view of our circumstances, as it did with our commitment to education. But we have been alike in our dedication to mastering subject matter and skills and our determination to help the students we teach.

In other respects, the contrasts between us are startling and reflect the vastly different courses our lives have taken. My brother is a preacher. In this capacity he exhorts the people in his care to right behavior, officiates in their marriages, shares their joy in births, visits them when they are sick, comforts them in trouble and loss, holds their hands and prays with them while they are dying, and officiates again at their burials—all with courage, compassion, and conviction.

I travel a much darker path. In a women's detox center where I have completed four thousand contact hours, I steady some woman while she shakes and vomits or maneuver her through her terror during delirium tremens. Sometimes—much too often—I eventually help identify her body at the morgue. I talk to a group of two hundred white-jacketed young men in a prison chemical dependency unit and afterward—with some mild trepidation—hug them and manage quick words of encouragement as they file past. Walking through the cellblocks at Eastham Unit, perhaps, intensely aware of the resentment, anger, hopelessness, and frustration in the stares of the hundreds of men standing like cattle in their chest-high stalls, I am most aware that place for me is very portable, and that it needs to be.

Epilogue

Whether I have wished it or not, *change* has been a recurrent theme in this book. Writing about life as it was in Cumby and Hopkins County when I was a child has been like trying to take a picture with an old-fashioned tripod camera when the subject will not sit still. And change is ongoing.

While I was working on revisions prior to publication, my niece Shannon got married, and Aunt Minnie and Aunt Lucille both died. Aunt Minnie is buried in Long Cemetery, and Aunt Lucille has taken her place beside Aunt Lynna in the Winniford plot in Cumby. When my niece and I made a recent trip to Hopkins County for last minute research and picture taking, we had to track the Hopkins County Genealogical Society to its new location on Sulphur Springs' old Main Street in a larger building in which materials can be displayed and examined with greater ease and efficiency. Furthermore, we found the old Winniford homeplace where my grandparents once lived so deteriorated and overgrown that taking pictures seemed not only impossible but pointless.

The most disturbing changes, however, had occurred in Long Cemetery. I recall when Long Cemetery seemed quite filled to capacity, laid out in neat rows of mounded graves marked by modest monuments, posts or fieldstones—and this is how I had described it in three chapters of my book. Now grave placement appears almost random due to the leveling of mounds and the gradual loss or erasure of uninscribed graves. For instance, Great Uncle Fate and a wife who outlived him share a new double monument, and all signs of other burials in that plot have vanished. Similar vacant spaces are obvious in other areas of the graveyard as well. The occupants of these uninscribed, now unmarked and leveled, *lost* graves were not "sharers" or informants in the usual sense, yet I am deeply aware that they informed the nature and message of my book in subtle but powerful ways. As my Houston-bound Greyhound lumbered through a Texas landscape green with spring, I grieved for them—people whose faces I never saw, whose voices I never heard, whose names I never knew or have forgotten.

In high school, my world history textbook started each successive section with the adage *"Time is. Man marches on."* Working on this book has reinforced for me the truth of that observation. My Macintosh and I together cannot keep up, hard as we try. But I have done the best I could, so I will settle for that and square my shoulders and have no regrets. Forward march!

Notes

Chapter One
Introduction

1. Gladys St. Clair, *A History of Hopkins County, Texas,* p. 3.
2. Lewis P. Simpson, "The Southern Aesthetic of Memory," *Tulane Studies in English* 23 (1978): 215.
3. See J. N. Winniford, "Pioneer Days in Black Jack Grove," *The Cumby (Tex.) Rustler,* March 14, 1934.
4. Carl Lindahl, "Folklore/Oral Tradition," in *Encyclopedia of Social History,* ed. Peter N. Stearns, p. 282.
5. Barre Toelken, *The Dynamics of Folklore,* pp. 10, 32.
6. Zora Neale Hurston, *Mules and Men.*
7. Rosan Augusta Jordan, "Not into Cold Space: Zora Neale Hurston and J. Frank Dobie As Holistic Folklorists," *Southern Folklore* 49 (1992): 109-31; John Dorst, "Zora Neale Hurston's *Mules and Men* and the Death of the Ethnographer," *Contemporary Anthropology,* 1989.
8. Zora Neale Hurston, *Dust Tracks on a Road,* p. 97.
9. Lucinda M. MacKethan, "Prodigal Daughters: The Journeys of Ellen Glasgow, Zora Neale Hurston, and Eudora Welty," in *Daughters of Time: Creating Woman's Voice in Southern Story,* pp. 40–63.
10. Robert E. Hemenway, *Zora Neale Hurston: A Literary Biography,* and introduction to Hurston, *Mules and Men,* p. xxii.
11. Karla F. C. Holloway, *The Character of the Word: The Texts of Zora Neale Hurston,* p. 105.

Chapter Two
Getting a Handle on the Past

1. Bruce Jackson, *Fieldwork,* p. 7.
2. Ibid., p. 39.
3. Kenneth S. Goldstein, *A Guide for Field Workers in Folklore.*
4. Edward D. Ives, *The Tape-Recorded Interview: A Manual for Field Workers in Folklore and Oral History.*
5. George E. Marcus and Michael M. J. Fischer, *Anthropology As Cultural Critique: An Experimental Moment in the Human Sciences,* pp. 45–71.
6. David Jacobson, *Reading Ethnography,* p. 115.
7. Florene Chapman Adams, *Hopkins County and Our Heritage,* p. 41; Sue Via Brazell, "Pioneer Days in Black Jack Grove," in *Pioneers of Hopkins County, Texas,* vol. 1, ed. Sylvia M. Kibart and Rita M. Adams, p. 298–99; and Gladys St. Clair, *A History of Hopkins County, Texas,* p. 21.
8. Adams, *Hopkins County,* p. 41.
9. From the Celia M. Wright Collection, Library Archives, James Gilliam Gee Library, East Texas State University (Commerce), "Cumby Masons Climax Centennial Programs," *Commerce (Tex.) Journal,* Jan., 1956.
10. Tommy Ayres, "Ladies' March on Saloons Still a Legend in Cumby," *Dallas Times Herald,* Friday, Feb. 11, 1966, 2nd ed., sec. A., p. 12.
11. E. B. Fleming, *Early History of Hopkins County, Texas,* pp. 35–36.
12. David Hugh ("Dick") Hare, *To Tell of Time: People, Places, and Things of Sulphur Bluff and Hopkins County, Texas,* pp. 93–94.
13. From the Celia M. Wright Collection, *News Telegram* (Greenville, Tex.), Fall Festival Section, Sept. 6, 1977.
14. From the Celia M. Wright Collection, "Going with Summer Term," *Times Tribune* (Sulphur Springs, Tex.), Aug. 29, 1954.
15. From the Celia M. Wright Collection, "Cumby Enjoys Neighbor Cities," *Commerce (Tex.) Journal,* Apr. 18, 1978.

Chapter Three
Picking Cotton, Killing Hogs, and Stretching the Truth

1. Gladys St. Clair, *A History of Hopkins County, Texas,* pp. 6–9.
2. James Winniford, tape-recorded interview with author, Gilmer, Tex., Jan., 1993.
3. Ibid.
4. Elliott Oring, *Folk Groups and Folklore Genres: An Introduction,* p. 39.
5. Mody C. Boatright, "The Family Saga As a Form of Folklore," in *The Family Saga and Other Phases of American Folklore,* ed. Mody Boatright, p. 2.
6. St. Clair, *History of Hopkins County,* p. 36.
7. James Winniford, taped narration, shipped to author from home near Longview, Tex., spring, 1993.

8. Ibid.

9. Ibid.

10. Oring, *Folk Groups and Folklore Genres.*

Chapter Four
Telling Storm-Cellar Tales in Cyclone Country

1. James Winniford, tape-recorded interview with author, Gilmer, Tex., Jan., 1992.

2. Ibid.

3. James Winniford, taped narration, shipped to author from farm near Gilmer, Tex., spring, 1993.

Chapter Five
Place Permanent and Place Portable

1. Gladys St. Clair, *A History of Hopkins County, Texas,* p. 11.

2. Morris L. A. Wardell, *A Political History of the Cherokee Nation, 1838–1907,* pp. 320–34.

3. Grace Steele Woodward, *The Cherokees,* pp. 322–23.

4. Terry G. Jordan, *Texas Graveyards: A Cultural Legacy.*

5. Karen Baldwin, "'Woof!' A Word on Women's Roles in Family Storytelling," in *Women's Folklore, Women's Culture,* ed. Rosan A. Jordan and Susan Kalcik.

6. Joan N. Radner and Susan S. Lanser, "Strategies of Coding in Women's Cultures," in *Feminist Messages: Coding in Women's Folk Culture,* ed. Joan Newlon Radner; Sandra M. Gilbert and Susan Gubar, *The Madwoman in the Attic: The Woman Writer and the Nineteenth-Century Imagination.*

7. Judith Lowder Newton, *Women, Power, and Subversion: Social Strategies in British Fiction, 1778–1860.*

8. June England Tuck and Deborah Tuck Young, *Cemetery Inscriptions,* vol. 1.

9. *Census of the United States, 1870,* microfilm copy, prect. 4, Black Jack Grove, Hopkins County, Tex., Sept. 29, 1870.

10. James Winniford, taped narration, shipped to author from farm near Gilmer, Tex., spring, 1993.

11. Cumberland County, Virginia, records, circuit court, "Appraisement, George Winneford," *Will Book 1,* p. 144.

12. Cumberland County, Virginia, records, circuit court, "Deed, Wineford to Mayo," *Deed Book 3,* p. 246.

13. Cumberland County, Virginia, records, circuit court, "Will of David Winniford," *Will Book 2,* p. 203.

14. W. J. Winniford, "In Search of Gold," *Lancaster (Tex.) Herald,* Friday, Nov. 26, 1909, sec. 4, p. 3.

15. Ibid., Friday, Nov. 19, 1909, sec. 3, p. 3, 4.

16. A. C. Greene and Ella Winniford Taylor, "The Gold Rush: From Dallas

County to California by Wagon Train," *The Dallas Morning News,* Jan. 19, 1986, pp. 24–25.

17. Sylvia M. Kibart and Rita M. Adams, eds., *Pioneers of Hopkins County, Texas,* vol. 2, p. 175.
18. Mamie Winniford Robertson, tape-recorded interview with author, Cumby, Tex., Aug., 1991.
19. June E. Tuck, *Civil War Shadows in Hopkins County, Texas,* p. 346.
20. Kibart and Adams, *Pioneers of Hopkins County,* p. 176.
21. James Winniford, taped narration, spring, 1993.
22. Kibart and Adams, *Pioneers of Hopkins County,* p. 176.
23. Douglas Hale, *The Third Texas Cavalry,* pp. 5–28.
24. Ibid., p. 8.

Chapter Six
Two Graveyards

1. Stanley French, "The Cemetery As Cultural Institution: The Establishment of Mount Auburn and the 'Rural Cemetery' Movement," in *Death in America,* ed. David E. Stannard, p. 176.
2. Anita Pitchford, "The Material Culture of the Traditional East Texas Graveyard," *Southern Folklore Quarterly* 43 (1978): p. 277–90.
3. Ibid., p. 280.
4. Terry G. Jordan, *Texas Graveyards: A Cultural Legacy,* pp. 15, 16.
5. D. Gregory Jeane, "The Upland South Folk Cemetery Complex: Some Suggestions of Origin," in *Cemeteries and Gravemarkers: Voices of American Culture,* ed. Richard E. Meyer, p. 121.
6. Pitchford, "Material Culture of the Traditional East Texas Graveyard," p. 290.
7. Fred Tarpley, "Southern Cemeteries: Neglected Archives for the Folklorist," *Southern Folklore Quarterly* 27 (1963): 330.
8. Minnie Martin Foster, tape-recorded interview with author, Jan. 4, 1994.
9. Sir James George Frazer, *The Golden Bough: A Study in Magic and Religion,* vol. 1, abridged ed., p. 13.
10. Pitchford, "Material Culture of the Traditional East Texas Graveyard," p. 284.
11. Ibid., p. 283.
12. Richard V. Francaviglia, "The Cemetery As an Evolving Cultural Landscape," *Annals of the Association of American Geographers* 61 (1971): 503.
13. Ibid., pp. 501–502.
14. E. B. Fleming, *Early History of Hopkins County, Texas.*
15. Larry McMurtry, *In a Narrow Grave: Essays on Texas,* p. 68.
16. W. Lloyd Warner, *The Living and the Dead: A Study of the Symbolic Life of Americans,* p. 293.

17. Margaret R. Yocom, "Woman to Woman: Fieldwork and the Private Sphere," in *Women's Folklore, Women's Culture,* ed. Rosan A. Jordan and Susan J. Kalcik, p. 48.
18. Ibid., p. 50.

Chapter Seven
"Home Is Where You Bury"

1. "Home Is Where You Bury," quote from William Humphrey, *Home From the Hills.* See Terry Jordan, *Texas Graveyards: A Cultural Legacy;* D. Gregory Jeane, "The Upland South Folk Cemetery Complex: Some Suggestions of Origin," in *Cemeteries and Graveyards: Voices of American Culture,* ed. Richard E. Meyer; Joey Brackner, "'Decoration Day': Alabama's Day of the Dead," unpub. paper presented to the American Folklore Society, Eugene, Oregon, Oct., 1993; and Anita Pitchford, "The Material Culture of the Traditional East Texas Graveyard," *Southern Folklore Quarterly* 43 (1978).
2. Brackner, "'Decoration Day.'"
3. Pitchford, "Material Culture of the Traditional East Texas Graveyard."
4. William Lynwood Montell, *Ghosts along the Cumberland: Deathlore in the Kentucky Foothills.*
5. Lewis O. Saum, "Death in the Popular Mind of Pre–Civil War America," in *Death in America,* ed. David E. Stannard, pp. 30–48.
6. Ann Douglas, "Heaven Our Home," in *Death in America,* ed. David E. Stannard, p. 63.
7. Richard V. Francaviglia, "The Cemetery As an Evolving Cultural Landscape," *Annals of the Association of American Geographers* 61 (1971): 503–505.
8. Leroy Bowman, *The American Funeral: A Study in Guilt, Extravagance, and Sublimity,* p. 123.
9. Sir James George Frazer, *The Golden Bough: A Study in Magic and Religion,* vol. 1, abridged ed., p. 43.
10. Robert W. Habenstein and William M. Lamers, *The History of American Funeral Directing,* pp. 287–91.
11. Ibid.
12. Mody C. Boatright, "The Family Saga As a Form of Folklore," in *The Family Saga and Other Phases of American Folklore,* ed. Mody Boatright, p. 7.
13. Judith Lowder Newton, *Women, Power, and Subversion: Social Strategies in British Fiction, 1778–1860,* p. 169.
14. Joan N. Radner and Susan S. Lanser, "Strategies of Coding in Women's Cultures," in *Feminist Messages: Coding in Women's Folk Culture,* ed. Joan Newlon Radner, p. 6.
15. Ibid., p. 8.
16. Sabine Broeck-Sallah, "Plots to a Happy Ending: Re-Reading Closure," in

Feminine Critical Negotiations, ed. Alice A. Parker and Elizabeth A. Meese; Rachel M. Brownstein, *Becoming a Heroine: Reading about Women in Novels.*

17. John G. Cawelti, *Adventure, Mystery, and Romance: Formula Stories As Art and Popular Culture,* p. 35.
18. Nancy Chodorow, *The Reproduction of Mothering: Psychoanalysis and the Sociology of Gender,* p. 200. See also William Humphrey, *Home from the Hill;* and Humphrey, *The Ordways.*

Chapter Eight
Coming Home Feet First

1. Robert W. Habenstein and William M. Lamers, *The History of American Funeral Directing,* pp. 354, 384–85.
2. James Winniford, tape-recorded narration, shipped to author from home near Gilmer, Tex., spring, 1993.
3. W. Lloyd Warner, *The Living and the Dead: A Study of the Symbolic Life of Americans,* pp. 309–10.
4. Ibid., p. 310.
5. Leroy Bowman, *The American Funeral: A Study in Guilt, Extravagance, and Sublimity,* pp. 102–103.
6. James Winniford, taped narration, spring, 1993.
7. Ibid.
8. Ibid.
9. Warner, *The Living and the Dead,* pp. 74–75.
10. Minnie Martin Foster, taped-recorded interview with author, Gilmer, Tex., Jan. 4, 1994.
11. James J. Farrell, *Inventing the American Way of Death, 1830–1920,* p. 154.
12. Bowman, *The American Funeral,* p. 166.
13. James Winniford, taped narration, spring, 1993.
    See also Linda Degh, *Folktales and Society: Story-Telling in a Hungarian Peasant Community,* trans. Emily M. Schossberger, 2d ed.; W. C. McNeil, *Ozark Mountain Humor;* and Sean O'Sullivan [O Suilleabhain], *Irish Wake Amusements,* trans. Caitheamh Aimsire Arrhorraimh.

Chapter Nine
Conclusion

1. Elliott Oring, *Folk Groups and Folklore Genres: An Introduction,* p. 125.

Bibliography

Abernethy, Francis E., ed. *Tales from the Big Thicket.* Austin and London: University of Texas Press, 1968.

Abrahams, Roger C. *Deep Down in the Jungle: Negro Narrative Folklore from the Streets of Philadelphia.* 1st rev. ed. New York: Aldine, 1970.

Adams, Florene Chapman. *Hopkins County and Our Heritage.* American Revolution Bicentennial, 1776–1976. Hopkins County Historical Commission. Wolfe City, Tex.: Henington Publishing Co., 1976.

Ayres, Tommy. "Ladies' March on Saloons Still a Legend in Cumby." *Dallas Times Herald,* Friday, February 11, 1966, 12-A, 2.

Baldwin, Karen. "'Woof!' A Word on Women's Roles in Family Storytelling." In *Women's Folklore, Women's Culture.* Edited by Rosan A. Jordan and Susan Kalcik. Philadelphia: University of Pennsylvania Press, 1985.

Boatright, Mody C. "The Family Saga As a Form of Folklore." In *The Family Saga and Other Phases of American Folklore.* Edited by Mody Boatright. Urbana: University of Illinois Press, 1958, pp. 1–26.

Bowman, Leroy. *The American Funeral: A Study in Guilt, Extravagance, and Sublimity.* Washington, D.C.: Public Affairs Press, 1959.

Brackner, Joey. "'Decoration Day': Alabama's Day of the Dead." Unpublished paper presented to the American Folklore Society, Eugene, Oregon, October, 1993.

Brazell, Sue Via. "Pioneer Days in Black Jack Grove." In *Pioneers of Hopkins County, Texas.* Edited by Sylvia M. Kibart and Rita M. Adams. Vol. 1. Wolfe City, Tex.: Henington Publishing Co, 1986.

Brewer, J. Mason. *Dog Ghosts and Other Negro Folk Tales; The Word on the Brazos: Negro Preacher Tales from the Brazos Bottoms of Texas.* Austin: University of Texas Press, 1976.

Broeck-Sallah, Sabine. "Plots to a Happy Ending: Re-Reading Closure." In *Feminine Critical Negotiations*. Edited by Alice A. Parker and Elizabeth A. Meese. Amsterdam and Philadelphia: John Benjamins Publising Co., 1992.

Brownstein, Rachel M. *Becoming a Heroine: Reading about Women in Novels*. New York: Penguin Books, 1982.

Cawelti, John G. *Adventure, Mystery, and Romance: Formula Stories As Art and Popular Culture*. Chicago and London: University of Chicago Press, 1980.

Chodorow, Nancy. *The Reproduction of Mothering: Psychoanalysis and the Sociology of Gender*. Berkeley: University of California Press, 1978.

Clifford, James, and George E. Marcus, ed. *Writing Culture: The Poetics and Politics of Ethnography*. Berkeley, Los Angeles, London: University of California Press, 1986.

Cumberland County, Virginia. Records, circuit court. "Appraisement, George Winneford." *Will Book 1*, p. 144.

———. "Will of David Winniford." *Will Book 2*, p. 203.

———. "Deed, Wineford to Mayo." *Deed Book 3*, p. 246.

Degh, Linda. *Folktales and Society: Story-Telling in a Hungarian Peasant Community*. Translated by Emily M. Schossberger. 2nd ed. Bloomington and Indianapolis: Indiana University Press, 1989.

Dorst, John. "Zora Neale Hurston's *Mules and Men* and the Death of the Ethnographer." *Contemporary Anthropology*, 1989.

Douglas, Ann. "Heaven our Home." In *Death in America*. Edited by David E. Stannard. Philadelphia: University of Pennsylvania Press, 1975.

Farrell, James J. *Inventing the American Way of Death, 1830–1920*. Philadelphia: Temple University Press, 1980.

Fleming, E. B. *Early History of Hopkins County, Texas*. N.p., 1902.

Foster, Minnie Martin. Tape-recorded interview. Gilmer, Tex., January 4, 1994.

Fowler, Bridget. *The Alienated Reader: Women and Romantic Literature in the Twentieth Century*. New York, London: Harvester Wheatsheaf, 1991.

Francaviglia, Richard V. "The Cemetery As an Evolving Cultural Landscape." *Annals of the Association of American Geographers* 61 (1971): 501–509.

Frazer, Sir James George. *The Golden Bough: A Study in Magic and Religion*. Vol. 1. Abridged edition. New York: The Macmillan Co., 1953.

French, Stanley. "The Cemetery As Cultural Institution: The Establishment of Mount Auburn and the 'Rural Cemetery' Movement." In *Death in America*. Edited by David E. Stannard. Philadelphia: University of Pennsylvania Press, 1975.

Gammel, H. P. N. *The Laws of Texas, 1822–1897*. Vol. 2, p. 1330.

Gilbert, Sandra M., and Susan Gubar. *The Madwoman in the Attic: The Woman Writer and the Nineteenth-Century Imagination*. New Haven: Yale University Press, 1979.

Glassie, Henry. *Passing the Time in Ballymenone.* Philadelphia: University of Pennsylvania Press, 1982.

Goldstein, Kenneth B. *A Guide for Field Workers in Folklore.* Published for the American Folklore Society by Folklore Associates, Inc., Hatboro, Penn., 1964. Book Tower, Detroit: Gale Research Co., 1974.

Greene, A. C., and Ella Winniford Taylor. "The Gold Rush: From Dallas County to California by Wagon Train." *The Dallas Morning News,* January 19, 1986, pp. 24–25.

Grimes, Ronald L. *Marrying and Burying: Rites of Passage in a Man's Life.* Boulder, Colo.: Westview Press, 1995.

Habenstein, Robert W., and William M. Lamers. *The History of American Funeral Directing.* Milwaukee: Bulfin, 1955.

Hare, David Hugh ("Dick"). *To Tell of Time: People, Places, and Things of Sulphur Bluff and Hopkins County, Texas.* Hereford, Tex.: Pioneer, 1972.

Helias, Pierre-Jakez. *The Horse of Pride: Life in a Breton Village.* Translated by June Guicharnaud, 1978. New Haven: Yale University Press.

Hemenway, Robert E. *Zora Neale Hurston: A Literary Biography.* Urbana: University of Illinois Press, 1977.

Holloway, Karla F. C. *The Character of the Word: The Texts of Zora Neale Hurston.* New York: Greenwood, 1987.

Humphrey, William. *Home from the Hill.* New York: Knopf, 1958.

———. *The Ordways.* New York: Knopf, 1965.

Hurston, Zora Neale. *Dust Tracks on a Road.* 1942. Reprint, New York: Arno, 1969.

———. *Mules and Men.* Bloomington: Indiana University Press, 1978.

———. *Their Eyes Were Watching God.* Reprint, Urbana and Chicago: University of Illinois Press, 1978.

Ives, Edward D. *The Tape-Recorded Interview: A Manual for Field Workers in Folklore and Oral History.* Knoxville: University of Tennessee Press, 1974.

Jackson, Bruce. *Fieldwork.* Urbana and Chicago: University of Illinois Press, 1987.

Jacobson, David. *Reading Ethnography.* New York: State University of New York Press, 1991.

Jeane, D. Gregory. "The Upland South Folk Cemetery Complex: Some Suggestions of Origin." *Cemeteries and Gravemarkers: Voices of American Culture.* Edited by Richard E. Meyer. Ann Arbor: University of Michigan Institute of Research Press, 1989, pp. 107–36.

Jordan, Rosan Augusta. "Not into Cold Space: Zora Neale Hurston and J. Frank Dobie As Holistic Folklorists." *Southern Folklore* 49 (1992): 109–31.

Jordan, Terry. *Texas Graveyards: A Cultural Legacy.* Austin: University of Texas Press, 1982.

Kibart, Sylvia M., and Rita M. Adams, eds. *Pioneers of Hopkins County, Texas.* Vol. 2. Wolfe City, Tex.: Henington Publishing Co., 1989.

Lindahl, Carl. *Earnest Games: Folkloric Patterns in the Canterbury Tales.* Bloomington and Indianapolis: Indiana University Press, 1986.

———. "Folklore/Oral Tradition." *Encyclopedia of Social History.* Edited by Peter N. Stearns. New York and London: Garland Pub., 1994.

MacKethan, Lucinda H. "Prodigal Daughters: The Journeys of Ellen Glasgow, Zora Neale Hurston, and Eudora Welty." In *Daughters of Time: Creating Woman's Voice in Southern Story.* Athens: University of Georgia Press, 1990, pp. 40–63.

McMurtry, Larry. *In a Narrow Grave: Essays on Texas.* Albuquerque: University of New Mexico Press, 1968.

McNeil, W. C. *Ozark Mountain Humor.* Little Rock: August House, 1989.

Marcus, George E., and Michael M. J. Fischer. *Anthropology As Cultural Critique: An Experimental Moment in the Human Sciences.* Chicago and London: University of Chicago Press, 1986.

Miles, Elton. *Tales of the Big Bend.* College Station: Texas A&M University Press, 1976.

———. *More Tales of the Big Bend.* College Station: Texas A&M University Press, 1988.

———. *Stray Tales of the Big Bend.* College Station: Texas A&M University Press, 1993.

Montell, William Lynwood. *Ghosts along the Cumberland: Deathlore in the Kentucky Foothills.* Knoxville: University of Tennessee Press, 1975.

Mullen, Patrick. *I Heard the Old Fishermen Say: Folklore of the Texas Gulf Coast.* Logan: Utah State University Press, 1988.

Newton, Judith Lowder. *Women, Power, and Subversion: Social Strategies in British Fiction, 1778–1860.* New York and London: Methuen, 1981.

Oring, Elliott. *Folk Groups and Folklore Genres: An Introduction.* Logan: Utah State University Press, 1986.

O'Sullivan [O Suilleabhain], Sean. *Irish Wake Amusements.* Translated by Caitheamh Aimsire Arrhorraimh. Dublin: Mercer, 1967.

Pitchford, Anita. "The Material Culture of the Traditional East Texas Graveyard." *Southern Folklore Quarterly* 43 (1978): 277–90.

Radner, Joan N., and Susan S. Lanser. "Strategies of Coding in Women's Cultures." *Feminist Messages: Coding in Women's Folk Culture.* Edited by Joan Newlon Radner. Urbana: University of Illinois Press, 1993.

Ritchie, Jean. *Singing Family of the Cumberlands.* New York: Oak Publications, 1955.

Robertson, Mamie Winniford. Tape-recorded interview. Cumby, Tex., August, 1991.

St. Clair, Gladys. *A History of Hopkins County, Texas.* Waco: Texian, 1965.

Saum, Lewis O. "Death in the Popular Mind of Pre–Civil War America." In *Death in America*. Edited by David E. Stannard. Philadelphia: University of Pennsylvania Press, 1975, pp. 30–48.

Simpson, Lewis P. "The Southern Aesthetic of Memory." *Tulane Studies in English* 23 (1978): 207–27.

Stahl, Sandra K. Dolby. *The Personal Narrative As a Folklore Genre*. Ph.D. thesis, authorized facsimile. Indiana University. Ann Arbor: University Microfilms, 1975.

Tarpley, Fred. "Southern Cemeteries: Neglected Archives for the Folklorist." *Southern Folklore Quarterly* 27 (1963): 323–33.

Thompson, Sharyn, Joey Brackner, and Alfred E. Lemmon. *A Preliminary Bibliography: Historic Cemetery Preservation in the Southern United States*. Compiled for the National Trust for Historic Preservation Conference, Charleston, S.C., June 23–24, 1989.

Toelken, Barre. *The Dynamics of Folklore*. Boston: Houghton Mifflin Co., 1979.

Tuck, June England. *Civil War Shadows in Hopkins County, Texas*. Sulphur Springs, Tex.: Walsworth, 1993.

Tuck, June England, and Deborah Tuck Young. *Cemetery Inscriptions*. Vol. 1. Wolfe City, Tex.: Henington Publishing Co., 1985.

U.S. Bureau of the Census. *Census of the United States, 1870*. Microfilm copy. Prect. 4. Black Jack Grove, Hopkins County, Tex., September 29, 1870.

———. *Census of the United States, 1880*. Microfilm copy. Prect. 4. Black Jack Grove, Hopkins County, Tex., June 4, 1880, p. 173.

———. *Census of the United States, 1890*. Microfilm copy. Prect. 6. part, Hunt County, Tex. Supv. dist. no. 261, Enum. dist. no. 135. Sheet 22, 124-A.

Tyler, Stephen. *The Unspeakable: Discourse, Dialogue, and Rhetoric in the Postmodern World*. Madison: University of Wisconsin Press, 1987.

Vidutis, Ricardas, and Virginia Lowe. "The Cemetery As a Cultural Text." *Kentucky Folklore Record* 26: 2.

Wardell, Morris L. A. *A Political History of the Cherokee Nation, 1838–1907*. Norman: University of Oklahoma Press, 1938.

Warner, W. Lloyd. *The Living and the Dead: A Study of the Symbolic Life of Americans*. New Haven: Yale University Press, 1959.

Williams, Melvin D. *On the Street Where I Lived*. New York: Holt, 1981.

Winniford, J. N. "Pioneer Days in Black Jack Grove." *The Cumby (Tex.) Rustler*, March 14, 1934.

Winniford, James R. Tape-recorded consultations, interviews, and fieldwork expeditions, January, 1992, 1993, 1994.

Winniford, Shannon. Interview and fieldwork expedition, January, 1994.

Winniford, W. J. "The Rush for Gold." *Lancaster (Tex.) Herald*. Eleven installments: Friday, November 26, 1909–Friday, January 28, 1910.

Woodward, Grace Steele. *The Cherokees*. Norman: University of Oklahoma Press, 1990.

Wright, Celia M. *Heritage from the Past: Sketches from Hopkins County History.* Sulphur Springs, Tex.: Shining Path, 1959.

Wright, Celia M. Collection. Library Archives. James Gilliam Gee Library, East Texas State University, Commerce.

———. "Going with Summer Term." *Times Tribune* (Sulphur Springs), August 29, 1954.

———. "Cumby Masons Climax Centennial Programs." *Commerce (Tex.) Journal,* January, 1956.

———. *News Telegram* (Greenville, Tex.), Fall Festival Section, September 6, 1977.

———. "Cumby Enjoys Neighbor Cities." *Commerce (Tex.) Journal,* April 18, 1978.

Yocom, Margaret R. "Woman to Woman: Fieldwork and the Private Sphere." In *Women's Folklore, Women's Culture.* Edited by Rosan A. Jordan and Susan J. Kalcik. Philadelphia: University of Pennsylvania Press, 1985.